At Home and Abroad

At Home and Abroad

*U.S. Labor-Market Performance in
International Perspective*

Francine D. Blau and Lawrence M. Kahn

Russell Sage Foundation • New York

The Russell Sage Foundation

The Russell Sage Foundation, one of the oldest of America's general purpose foundations, was established in 1907 by Mrs. Margaret Olivia Sage for "the improvement of social and living conditions in the United States." The Foundation seeks to fulfill this mandate by fostering the development and dissemination of knowledge about the country's political, social, and economic problems. While the Foundation endeavors to assure the accuracy and objectivity of each book it publishes, the conclusions and interpretations in Russell Sage Foundation publications are those of the authors and not of the Foundation, its Trustees, or its staff. Publication by Russell Sage, therefore, does not imply Foundation endorsement.

Library of Congress Cataloging-in-Publication Data

Blau, Francine D.
    At home and abroad: U.S. labor-market performance in international perspective / Francine D. Blau and Lawrence M. Kahn.
      p. cm.
    Includes bibliographical references and index.
    1. Labor market—United States.   2. Labor policy—United States.
  I. Kahn, Lawrence M. II. Title.

HD5724 .B546 2002
331.12′0973—dc21   2001055711

Text design by Suzanne Nichols

RUSSELL SAGE FOUNDATION
112 East 64th Street, New York, New York 10021
10 9 8 7 6 5 4 3 2 1

For Daniel Blau Kahn and Lisa Blau Kahn

— Contents —

About the Authors

Francine D. Blau is the Frances Perkins Professor of Industrial and Labor Relations and Labor Economics at Cornell University. She is also a research associate of the National Bureau of Economic Research (Cambridge, Mass.) and a research fellow of CESifo (Munich).

Lawrence M. Kahn is Professor of Labor Economics and Collective Bargaining in the School of Industrial and Labor Relations at Cornell University. He is also research fellow of CESifo (Munich).

Acknowledgments

We thank Karin Garver, Lisa Kahraman, and Abhijay Prakash for excellent research assistance and two anonymous reviewers for many helpful comments and suggestions. Portions of this book were written while we were Visiting Scholars at the Russell Sage Foundation, to which we are grateful for research support. We would also like to thank the extremely helpful team at the Russell Sage Foundation who worked with us on this volume: Suzanne Nichols, director of publications; Emily Chang, production editor; and Joseph Brown, copy editor. Finally, we are deeply indebted to Eric Wanner for his support and encouragement.

—— Chapter 1 ——

Introduction: The Labor-Market Performance of the United States in an International Context

THE CONTRAST BETWEEN the labor-market performance of the United States and that of most other advanced economies over the 1980s and 1990s has been striking. In 1973, the unemployment rate standardized to a common OECD definition was 4.8 percent in the United States but 3.2 percent or below in Australia, Austria, Belgium, France, Japan, the Netherlands, Norway, Spain, Sweden, the United Kingdom, and West Germany. The unweighted average unemployment rate among these countries was 2.1 percent, an astonishingly low figure by today's standards.[1] American economic observers pondered the explanation for the persistently higher U.S. unemployment levels. This concern was well captured in the title of an influential paper about the U.S. experience that appeared at this time, "Why Is the Unemployment Rate So High at Full Employment?" (Hall 1970). High turnover rates among U.S. workers accompanied by spells of unemployment were seen as an important part of the story (Flanagan 1973).

Since the early 1970s, after two oil crises, vastly increased globalization, and rapid technological change, the unemployment position of the United States and the other Western countries has dramatically reversed. By 1999, the U.S. unemployment rate had fallen to 4.2 percent and was as low as 3.9 percent as of October 2000.[2] In contrast, beginning in the 1970s, unemployment rose sharply in virtually every other Western country. By 1999, it aver-

1

aged 8.7 percent in the European Union, such levels having prevailed for nearly twenty years (OECD 2000). Unemployment rates were particularly high in Finland (10.3 percent), France (11.3 percent), Italy (11.4 percent), and Spain (15.9 percent).

By the 1980s and 1990s, it was European observers who were searching for explanations for persistently high unemployment rates. Increasing labor-market flexibility—freeing up the forces of supply and demand to determine pay and employment and diminishing the role of union contracts or government regulations—was seen by some as the key to lowering European unemployment (OECD 1994b). Interestingly, this reasoning implies that the high worker mobility in the United States that had been a concern in the earlier period could now be viewed as one component of the more flexible U.S. labor-market package that, taken as a whole, was associated with lower unemployment rates. Others, however, questioned whether greater flexibility would, in fact, achieve lower unemployment and pointed instead to low levels of demand for labor as the culprit behind Europe's higher unemployment (Glyn and Salverda 2000).

There is, however, another side to this comparison. While the United States has fared well in recent years in creating jobs and maintaining low unemployment, its wage levels have deteriorated relative to those overseas, and wage inequality, always higher in the United States than in other advanced countries, has risen more sharply than it has elsewhere. In 1979 to 1981, median weekly earnings of male full-time workers in the United States were $609 (in 1998 U.S. dollars), while, across six major OECD countries for which comparable data are available (Australia, Austria, Canada, Sweden, the United Kingdom, and West Germany), men earned only $419.[3] By 1994 to 1998, U.S. men's earnings had fallen to $576 in real terms (a 5.5 percent decline), while men's earnings in the other countries rose to $514 (a 22.6 percent increase). Similar trends prevailed among women. However, in contrast to men, U.S. women experienced rising, rather than stagnating, real earnings, and women in the other countries did not gain on U.S. women as rapidly: women's wages rose from $381 in 1979 to 1981 to $439 in 1994 to 1998 in the United States (a 15.3 percent increase), compared to an increase from $292 to $384 in the other countries (a 31.6 percent rise).

At the same time as the real wages of the median worker in the United States deteriorated relative to those of the median worker in other Western nations, Americans at the bottom fared even worse, both absolutely and relatively. U.S. men at the 10th percentile saw a decline in their real wages of 16.3 percent between 1979 to 1981 and 1994 to 1998, while workers at the 10th percentile in the six OECD countries listed earlier saw an increase of 18.7 percent. Among women, real wages at the 10th percentile fell by 2.8 percent in the United States but increased by 28.2 percent in the other countries. In 1979 to 1981, workers at the 10th percentile in the United States outearned comparable workers in these other countries by 20.0 percent (men) to 27.7 percent (women), but, by the mid-1990s, their foreign counterparts outearned U.S. workers by 3.3 percent (women) to 18.3 percent (men).

Thus, while the U.S. economy may have been an impressive job-creation machine since the 1970s, real wages in the United States have not kept pace with those in other countries, and workers at the bottom have fared particularly poorly. If unemployment was a signature problem for much of Europe in the latter part of the twentieth century, low and declining real and relative wages for those at the bottom of the wage hierarchy were America's.[4]

FLEXIBILITY AND LABOR-MARKET INSTITUTIONS: THE UNIFIED THEORY

The U.S. labor market has long been much less subject to institutional intervention by unions or the government than have the labor markets of other Western countries, and some have pointed to these differences as key to understanding the differences in unemployment, wage levels, and wage inequality that we have just documented (see, for example, Siebert 1997). While some controversy surrounds the effort to link the institutional differences to differences in labor-market outcomes, the broad outlines of these differences are clear.

First, collective bargaining plays a much smaller role in determining workers' wages in the United States than it does elsewhere. In the 1990s, fewer than 20 percent of U.S. workers were covered by collective-bargaining agreements, while coverage averaged about 70 percent among other OECD countries (OECD 1997). In countries such as Australia, Austria, Belgium, Finland, France, Germany, Italy, the Netherlands, and Sweden, where collective-bargaining coverage is 80 percent or more, there is very nearly complete coverage of the workforce by union contracts. Moreover, whereas, in the United States, collective bargaining usually takes place at the single-firm level, collective bargaining in many of these other countries takes place at the industry or even the economy level. And legislated minimum-wage levels are also higher relative to average wages in these other countries than they are in the United States (OECD 1998b).

Second, unemployment-insurance (UI) benefits are much more generous in other countries than in the United States, and, while UI benefits usually run out after six months in the United States, unemployed workers can collect for much longer periods in other countries. In several countries, including Australia, Belgium, Germany, New Zealand, and Switzerland, individuals can collect UI benefits indefinitely. Other mandated benefits, including vacation and sick leave, disability leave, and family leave, also tend to be more generous in other countries than in the United States, and the payroll-tax rates used to pay for these benefits are correspondingly higher elsewhere as well (Nickell and Layard 1999).

Third, it is much more expensive and administratively cumbersome for firms to lay off or discharge workers in other countries than in the United States. And firms in other countries also face many more restrictions on the use of temporary workers (OECD 1999).

Finally, the government accounts for a much larger share of total employment in other OECD countries than in the United States. Moreover, while the public-sector share of employment has been falling steadily in the United States since the 1970s, the opposite is true in most other OECD countries (Gregory and Borland 1999, 3575).

As noted earlier, some have pointed to these major differences in the degree of intervention in the labor market as an important cause of the relatively high unemployment in other Western nations compared to that in the United States. However, one must remember that, in the 1960s and early 1970s, with largely the same differences in labor-market institutions between the United States and other Western nations, it was the United States that was the high-unemployment country. Thus, it cannot be true that interventionist institutions produce high unemployment all the time. However, consideration of the vast differences between the United States and other Western countries in wage-setting and other labor-market institutions has suggested a plausible interpretation of the relationship between these institutions and the unemployment disparities that have prevailed since the early 1970s. This view essentially posits an interaction between labor-market institutions and "shocks" to (strains on) the labor market.

Since the early 1970s, there have been a variety of shocks to which labor markets in all countries have been exposed, including the slowdown in productivity growth dating from the early 1970s, the oil-price increases of the 1970s and early 1980s, the fall in the relative demand for unskilled labor since 1980, and disinflation in the 1980s and 1990s (Layard, Nickell, and Jackman 1991; Freeman and Katz 1995; Blanchard and Wolfers 2000; Ball 1997, 1999). It has been hypothesized that the flexible U.S. labor market was able to accommodate these shocks by letting absolute and relative real-wage levels adjust, allowing its unemployment rate to stay low. In contrast, in most other OECD countries, labor-market institutions kept overall real wages rising and prevented unskilled workers' relative wages from falling as fast as they did in the less-restricted U.S. market (in some cases preventing any fall in low-skilled workers' relative pay), thus producing sharp increases in unemployment in these countries (Blanchard and Wolfers 2000; Freeman 1994).

This view has been termed the *unified theory* (Blank 1997), in recognition of the fact that the EU experience of rising unemployment, rising real wages, and comparatively stable relative-wage levels and the U.S. experience of falling unemployment, falling to steady real wages, and rapidly rising wage inequality are two sides of the same coin. The United States permitted real and relative wages to adjust, while, in other Western nations, employment took the brunt of the shocks. To illustrate the argument, consider the effect of productivity trends. From the 1960s to the 1990s, annual growth in total factor productivity in the OECD fell from 5 to

6 percent to 1 to 2 percent (Blanchard and Wolfers 2000). Total-factor-productivity growth is the growth in output per worker beyond that which can be explained by changes in the amounts of labor and capital used. It is, thus, a measure of technological progress. In the relatively flexible U.S. labor market, real wages were allowed to grow more slowly and even to decline, which eventually permitted unemployment to fall. In contrast, according to the unified theory, unions and other labor-market institutions kept real wages growing at their customary pace in other OECD nations, which led to higher unemployment.

We devote a considerable portion of this book to determining whether the weight of the evidence supports the unified theory. If the unified theory is true, it suggests that neither a policy of relative laissez-faire nor one of aggressive intervention in the labor market can produce both high employment and rising real wages in the face of the kind of economic forces that have been experienced over the last twenty to thirty years. We should also point out that, even if the unified theory is valid, differing views on the desirability of institutional interventions in the labor market are logically possible. On the one hand, as discussed in chapter 4, some institutions may enhance economic efficiency by solving problems of market failure in addition to raising wage levels or compressing the distribution of wages. In this case, even if institutions produce unemployment in some circumstances, it is possible that this cost is outweighed by the economic benefits of institutional intervention. On the other hand, as also mentioned in chapter 4, some institutions may have adverse economic effects other than any effect on unemployment. These possible negative effects include adverse incentives and a reduction in the degree to which prices are allowed to serve as a signal for efficiently allocating resources. In this instance, possible adverse employment effects of institutional intervention add to other negative economic effects of institutional intervention.

THE SCOPE OF THE STUDY

The purpose of this book is to evaluate alternative explanations for the divergence between the labor-market performance of the United States and that of the rest of the OECD. In the interest of manageability, we have placed certain limits on the types of institutions examined and the contexts in which those institutions are studied. We focus primarily on the effect of direct attempts to change market outcomes with respect to pay setting and firms' utilization of labor. These institutions and laws directly regulate what workers and firms are permitted to do in setting wages and allocating labor. In addition, there are a number of policies designed to ameliorate the outcomes produced by unrestricted markets that indirectly affect worker-firm interactions. Such policies may also have important effects on wages and employment. Thus, we consider several of them as well.

Examples of direct intervention in the wage-setting process include collective-bargaining agreements as well as policy interventions regulating wage determination. Government policies include rulings extending the terms of collective-bargaining contracts to workers not initially covered by those agreements, antidiscrimination policy as it relates to pay, minimum-wage laws, and the behavior of the government as an employer. In addition to regulating wages, governments in each of the countries that we examine have placed some limits on the right of firms to fire workers. For example, most European countries require severance pay and advanced notice in the event of layoffs. Antidiscrimination policy also affects firms' employment decisions, both directly and indirectly. Policies having a more indirect effect on labor utilization and wage determination include payroll taxes, UI, industrial subsidies, and active labor-market policies, including public-employment and training programs, and we review important evidence on these as well. However, we do not examine in detail every intervention that could conceivably affect wages or employment. So, for example, we do not discuss in detail the effect of international differences in income-tax systems, policies toward imports, occupational safety and health, or regulations governing firm entry or rate of return. This decision reflects considerations of space as well as a paucity of internationally comparable data on the effect of such policies.

Comparing outcomes across culturally similar countries provides a very attractive research design for evaluating the effect of institutions. For this reason, we limit the countries considered here primarily to the roughly twenty Western industrialized OECD member nations.

Not only does this limitation keep our review manageable, but it also permits us to utilize the similarity in education levels, technology, living standards, and cultures among these countries as de facto controls in examining the effects of institutions. It should be noted that we frequently use the term *European* in referring to institutional arrangements or outcomes that are highly characteristic of that region, although some OECD countries outside Europe, notably Australia and New Zealand, share the major features of this model.

While our focus on the OECD nations provides an attractive degree of comparability across countries along a number of important dimensions, significant noncomparabilities remain, some of which reflect labor-market institutions themselves. For example, it is likely that many people who would be classified as out of the labor force in the United States would be classified as long-term unemployed in Europe because they would be receiving long-term unemployment benefits there that are not available in the United States. Using standardized unemployment definitions does not completely solve this problem since comparably situated individuals may respond to the same questions differently in Europe than they would in the United States. The situation is further complicated by the fact that eligibility for long-duration benefits may be expected to drive up the true incidence of long-term unemployment in Europe compared to that in the United States, all else equal. While correctly classifying the long-term employed and other similar issues of data comparability is a matter of serious concern, we do not believe that such issues unduly affect our examination of the effect of institutions in this study. This is because the "differences-in-differences" approach employed by many, although certainly not all, of the studies that we consider nets out the effect of such factors, by comparing within-country changes over time rather than levels.

In addition, precisely because of the importance of institutions and cultural factors in influencing measured unemployment rates, even within countries, we tend to prefer studies that focus on employment-to-population ratios. With some exceptions, the results of studies using the latter concept are generally consistent with those focusing on the unemployment rate. Nonetheless, the way in which institutions and other factors affect labor-market concepts like unemployment or disability, as another example, would make for an interesting research question, one that we hope will receive greater attention now that international comparisons are becoming more prevalent.

THE PLAN OF THE BOOK AND OUR MAJOR FINDINGS

We begin in chapter 2 with an overview of economic performance across the OECD from the 1970s to the 1990s, followed in chapter 3 by an examination of international differences in labor-market institutions. Our review of the data on unemployment, employment, real-wage levels, wage inequality, and the gender pay gap in chapter 2 leads to the following conclusions about these patterns.

By the late 1990s, the United States had a considerably higher incidence of employment than did other Western nations across a number of dimensions:

- Unemployment was considerably lower in the United States. Not only had the U.S. aggregate-unemployment rate fallen to about half that of other advanced countries, but the incidence of long-term unemployment was also far lower in the United States than elsewhere.
- Employment-to-population ratios were higher in the United States. This was the case for both men and women, with especially large differences between the United States and other countries for women. Similarly, employment-to-population ratios within age groups were higher in the United States, and the differences between the United States and other countries were especially pronounced for the young and the elderly. Moreover, employment-to-population ratios of the young relative to those of prime age have deteriorated much less in the United States than elsewhere.
- A major exception to the pattern of more-favorable employment in the United States was that, within education groups, U.S. employment-to-population ratios were fairly similar to those in other Western countries. And, while unemployment rates were lower within education groups in the United States than in other

Western countries, the *differences* in unemployment rates between education groups were similar, and changes in relative-unemployment rates by education group from the 1970s to the 1990s were about the same in the United States as elsewhere.

- Work hours tended to be longer in the United States. OECD data suggest that annual work hours per employed person were higher in the United States than in other countries, and the U.S. advantage rose considerably between 1979 and 1999. Moreover, while, in all countries, women were more likely than men to work part-time, this gap in the incidence of part-time work was much smaller in the United States than elsewhere.
- The incidence of temporary employment tends to be lower in the United States than in many of the other OECD countries. This means that a higher share of employed workers in the United States hold "regular" jobs.

Our review of the wage data suggests that wage inequality tends to be significantly higher in the United States than in other Western nations, and this disparity has increased in recent years. Real wage growth has also lagged in the United States compared to other OECD countries:

- Between 1979 and 1998, the real wages of both men and women rose substantially in other Western nations. In the United States, in contrast, men's real wages declined, and, while women's rose, that increase was smaller than the increase in women's real wages in other OECD countries.
- Although, on average, labor productivity grew more rapidly in other OECD countries than in the United States from the late 1970s through the late 1990s, this growth was not sufficient to offset the effect of larger real-wage increases on unit labor costs in those other countries. As a result, from 1977 to 1999, unit labor costs rose more rapidly in most other Western nations than in the United States.
- Wage inequality has long been higher in the United States than elsewhere and rose more sharply for both men and women over the 1980s and 1990s in the United States than elsewhere. On average, wage inequality rose only modestly in other Western countries during this period. The real wages of U.S. men and

women at the bottom of the wage distribution fell relative to those of their foreign counterparts.

• In 1979, the gender pay gap was substantially higher in the United States than the average gender pay gap in the other OECD countries, but it decreased more rapidly in the United States than elsewhere over the 1980s and 1990s. By 1998, the U.S. gender pay gap was about the same as the average for the other OECD countries. The more rapidly declining gender pay gap in the United States is an important exception to the pattern of more rapidly rising wage differentials in the United States than elsewhere over this period. Nonetheless, the U.S. gender pay gap remained higher than that in half the other countries, often considerably so.

Overall, these findings suggest a pattern of relatively flexible wages and better employment outcomes in the United States. Some of our results for subgroups are consistent with the unified theory, for example, the better employment outcomes for U.S. youths, who are less affected by wage floors than are younger workers in other countries. And the larger incidence of temporary employment in other OECD countries may reflect an effort to introduce some flexibility into their more rigid systems. But other results are less consistent. For example, relative employment by education group behaved similarly in the United States and other OECD countries, even though wage differentials by education increased more in the United States. Of course, more-definitive research results can be obtained only when we use micro data that allow us to control for differences in the composition of workers in these subgroups, as we do in later chapters.

Our comparison in chapter 3 of the labor-market institutions in the United States and those in other OECD countries documents the following important differences:

• Workers in the United States are considerably less likely to have their wages determined by collective bargaining than are workers elsewhere in the OECD. And this disparity increased over the 1980s and 1990s. Not only do union members constitute a much smaller fraction of workers in the United States (16 percent) than in other countries (41 percent on average), but contrasts between the United States and other countries in the extent of collective-bargaining coverage are even more extreme: about half of nonunion members in other countries, but only about 2 percent of such workers in the United States, are covered by collective-bargaining agreements. Moreover, collective bargaining is much more highly coordinated and centralized in other Western countries than in the United States, and, although centralization and coordination have been falling both in the United States and in many other countries, this disparity remains.

- Statutory minimum wages pose less of a constraint on the U.S. labor market than is the case elsewhere.
- While in 1975 a larger fraction of workers were employed by the government in the United States than in the other OECD countries, by 1995 the reverse held. This reflects a declining incidence of public employment in the United States compared to a rising incidence elsewhere.
- Employment-protection regulations are much more stringent in other OECD countries than in the United States, although many of these other countries endeavored to loosen such restrictions during the 1980s and 1990s.
- Government expenditures on active labor-market policy per unemployed worker are much lower in relation to GDP per worker in the United States than in all the other OECD countries.
- UI-benefit systems are much less generous in the United States than elsewhere, with respect to both the level and the duration of benefits. Further, UI systems in several other countries became more generous in the 1970s and 1980s, while the UI system in the United States remained fairly stable.
- Pension systems generally provide more incentives for early retirement in other countries than in the United States.
- Vacation and parental-leave entitlements are much less generous in the United States than elsewhere, as are benefit entitlements for sickness and disability.
- Payroll-tax rates and the level of industrial subsidies for failing firms are considerably lower in the United States than elsewhere.

Our review of these institutional differences strongly suggests that the U.S. labor market is, indeed, much closer to a laissez-faire model than are labor markets elsewhere in the OECD. Of course, whether these institutional differences actually cause the major differences in labor-market outcomes documented in chapter 2 is an empirical question. The mere juxtaposition of data on outcomes and institutions is not sufficient to provide fully convincing evidence on the importance of institutions. To start with, we must be clear on the anticipated effect of institutional intervention on these outcomes from a theoretical perspective. We must also probe empirical evidence in greater detail, making full use of micro data on individuals, which allow us to adjust for international differences in the composition of the population that may also affect employment and wage outcomes, as well as of sophisticated statistical analyses of these data. This is important because there are other factors besides institutions—such as macroeconomic shocks—that can influence wage and employment outcomes, and it is essential to account for their effects before reaching conclusions about the effect of institutions. Moreover, the employment problems created by these other factors may then cause a country to alter the character of its institutions. For example, high unemployment may lead some countries to increase the generosity of their UI systems, as appears to have occurred in Switzerland (Sheldon 1997). In this case, the greater generosity of the UI system is a response to a country's employment problems rather than the cause of them, although it may, in turn, contribute to the persistence of these problems.

In chapter 4, we present the economic analyses that provide a theoretical framework for studying the effect of institutions on labor markets. We first discuss the role that institutions can play in creating desirable or undesirable wage, productivity, and employment outcomes. Under some circumstances, institutional intervention may correct market failures and, thus, produce superior economic outcomes. And, while there are circumstances under which institutional interventions will contribute to overall unemployment or exacerbate relative-employment problems for particular groups, economic theory does not unambiguously predict that wage interventions, employment protection, mandated benefits, or high taxes will produce such employment problems. Thus, empirical evidence is especially crucial in determining what the effect of these labor-market institutions has actually been. We then address the difficult issues of research design that can potentially allow us to separate out cause and effect and to account for other influences on labor-market outcomes besides institutional interventions. With this framework in hand, we turn in subsequent chapters to an evaluation of the available evidence on the effect of institutions on labor-market performance.

In chapter 5, we focus on the macroeconomic evidence on the effect of labor-market institutions on unemployment, paying particular attention to the remarkable reversal in the position of the United States from a high-unemployment to a low-unemployment country since the early 1970s.

Early research on the effect of centralized wage-setting institutions on unemployment reached somewhat mixed conclusions. Some early studies found an inverted U-shaped relationship between centralization and unemployment for the 1970s and 1980s: low unemployment was observed for countries with very decentralized and very centralized wage-setting institutions, with high unemployment in countries with moderate degrees of centralization. This was believed to be due to opposing effects of centralization on the aggressiveness of unions in pushing for higher wages. On the one hand, larger units have more bargaining power since there is less room for competition from other workers in the labor market. On the other hand, unions in larger units are more likely to take into account the effect of their bargains on other workers since the price and tax effects of the union's pay policies are likely to be felt by union members themselves. Thus, decentralized units are expected to result in wage restraint since the union has little power, but highly centralized units are also expected to result in wage restraint, on net. In contrast, other researchers examining these issues found a monotonic negative relation between the centralization of wage setting and unemployment. However, all these conclusions were found to be fragile with respect to the classification of countries according to the degree to which wage setting is centralized and to the time period examined (Flanagan 1999). Moreover, this research did not, by and large, control for other influences, both institutional and macroeconomic, on a country's unemployment rate.

More recent work has advanced our understanding of the causes of international differences in unemployment. First, Stephen Nickell and Richard Layard (Nickell 1997, 1998; Nickell and

Layard 1999) have examined the determinants of average unemployment in the 1980s and 1990s. They find a strong association between labor-market institutions such as collective bargaining, decentralized wage setting, generous UI, high labor taxes, and the like, and high unemployment. Our calculations based on their estimates imply that lower U.S. unemployment is explained by the lower labor taxes, less-generous UI system, and low level of unionization in the United States, with decentralized union wage setting in the United States having a somewhat offsetting effect.

Second, Olivier Blanchard and Justin Wolfers (2000) studied unemployment over the period 1960 to 1996 and found evidence consistent with the idea that macroeconomic shocks interact with labor-market institutions to affect unemployment. In a recent paper coauthored with Giuseppe Bertola (Bertola, Blau, and Kahn 2002), we estimated a model drawing on Blanchard and Wolfers's work in order to account for the reversal between 1970 to 1975 and 1995 to 1996 in the U.S. unemployment position, compared to that of other Western countries. We found that macroeconomic shocks, demographic trends in which the youth-population share fell more quickly in the United States than elsewhere, and institutional changes such as a more slowly rising UI replacement ratio since 1970 in the United States did contribute to the observed decline in the U.S. unemployment rate relative to that in other Western nations. And, while these macroeconomic, demographic, and institutional shocks could by themselves account for only a modest portion (30 percent) of this fall, the model accounted for fully 63 percent of the decrease in the U.S. relative unemployment rate when we allowed for interactions between macroeconomic and demographic shocks and institutions. These shocks were found to have a much larger effect in raising unemployment in other countries than in the United States. This is consistent with a large role for the more flexible labor-market institutions in the United States, which we believe permitted real wages rather than employment to bear the burden of adjustment.

While the findings reported in chapter 5 are remarkably consistent with the unified theory, the concerns about research design that we discussed earlier are applicable to these studies. For example, many of the explanatory variables themselves can be affected by unemployment: higher unemployment may lead to changes in monetary policy and might affect productivity growth through changes in workforce composition or incentives to innovate. Moreover, the generosity of UI benefits and even the decisions of individual workers to become union members may be affected by the extent of unemployment. These considerations suggest that the regressions discussed in chapter 5 may suffer from endogeneity biases and that, therefore, so may our estimates of the importance of shocks and institutions in explaining U.S. unemployment performance.

In addition to these potential problems of endogeneity, the macroeconomic research designs discussed in chapter 5 do not directly test the mechanisms that are, in principle, behind the unified theory. First, the theory holds that some labor-market institutions affect absolute and relative wages and keep them rigid in the face of economic forces that would otherwise change absolute and relative pay levels. Second, the unified theory posits that these rigid wages lead to unemployment as firms move along their labor-demand curves. There is nothing in the macroeconomic evidence examined in chapter 5 that demonstrates these links in the causal chain directly, even if the data do provide some plausible evidence consistent with the unified theory. In chapters 6 and 7, therefore, we examine microeconomic evidence that sheds light on the specific mechanisms that macroeconomic observers believe underlie the effect on aggregate unemployment.

We begin chapter 6 by asking whether the higher level of U.S. wage inequality is, indeed, caused by higher labor-market prices—that is, higher returns to skills and higher wage differentials associated with more-favorable locations (that is, industries and occupations) in the labor market—as the U.S. labor market's noninterventionist institutions would suggest. The only way in which to answer this question convincingly is to use micro data that allow us to account for population heterogeneity. We find that, although the United States does have a more diverse population with respect to educational attainment and cognitive skills, these differences explain only a portion of the higher wage inequality in the United States. We infer that the United States does, indeed, have higher labor-market prices than other countries do. These higher prices of skill could be due in part to the greater abundance of relatively less skilled workers in the United States. However, we present extensive evidence that collective bargaining and minimum-wage laws lead to wage compression and thus also help explain the higher level of wage inequality in the United States. Collective bargaining has stronger effects on the overall labor market than minimum wages do. Thus, while market-oriented factors (that is, population heterogeneity and the relative supply of less-skilled workers) are important, there is still a strong, independent effect of wage-setting institutions on the wage structure as well.

Our examination of the effect of institutions on employment yielded less clear-cut results than did our examination of wage structure. In many studies, union- or minimum-wage-induced wage compression was seen to lower the relative employment of the less skilled. In other studies, such effects were not evident. Where negative relative-employment effects of unions are found, there is some evidence that these effects are concentrated on the young. Moreover, in chapter 2, we show that youths had lower relative employment in 1999 and more adverse changes in their relative employment over the period 1979 to 1999 in the European Union than in the United States. Increasingly, in the high-unemployment European economy of the 1980s and 1990s, the young were outside the protected labor markets that provide high wages and benefit levels. Integrating youths into work is a major challenge facing these countries in the coming years (Blanchflower and Freeman 2000). Conversely, wage inequality has grown in the United States over the 1980s and the 1990s both absolutely and relatively and is higher there than anyplace else in the industrialized world. Young workers have been particularly adversely affected by these trends. Raising the living standards of the less skilled in the United States, without causing major damage to the job-generation process, is one of our major challenges.

Chapter 7 continues our examination of the labor-market effects of institutions by examining their effects on the gender pay gap. Until the 1990s, the United States had a higher gender pay gap than did most other Western countries. But, throughout the 1980s and 1990s, the qualifications of women relative to those of men appeared to be at least as favorable, and generally more favorable, in the United States as they were elsewhere. Specifically, women in the United States have higher labor-force-participation rates, are more likely to work full-time, and are segregated to a lesser degree into what are traditionally considered female occupations than are women in most other Western countries. Yet, somewhat paradoxically, the gender pay gap has, until recently, been higher in the United States than elsewhere. And, even by the mid-1990s, the U.S. gender pay gap was only about the same as the average of other Western countries.

In chapter 7, we present a variety of evidence indicating that the major factor raising the gender pay gap in the United States relative to that in other countries (or preventing the United States from having a lower gender pay gap) is the far higher degree of overall wage inequality there. In many other advanced countries, where wages are more compressed, women's wages are swept up by centrally negotiated wage floors. We also examine research on some specific interventions on behalf of women, including anti-discrimination laws and mandated changes designed to raise the pay in women's occupations to the level of that in men's occupations having a similar value to the employer ("comparable worth"). We find that, while these interventions can lower the gender pay gap, in several instances (but not all) they also reduced the growth of women's employment.

Finally, in chapter 8, we discuss the policy implications of our study and suggest some future research directions. In the area of policy, we are concerned with finding policies that can lead to sustained high employment levels while at the same time improving the living standards of the less skilled. As the unified theory suggests, there are no easy answers. Many of the policies that have been pursued by other Western nations do raise the wages of people who have jobs, but quite possibly at the cost of employment problems for affected groups as well as higher aggregate unemployment rates. Contrasted with these are policies such as the earned-income tax credit in the United States that can raise living standards among those at the bottom of the income distribution without threatening employment levels. But these programs can be very expensive. Society will pay a price whatever the path chosen, but we can have some influence on what that price will be.

—— Chapter 2 ——

Labor-Market Performance: How Does Labor-Market Performance in the United States Compare to That in Other Countries?

L ABOR-MARKET PERFORMANCE in the United States diverged sharply from that in other advanced industrialized countries in the 1980s and 1990s. In this chapter, we chart this divergent experience in detail using data gathered by the OECD and the U.S. Bureau of Labor Statistics (BLS), data that are, as far as possible, comparable across countries. We first examine indicators of employment, such as the unemployment rate, employment-to-population ratios, and work hours among the employed. Next, we compare real wages, labor productivity, labor costs, wage inequality, and the gender pay gap across countries and over time.

While there is some diversity in outcomes across countries, we conclude that the aggregate data reported in this chapter are broadly consistent with the unified theory discussed in chapter 1. In particular, overall wage levels and relative wages among groups appear to have been more flexible in the United States than in other OECD countries since the 1970s. This is suggested by the slower real-wage growth relative to productivity and greater increases in wage inequality that the United States has experienced. At the same time, the U.S. unemployment rate has declined, while the unemployment rate has risen sharply, on average, in other OECD countries. A rosier employment picture prevails in America for virtually all subgroups and most especially for youths.[1] This outcome would be predicted to the extent that collective bargaining and other institutions in the other OECD countries resulted in faster real-wage growth and smaller increases in wage inequality in the face of the macro shocks of the 1980s and 1990s than would have been dictated by market forces. However, the "flexibility" of real and relative wages in the United States has meant falling real-wage levels overall, with especially large negative effects on workers at the bottom of the wage distribution. While much of the evidence presented in this chapter is consistent with the unified theory, sharper tests can be implemented only when micro data are utilized. We carefully examine such research in later chapters.

EMPLOYMENT PERFORMANCE

In this section, we examine evidence on a variety of indicators of employment performance. These include unemployment rates, employment-to-population ratios, unemployment duration, work hours, and the incidence of temporary employment. As we will see, there are dramatic differences between the United States and other countries along these dimensions.

Unemployment Rates and Employment-to-Population Ratios

Evidence on the unemployment rate over the period 1973 to 1998 for the United States and eighteen other industrialized countries is provided in table 2.1. Each country's unemployment rate has been standardized to the U.S. definition by the OECD, an essential adjustment since different countries define unemployment in different ways.

As may be seen in the table, in 1973, around the time of the first oil crisis, the U.S. unemployment rate of 4.8 percent was nearly double the average for the other countries. By 1984, after two oil crises, unemployment had moved up virtually everywhere, but the increases were far larger in the other countries. The non-

TABLE 2.1 **Standardized Unemployment Rates in Selected OECD Countries, 1973, 1984, 1995, and 1999**

	1973	1984	1995	1999
Australia	2.3	8.9	8.5	7.2
Belgium	2.8	12.1	9.9	9.0
Canada	5.5	7.8	9.4	7.6
Finland	2.3	5.2	15.3	10.3
France	2.6	9.7	11.7	11.3
Germany[a]	.8	7.1	8.2	8.7
Italy	6.2	9.9	11.6	11.4
Japan	1.3	2.7	3.2	4.7
Netherlands	2.2	11.8	6.9	3.3
Norway	1.5	3.1	5.0	3.3
Spain	2.5	20.1	22.9	15.9
Sweden	2.5	3.1	8.8	7.2
United Kingdom	3.2	11.7	8.7	6.1
Non-U.S. average (unweighted)	2.7	8.7	10.0	8.2
European Union	. . .	. . .	10.7	9.2
United States	4.8	7.4	5.6	4.2

Sources: OECD (1983, 23); OECD (1989, 19); OECD (2000, 202). Data in table 2.1 © OECD; for full citation see references.
[a]Prior to 1991, data are for West Germany only.

U.S. average rose to 8.7 percent, over a percentage point higher than the U.S. rate of 7.4 percent. Since then, unemployment has come down dramatically in the United States while remaining at very high levels in much of the OECD. By 1999, the U.S. rate was 4.2 percent (and had fallen to 3.9 percent by September 2000),[2] while it averaged 8.2 percent elsewhere. The reversal of the relative position of the United States from the 1970s to the 1990s has been dramatic indeed.

While the more favorable unemployment performance of the United States since the mid-1970s could be taken as evidence in favor of the laissez-faire labor-market institutions that prevail in the United States, a closer look at the data presented in table 2.1 shows that not all the other OECD countries had the same unemployment experience during this time. On the one hand, especially large increases in unemployment rates occurred in a number of European countries by the mid-1980s, including Belgium, Finland, France, the Netherlands, Spain, and the United Kingdom, as well as in Australia. On the other hand, there were more modest increases during that time in a number of other European nations, such as Norway and Sweden, as well as in Japan. Moreover, the unemployment rate fell dramatically by the mid- to late 1990s in some nations, including Finland, the Netherlands, Spain (from a very high level of 23 percent to 16 percent), and the United Kingdom. Any study of the effect of institutions on unemployment performance must be able to explain this diversity of outcomes across the OECD in addition to the remarkable change in the relative position of the United States.

While unemployment is one measure of the degree to which the economy provides jobs for those willing to work, it does not count people who are not currently looking for work but would be in the labor market if jobs were available, the so-called discouraged workers. If each country had the same incidence of discouraged workers, then comparing unemployment rates would be sufficient for the purposes of measuring the extent of joblessness. However, evidence consistently shows that the labor force decreases in size or grows more slowly when the unemployment rate rises (Ehrenberg and Smith 2000).[3] This implies that the incidence of discouraged workers increases when unemployment is high and decreases when unemployment is low. Comparing unemployment rates may, thus, give an incomplete picture of the extent of international differences in joblessness. Such differences are likely to be even larger than the unemployment-rate differences in table 2.1 suggest.

Table 2.2 provides some evidence on this question by showing data on employment-to-population ratios, labor-force-participation rates, and unemployment rates by gender as of 1999. The numbers are consistent with our discussion of the effect of unemployment on labor-force participation. Not only are the unemployment rates of both men and women lower in the United States than they are on average in the other OECD countries, but the labor-force-participation rates of both are higher. For example, men's labor-force-participation rate is 84.0 percent in the United States, compared to 78.4 percent in the European Union, while the women's rate is 70.7 percent in the United States, compared to 59.5 percent in Europe. Of course, there may be other reasons for higher labor-force-participation rates in the United States besides the greater availability of jobs. Particularly in the case of women, cultural factors are likely to play a role. But, when combined with lower U.S. unemployment rates for both men and women, in an

TABLE 2.2 **Employment to Population (E/P) Ratios, Labor-Force-Participation (LFP) Rates, and Unemployment Rates by Gender for Persons Aged Fifteen to Sixty-Four Years, 1999**

	Men			Women		
	E/P Ratio	LFP Rate	Unemployment Rate	E/P Ratio	LFP Rate	Unemployment Rate
Australia	76.5	82.7	7.5	59.9	64.5	7.2
Austria	76.7	80.5	4.7	59.7	62.7	4.8
Belgium	67.5	73.0	7.5	50.2	56.0	10.3
Canada	75.5	82.0	7.9	64.7	69.8	7.3
Denmark	81.2	85.0	4.5	71.6	76.1	5.9
Finland	68.4	75.9	9.8	63.5	71.2	10.8
France	66.8	74.4	10.3	52.9	61.3	13.7
Germany	73.1	79.7	8.3	56.5	62.3	9.3
Greece[a]	71.6	77.1	7.2	40.3	48.5	16.8
Iceland[b]	88.2	89.4	1.4	80.2	82.3	2.5
Ireland	73.5	78.3	6.1	51.3	54.3	5.5
Italy	67.1	73.7	9.0	38.1	45.6	16.4
Japan	81.0	85.3	5.0	56.7	59.5	4.7
Luxembourg	74.4	75.7	1.7	48.5	50.2	3.3
Netherlands	80.3	82.6	2.7	61.3	64.4	4.9
New Zealand	77.3	83.2	7.1	63.0	67.4	6.6
Norway[b]	82.1	85.0	3.4	73.8	76.1	3.0
Portugal	75.5	78.7	4.0	59.4	62.8	5.3
Spain[b]	69.6	78.3	11.1	38.3	49.9	23.2
Sweden[b]	74.8	80.9	7.5	70.9	76.0	6.7
Switzerland	87.2	89.6	2.7	71.8	74.5	3.6
United Kingdom[b]	78.4	84.1	6.8	64.9	68.4	5.1
Non-U.S. average (unweighted)	75.8	80.7	6.2	59.0	63.8	8.0
European Union	72.0	78.4	8.2	53.1	59.5	10.9
United States[b]	80.5	84.0	4.1	67.6	70.7	4.4

Source: OECD (2000, table B, 204–5). Data in table 2.2 © OECD; for full citation see references.
[a]Refers to 1998.
[b]Refers to ages sixteen to sixty-four.

accounting sense the higher U.S. labor-force-participation rates imply even larger differences in the employment-to-population ratios.

In the United States, 80.5 percent of men and 67.6 percent of women in the population have jobs, compared to only 72.0 percent of men and 53.1 percent of women in the European Union. Employment is, thus, substantially more prevalent in the United States than elsewhere, and focusing on unemployment rates leads one to understate these differences. Moreover, the differences are especially large for women, although we again note that international differences in participation rates may well reflect cultural factors as well as economic conditions. Of course, our earlier comments about the diversity of experience across countries apply here as well since individual countries such as Denmark, Iceland, Norway, and Switzerland have employment and labor-force-participation rates that are as high as or higher than the U.S. rates. However, there can be no doubt that, on average, joblessness is more prevalent outside the United States.

While unemployment is a serious problem in any economy, it may have different consequences for individuals' economic well-being depending on whether the unemployed are typically without work for only a short time or unemployment spells are typically long lasting. A simple accounting identity that holds in a steady state serves to highlight this issue:

$$\text{unemployment rate} = \text{frequency} \times \text{duration}, \qquad (2.1)$$

where the unemployment rate is the fraction of the labor force that is unemployed at a given point in time, frequency is the fraction of the labor force that becomes newly unemployed over a given time period (say, per week), and duration is the average number of weeks that an unemployed person remains unemployed in each spell.

Some simple examples serve to illustrate the relationship between unemployment, on the one hand, and frequency and duration, on the other. Suppose that 1 percent of the labor force becomes newly unemployed each week and that each unemployed person spends ten weeks unemployed; then, on any given survey date, 10 percent of the labor force will be unemployed. Alternatively, 10 percent of the labor force may become unemployed each week but spend only one week apiece unemployed, leading to the same 10 percent unemployment rate. In the first case, unemployment is concentrated among a few people and lasts a relatively long time, while, in the second case, unemployment is a more common occurrence but lasts for a relatively short time.

It is commonly believed that long-term unemployment potentially has more severe consequences for economic welfare and for the operation of labor markets than does short-term unemployment. Long-term unemployment may mean a more permanent disruption of family income, depending on the availability of un-employment-insurance (UI) benefits. And being without a job for a long time may be associated with deteriorating labor-market skills and, thus, lead to more long-term problems for the indi-vidual than do short spells of unemployment (see Machin and Manning 1999). If people are risk averse, then a short-duration, high-incidence combination may be preferable to a long-duration, low-incidence combination. Moreover, for a given unemployment rate, shorter duration is associated with a more equal distribution of income loss across workers than is longer duration. On the other hand, for a given unemployment rate, the problems of un-employment are concentrated among fewer people when average unemployment duration is longer. This outcome may be prefer-able from the government's point of view to the extent that it is easier to provide targeted assistance to the unemployed under this scenario than to a large number of unemployed workers in the high-incidence, short-duration situation.

Table 2.3 provides some evidence on the duration of unem-ployment. The differences between the United States and other countries are even more dramatic than are the contrasts in unem-ployment rates. In the United States, long-term unemployment is very rare, affecting only 12 to 13 percent of the unemployed using a six-month definition and 6 to 7 percent using a more stringent twelve-month definition. In contrast, in the European Union, long-term unemployment is the rule, with corresponding figures of 62 to 66 percent (six months or more) and 46 to 49 percent (twelve months or more). In Belgium, Italy, and the Netherlands, over 70 percent of the unemployed are out of work for at least six months! While table 2.2 showed that a few countries have lower unem-ployment rates for men or women than does the United States (for example, Iceland, Luxembourg, the Netherlands, Norway, Portu-gal, and Switzerland), table 2.3 indicates that long-term unemploy-ment is everywhere at least as prevalent as it is in the United States and, in most cases, much more prevalent. This observation includes these low-unemployment countries. Considering the du-ration of unemployment implies even less favorable performance in other countries on average than does looking at unemployment rates alone: not only is unemployment less prevalent in the United

TABLE 2.3 **Long-Term Unemployment as a Percentage of Total Unemployment, 1999 (Ages Fifteen and Over)**

	Men		Women	
	Six Months +	Twelve Months +	Six Months +	Twelve Months +
Australia	50.9	31.8	44.9	25.8
Austria	40.2	28.1	56.9	36.1
Belgium	73.2	60.1	73.8	60.9
Canada	23.3	12.8	18.9	10.2
Denmark	38.6	20.9	38.5	20.1
Finland	49.2	33.1	43.7	26.2
France	53.7	39.0	57.3	41.6
Germany	65.3	49.9	69.4	54.0
Greece	68.9	44.7	78.6	61.5
Iceland	13.9	6.6	24.5	15.2
Ireland	77.9	63.3	66.6	46.9
Italy	76.6	62.1	77.7	60.7
Japan	49.5	27.4	36.9	14.8
Luxembourg	61.6	38.6	47.5	27.2
Netherlands	75.1	47.7	84.9	40.4
New Zealand	42.5	23.0	34.3	17.9
Norway	17.1	7.3	15.6	6.3
Portugal	63.5	39.5	64.2	42.9
Spain	62.2	45.4	72.0	55.5
Sweden	52.2	36.3	45.6	30.1
Switzerland	59.3	40.7	62.7	39.0
United Kingdom	50.5	34.8	37.9	21.6
Non-U.S. average (unweighted)	53.0	36.1	52.4	34.3
European Union	61.8	46.2	65.6	48.9
United States	13.0	7.4	11.6	6.2

Source: OECD (2000, table G, 220). Data in table 2.3 © OECD; for full citation see references.
Note: Ages fifteen and over, except for Iceland, Spain, the United Kingdom, and the United States (sixteen and over), Finland (fifteen to sixty-four), Norway (sixteen to seventy-four), and Sweden (sixteen to sixty-four). 1998 data are used for Greece and Sweden, and 1997 data are used for Ireland.

States, but it is also of much shorter duration. As we discuss in chapter 6, these differences in long-term unemployment are also of interest because they serve as important evidence on the effect of labor-market interventions such as UI benefits as well as systems of job protection.

So far, we have considered the incidence of employment and unemployment either for all workers or for all men and women in the aggregate. This information is clearly of prime importance in evaluating labor-market performance. However, examining the relative employment of particular subgroups can provide further evidence on performance as well as shedding light on the effect of institutions on labor-market outcomes.

When evaluating labor-market performance, it is crucial to understand how disadvantaged groups, such as the less educated, fare. Moreover, to the extent that some of the adverse social consequences of joblessness, such as crime, are concentrated among particular subgroups, such as young, out-of-work men (Freeman 1999), knowledge about the employment experience of particular groups can be quite important.

Disaggregated data on employment outcomes are useful in testing theories about the effect of institutions because many economic theories about the effect of institutions have sharper predictions for relative-employment outcomes than for overall employment. For example, systems of employment protection are likely to reduce layoffs as well as new hiring. While the effect on overall employment is unclear, we do expect such systems to make it especially hard for new entrants, such as youths or women, to find work (Bertola 1999). And government- or union-imposed wage floors are expected to have their largest effects on the employment of the young and less skilled, for whom they are binding (Brown 1999; Blau and Kahn 1999; Kahn 2000). Finally, even if labor-market institutions do not affect relative wages (for example, unions might raise everyone's wages by the same percentage), to the extent that there are queues of workers looking for jobs, employment problems may be disproportionately experienced by the low skilled. To see this, suppose, for example, that an economy experiences a reduction in the overall demand for labor. The least skilled will be at the end of the queue for the scarce jobs (Howell 1999). Of course, in the likely event that labor-market institutions disproportionately raise the pay of the less skilled, labor-demand effects on them will be even larger.[4]

We first provide some comparative evidence on relative-employment outcomes by age and then by education. Unemployment rates and employment-to-population ratios by age in 1999 are presented in table 2.4 for men and in table 2.5 for women. A general pattern revealed in these tables is that, among both men and women, unemployment rates are higher and employment-to-population rates lower for the young (those aged fifteen to twenty-four) than for those of prime working age (those aged twenty-five to fifty-four). This difference is expected given that youths are more likely to be in school, searching for their first jobs while unemployed, or affected by wage floors such as minimum wages. Moreover, while unemployment rates among older individuals (those aged fifty-five to sixty-four) are comparable to those of the prime aged for men and slightly less than those of the prime aged for women, the employment-to-population ratio among the elderly is lower than is that among the prime aged in every case, usually substantially so. Again, such employment differences are expected given individual preferences as well as retirement incentives offered to individuals in this age range. However, despite the expected direction of the differences in employment and unemployment experience by age, the extent of such differences can yield suggestive evidence about the effect of labor-market institutions.

The tables indicate that, among both men and women, a larger share of youths are employed in the United States than in other OECD countries. For example, in the European Union, on average, 43.4 percent of young men were employed, compared to 61.0 percent in the United States; the corresponding figures for women were 35.5 percent for the European Union and 57.0 percent for the United States. Moreover, the youth–prime-age differential in employment-to-population ratios is considerably larger in the European Union than in the United States whether we measure this gap in absolute or in relative terms. So, for example, in the European Union, the employment-to-population ratio of youths was 42.9 percentage points lower than that of the prime aged for men and 29.2 percentage points lower for women, compared to gaps of 28.0 percentage points for men and 17.1 percentage points for women in the United States. Similarly, young men's employment-to-population ratio was only 50 percent of that of the prime aged in the European Union, compared to 69 percent in the United States, and the comparable figures for women were 55 percent in the European Union and 77 percent in the United States.

While a low incidence of youth employment in Europe might not be considered an unfavorable outcome if it means that non-employed youths are in school, high youth unemployment may unambiguously be viewed as an adverse labor-market indicator. As may be seen in the tables, data on youth-unemployment rates show greater relative joblessness among youths in the rest of the OECD than in the United States, although the disparities are smaller than are those for the employment data. The youth-unemployment rate averaged 16.1 percent for men and 18.6 percent for women in the European Union, compared to 10.3 percent for men and 9.5 percent for women in the United States, with Belgium, France, Greece, Italy, and Spain all having unemployment rates in excess of 20 percent for both young men and young women. There is also a greater absolute gap between the unemployment rates of youths and those of the prime aged in the European Union than in the United States for both sexes: 9.2 percentage points in the European Union versus 7.3 percentage points in the United States for men and 8.8 percentage points in the European Union versus 6.1 percentage points in the United States for women. On the other hand, taking ratios of unemployment rates shows a higher youth–prime-age ratio among both men and women in the United States than in the European Union: for men, the ratios are 3.43 in the United States and 2.33 in the European Union, while, for women, they are 2.79 in the United States and 1.90 in the European Union.

We would argue that, for the purposes of measuring the demand for labor, it is employment that is relevant. From this perspective, the appropriate measure is either the share of the labor force that is employed (that is, 100 − the unemployment rate) or the employment-to-population ratio; the latter is the preferred measure if one is concerned about discouraged workers. As the following example suggests, unemployment-rate ratios may be misleading as an indicator of relative labor demand, although the absolute difference in unemployment rates may be more instructive. Suppose that, in one country (C), unemployment rates for prime-age and young workers are 4 and 8 percent, respectively, while, in another country (D), they are 10 and 20 percent. Employment rates are 96 and 92 percent for prime-age and young workers, respectively, in C, and 90 and 80 percent in D. A compar-

(Text continues on p. 34.)

TABLE 2.4 Unemployment Rates and Employment-to-Population (E/P) Ratios by Age for Men, 1999

	Unemployment Rate			E/P Ratio		
	Fifteen to Twenty-Four	Twenty-Five to Fifty-Four	Fifty-Five to Sixty-Four	Fifteen to Twenty-Four	Twenty-Five to Fifty-Four	Fifty-Five to Sixty-Four
Australia	14.5	5.7	6.5	62.0	85.3	57.0
Austria	5.5	4.5	5.3	59.2	89.6	41.6
Belgium	22.7	6.1	4.5	27.5	86.2	35.1
Canada	15.3	6.5	6.3	55.4	85.1	56.9
Denmark	9.5	3.7	3.2	69.5	89.3	59.9
Finland	21.0	7.9	10.9	39.3	83.4	40.1
France	24.2	9.0	8.7	24.3	85.7	38.9
Germany	9.1	7.3	12.8	50.7	87.0	48.0
Greece	21.4	5.7	2.9	34.2	89.0	55.8
Iceland[a,b]	4.4	.7	.9	63.3	96.4	93.2
Ireland	8.6	5.7	4.2	49.7	86.4	61.7
Italy	28.6	6.9	4.6	30.3	84.3	40.8

Japan	10.3	3.7	6.7	42.8	93.6	79.5
Luxembourg	6.2	1.4	.7	33.7	92.9	35.4
Netherlands	6.6	2.1	2.1	62.9	91.5	48.8
New Zealand	14.6	5.5	5.5	57.2	86.0	67.7
Norway[b]	9.6	2.6	1.3	60.2	89.4	73.6
Portugal	7.0	3.4	3.9	47.6	89.8	62.1
Spain[b]	21.7	9.2	9.4	41.3	84.2	52.4
Sweden[b]	14.8	6.5	7.3	44.8	84.5	67.1
Switzerland	5.6	2.2	2.5	64.1	95.1	78.9
United Kingdom[b]	14.1	5.4	6.4	63.0	86.7	59.4
Non-U.S. average (unweighted)	13.4	5.1	5.3	49.2	88.2	57.0
European Union	16.1	6.9	8.4	43.4	86.3	49.5
United States[b]	10.3	3.0	2.7	61.0	89.0	66.1

Source: OECD (2000, table C, 209–11). Data in table 2.4 © OECD; for full citation see references.

[a]1998 for Iceland.

[b]Refers to ages sixteen to twenty-four.

TABLE 2.5 Unemployment Rates and Employment-to-Population (E/P) Ratios by Age for Women, 1999

	Unemployment Rate			E/P Ratio		
	Fifteen to Twenty-Four	Twenty-Five to Fifty-Four	Fifty-Five to Sixty-Four	Fifteen to Twenty-Four	Twenty-Five to Fifty-Four	Fifty-Five to Sixty-Four
Australia	13.2	5.6	3.9	59.6	65.6	31.3
Austria	6.4	4.6	3.4	50.7	72.8	17.6
Belgium	22.4	9.0	8.1	23.4	66.4	14.8
Canada	12.6	6.3	5.3	53.9	73.2	37.3
Denmark	10.5	4.9	5.6	62.8	79.4	47.8
Finland	22.2	9.0	9.4	38.2	77.1	38.4
France	29.7	12.6	8.7	17.3	68.5	29.6
Germany	7.7	8.7	15.5	42.8	69.2	28.9
Greece[a]	39.3	13.9	3.7	22.2	51.6	23.6
Iceland[b]	4.4	2.1	1.9	67.0	85.1	78.8
Ireland	8.3	4.8	4.3	42.9	60.0	25.7
Italy	38.3	13.6	5.6	20.8	49.5	15.0

Japan	8.2	4.4	3.3	42.9	63.6	48.2
Luxembourg	7.4	2.9	1.5	29.5	60.2	17.5
Netherlands	8.2	4.1	3.9	62.5	69.4	21.9
New Zealand	12.8	5.3	4.2	52.0	69.6	46.3
Norway[b]	9.5	2.2	.8	55.2	81.4	61.1
Portugal	10.8	4.6	2.0	38.7	72.1	41.1
Spain[b]	37.3	21.0	11.2	26.2	47.6	19.1
Sweden[b]	13.6	5.9	5.9	42.8	80.6	61.0
Switzerland	5.7	3.2	2.8	65.4	75.1	62.2
United Kingdom[b]	10.2	4.3	3.2	58.5	72.6	39.8
Non-U.S. average						
(unweighted)	15.4	7.0	5.2	44.3	68.7	36.7
European Union	18.6	9.8	9.0	35.5	64.7	27.8
United States[b]	9.5	3.4	2.6	57.0	74.1	50.1

Source: OECD (2000, table C, 212–14). Data in table 2.5 © OECD; for full citation see references.
[a]1998 for Greece.
[b]Refers to ages sixteen to twenty-four.

ison of the employment-rate ratios by age (that is, 0.96 versus 0.88) will correctly indicate that young workers in C face a greater relative demand for their labor than do those in D, as will a comparison of the absolute differences in unemployment rates (that is, 4 percentage points versus 10 percentage points). This conclusion is not reflected in the ratios of the unemployment rates by age, which are the same in the two countries.[5]

Both measures, the share of the labor force that is employed and the employment-to-population ratio, show bigger differentials between youths and the prime aged for the European Union than for the United States.[6] And the absolute gaps in unemployment rates between the two groups tell the same story. Thus, we conclude that youths in the United States—whether in the population or in the labor force—are relatively and absolutely more likely to be at work than are youths in other OECD countries. It is important to note that, in addition to economic conditions, youth-employment and -unemployment rates may be influenced by other factors, including school attendance and cultural norms about working while in school. Nonetheless, the conjunction of findings for employment and unemployment differentials suggests greater employment problems for young people in the other OECD countries than in the United States.

The second age comparison shown in tables 2.4 and 2.5 is for older individuals. As in the case of youths, the data indicate that those aged fifty-five to sixty-four are more likely to be employed in the United States than elsewhere in the OECD, both absolutely and relative to the prime aged. The differences in the relative-employment-to-population ratios for the elderly between the United States and the European Union are comparable to those for youths. This could be due to greater employment problems for older workers in the European Union, although it could also be a result of the more-generous retirement systems in these countries or some combination of demand- and supply-side factors. Differences between the United States and the other OECD countries are less evident in a comparison of unemployment rates, perhaps because retirement systems in the OECD induce the elderly to leave the labor force if they lose their jobs and, thus, not be counted as unemployed.

The data reported in tables 2.4 and 2.5 for 1999 suggest that the young and the elderly have higher relative employment in the United States than elsewhere. This is consistent with more-extensive labor-market interventions in other OECD countries than in the United States, which would more adversely affect the unemployment of these groups than that of the prime aged. In addition, as we saw in the previous chapter, all advanced nations have likely been hit with similar global economic shocks, including those stemming from technological change and international trade. We would expect these shocks to result in larger relative-wage changes and smaller relative-employment changes in the United States than elsewhere, given the more flexible U.S. labor market. Some evidence on this conjecture may be gleaned by examining the data on changes in relative employment by age over the period 1979 to 1999 that are presented in table 2.6, data that suggest that the relative-employment picture of the young and the elderly deteriorated in the other OECD countries compared to that in the United States. Later in this chapter, we examine trends in relative wages and find that they did, indeed, change by more in the United States than in other countries during this period, as expected.

Table 2.6 shows employment-to-population ratios of younger and older individuals relative to those of the prime aged in 1979 and 1999 and the percentage change in this figure over the period 1979 to 1999. The data presented in the table are for a subset of countries for which 1979 data on employment-to-population ratios are available (for the 1979 ratios, see appendix table 2A.1). Looking first at men, a comparison of table 2.4 and table 2A.1 indicates that employment-to-population ratios of men generally declined in each age group. However, as may be seen in table 2.6, the decreases were larger for younger and older men than for the prime aged. And these decreases in relative employment were more pronounced in the other OECD countries than in the United States. The ratio of young men's employment-to-population ratios to prime-age men's decreased by 12 percent in other OECD countries, on average, compared to a decrease of 6 percent in the United States. Similarly the relative-employment ratio of older men fell by 14 percent in the other OECD countries but by only 4 percent in the United States.

Comparing table 2.5 and table 2A.1 for women indicates that

TABLE 2.6 **Employment-to-Population Ratios of Younger and Older Individuals Relative to the Prime Aged, 1979 and 1999**

Country	1979		1999		Percentage Change, 1979 to 1999	
	Fifteen to Twenty-Four	Fifty-Five to Sixty-Four	Fifteen to Twenty-Four	Fifty-Five to Sixty-Four	Fifteen to Twenty-Four	Fifty-Five to Sixty-Four
A. Men						
Australia	.731	.735	.727	.668	−.5	−9.1
Canada	.689	.806	.651	.669	−5.5	−17.1
Finland	.651	.622	.471	.481	−27.6	−22.7
France	.510	.718	.284	.454	−44.4	−36.8
Germany	.655	.680	.583	.552	−11.0	−18.8
Ireland	.698	.820	.575	.714	−17.6	−12.9
Italy	.419	.402	.359	.484	−14.1	20.3
Japan	.442	.852	.457	.849	3.5	−.3
Netherlands	.505	.700	.687	.533	36.1	−23.8
Norway[a]	.551	.880	.673	.823	22.2	−6.4
Portugal	.758	.813	.530	.692	−30.0	−14.9
Spain[a]	.647	.819	.490	.622	−24.2	−24.0
Sweden[a]	.726	.826	.530	.794	−27.0	−3.9
Non-U.S. average (unweighted)	.614	.744	.540	.641	−12.1	−13.8
United States[a]	.729	.776	.685	.743	−6.0	−4.3

B. Women

Australia	1.096	.406	.909	−17.1	.477	17.6
Canada	.996	.596	.736	−26.1	.510	−14.5
Finland	.607	.501	.495	−18.3	.498	−.6
France	.605	.622	.253	−58.3	.432	−30.5
Germany	1.017	.503	.618	−39.2	.418	−16.9
Ireland	1.894	.734	.715	−62.2	.428	−41.6
Italy	.765	.268	.420	−45.1	.303	13.1
Japan	.777	.812	.675	−13.2	.758	−6.6
Netherlands	1.279	.424	.901	−29.6	.316	−25.6
Norway[a]	.753	.755	.678	−10.0	.751	−.5
Portugal	.913	.635	.537	−41.2	.570	−10.2
Spain[a]	1.332	.747	.550	−58.7	.401	−46.3
Sweden[a]	.827	.668	.531	−35.8	.757	13.3
Non-U.S. average (unweighted)[a]	.989	.590	.617	−37.7	.509	−13.7
United States[a]	.929	.685	.769	−17.2	.676	−1.3

Source: Computed from data in OECD (2000, table C, 209–14; table 5, 232–33); OECD (table B, 188–9, 1996). Data in table 2.6 © OECD; for full citation see references.

Note: 1979 and 1999 entries are the indicated groups' employment-to-population ratio divided by that for ages twenty-five to fifty-four for the same sex.

[a]Refers to ages sixteen to twenty-four in 1999.

employment-to-population ratios rose in each age group in the United States while, in the other countries, on average, they rose among those aged twenty-five to fifty-four and fifty-five to sixty-four but declined among youths. More important, changes in employment-to-population ratios were relatively more favorable among both younger and older women in the United States than elsewhere. The ratio of young women's employment-to-population ratios to prime-age women's decreased by 38 percent in other OECD countries, on average, compared to a decrease of 17 percent in the United States, while older women's relative-employment-to-population ratio declined by 14 percent in the other OECD countries but by only 1 percent in the United States.

Computations based on tables 2.4, 2.5, and 2A.1 further indicate that, compared to prime-age unemployment, youth unemployment tended to rise in the other OECD countries but not in the United States. For example, among men, the average youth-unemployment rate increased in the other OECD countries by 6.3 percentage points, compared to an increase of 2.7 percentage points for the prime aged, but declined in the United States by 1.1 percentage points, compared to a decrease of 0.4 percentage points for the prime aged. Among women, the difference between the changes for the two age groups in the other OECD countries was smaller; the unemployment rate of young women increased by 3.7 percentage points, compared to an increase of 3.5 percentage points for prime-age women. But, in the United States, as was the case for men, unemployment declined for both age groups and fell by more for younger women (2.7 percentage points) than for prime-age women (1.8 percentage points). In contrast to the trends for youths, changes in the unemployment rates of older men and women were similar to those of the prime aged both in the United States and elsewhere. However, as noted earlier, we believe that movements in the relative-employment-to-population ratios are more appropriate for indicating changes in labor demand. By this yardstick, the young and the elderly fared relatively better in the United States than in the other OECD countries.

A second dimension along which relative-employment outcomes may be influenced by relative-wage flexibility is education level. Table 2.7 shows employment-to-population ratios and unemployment rates for those age twenty-five to sixty-four by education level in 1998 for men (panel A) and women (panel B). In contrast to the results for age groups, this table shows roughly similar employment-to-population ratios within education groups in the United States and the other countries, on average. For example, for less-educated men, the employment-to-population ratio was 69.3 percent in the United States, compared to an EU average of 72.5 percent; for those with the middle level of schooling, the figures were 83.7 percent for the United States and 79.3 percent, on average, for the European Union. And, while unemployment rates were lower within each education group in the United States than in the European Union for both men and women, the differences across education groups were usually at least as large in the United States as in the European Union. The data presented in table 2.7, thus, suggest that, on average, the less educated do not suffer any greater *relative*-employment or -unemployment problems in the other OECD countries than in the United States.

Other data show that, between the 1970s and the 1990s, relative unemployment across education groups rose similarly in the United States and other OECD countries. Nickell and Layard (1999, 3075) report that, during the period 1975 to 1978, men's unemployment rates in the United States for those with high and low education levels were 2.2 and 5.1 percent, respectively. An unweighted average of Nickell and Layard's data for Spain, Sweden, the United Kingdom, and West Germany shows very similar corresponding figures of 2.2 and 5.4 percent.[7] By 1991 to 1993, the rates for the United States were 4.7 percent (high education levels) and 12.5 percent (low education levels), with corresponding averages for the four other countries of 5.1 and 13.7 percent. Thus, relative unemployment by education group (either absolute or relative differences) rose similarly over this period in the United States and in these other countries.

Our examination of relative employment by age and education indicates that the young and the elderly fare better relative to the prime aged in the United States than elsewhere and that the relative advantage of the United States has been growing over the 1980s and 1990s. Yet relative employment or unemployment by education group is similar in the United States and other OECD countries, and the limited evidence that we have been able to adduce suggests a similar deterioration in the relative-employment

TABLE 2.7 Unemployment Rates and Employment-to-Population (E/P) Ratios by Education, Individuals Aged Twenty-Five to Sixty-Four, 1998

	Unemployment Rate			E/P Ratio		
	< Upper Secondary Education	Upper Secondary Education	Tertiary Education	< Upper Secondary Education	Upper Secondary Education	Tertiary Education
A. Men						
Australia	10.4	5.8	3.1	72.1	83.8	90.7
Austria[a]	7.0	3.3	2.3	66.7	83.2	89.8
Belgium	10.5	5.0	2.6	62.5	82.5	89.6
Canada	11.9	7.8	5.4	65.0	81.5	87.5
Denmark	4.2	3.3	2.9	73.8	83.2	90.2
Finland[a]	14.5	11.7	5.9	58.9	75.5	85.0
France	13.5	7.6	5.8	66.5	82.3	86.3
Germany	18.1	10.0	4.9	61.1	74.6	85.7
Greece[a]	4.5	5.9	5.2	80.8	83.8	85.6
Ireland	11.7	4.2	2.7	71.3	88.0	91.6
Italy	8.2	6.5	4.8	68.3	79.9	86.7
Japan	5.2	3.4	2.2	82.8	92.8	95.8
Netherlands	4.6	2.1	1.9	74.0	85.8	89.7
New Zealand	10.8	4.4	4.5	70.8	87.1	87.2

Norway[a]	4.2	2.9	1.8	75.4	88.2	92.0
Portugal	3.3	3.3	1.9	86.8	84.1	92.8
Spain	12.6	10.0	8.5	71.8	81.8	84.7
Sweden	9.8	7.7	4.2	71.9	81.8	89.2
Switzerland	6.2	2.9	2.0	84.2	91.2	94.3
United Kingdom	13.7	5.3	2.7	59.1	83.5	89.9
Non-U.S. average (unweighted)	9.2	5.7	3.8	71.2	83.7	89.2
European Union	8.8	7.4	4.7	72.5	79.3	86.6
United States	8.0	4.6	2.0	69.3	83.7	91.2
B. Women						
Australia	7.5	5.9	3.6	50.5	62.1	77.3
Austria[a]	6.5	3.6	2.9	44.7	65.9	80.7
Belgium	17.6	10.9	3.8	32.6	60.6	79.2
Canada	12.3	8.2	5.6	41.6	66.7	78.3
Denmark	10.1	6.3	3.6	50.3	74.2	84.9
Finland[a]	17.0	12.2	7.1	50.1	68.5	80.6
France	16.5	12.1	7.4	47.7	66.6	77.1
Germany	15.1	11.6	6.5	37.8	59.8	76.4
Greece[a]	10.2	15.0	10.2	36.5	45.5	73.5
Ireland	11.4	4.8	3.4	33.3	59.7	77.9

(Table continues on p. 42.)

TABLE 2.7 *Continued*

	Unemployment Rate			E/P Ratio		
	< Upper Secondary Education	Upper Secondary Education	Tertiary Education	< Upper Secondary Education	Upper Secondary Education	Tertiary Education
Italy	16.4	11.8	9.5	27.4	55.4	73.5
Japan	3.0	3.1	3.5	55.0	60.8	61.3
Netherlands	7.7	4.2	2.7	40.5	66.8	79.6
New Zealand	9.9	5.1	4.2	48.4	69.6	74.8
Norway[a]	3.8	3.4	1.6	58.5	78.2	88.3
Portugal	5.7	5.4	3.1	64.7	75.3	86.8
Spain	25.6	22.8	18.5	29.1	52.5	67.8
Sweden	11.1	6.6	3.0	59.9	78.4	88.8
Switzerland	5.3	2.7	5.2	61.4	72.5	80.2
United Kingdom	7.3	4.5	2.5	48.1	72.7	84.1
Non-U.S. average (unweighted)	11.0	8.0	5.4	45.9	65.6	78.6
European Union	13.5	11.4	7.5	34.4	60.1	76.5
United States	9.3	4.2	2.1	45.2	69.5	80.6

Source: OECD (2000, table D, 215–17). Data in table 2.7 © OECD; for full citation see references.
[a]Data are for 1997.

and -unemployment outcomes for the less educated in the United States and Europe. Thus, the aggregate evidence on relative employment is only partially consistent with the notion that the economic upheavals of the 1980s and 1990s have affected relative employment by more in other OECD countries than in the United States. However, while the aggregate data are suggestive, they are no substitute for micro data, which allow us to control for composition effects when examining, say, the outcomes of youths or the less educated. For example, the young in one country may face especially high unemployment because they are relatively less well educated than are the young elsewhere. In later chapters, we will carefully examine additional evidence on these questions that is based on micro data.

Work Hours

In this section, we consider information on work hours among the employed. By and large, the evidence shows that work hours are longer in the United States than elsewhere. Thus, the lower unemployment rates and higher employment-to-population ratios that we generally find for the United States understate the difference between the United States and other OECD countries in labor input.

Data on the incidence of part-time employment (defined as usually working fewer than thirty hours per week) are presented in table 2.8. We find that part-time employment is substantially less prevalent among women in the United States than among women elsewhere and slightly more prevalent among men in the United States than among men in other countries. For example, in the European Union, 6 percent of men and 30 percent of women work part-time, while the corresponding figures for the United States are 8 and 19 percent. Taking all employees together, the incidence of part-time employment was lower in the United States than in other countries, with 13 percent of American workers and 16 percent of those in the European Union working part-time (OECD 2000, 218). Notably, the gender gap in the incidence of part-time work is much smaller in the United States than elsewhere, a finding that will inform our later discussion of gender differences in pay. However, as in the case of differences in

TABLE 2.8 **Part-Time Employment as a Percentage of Total Employment, 1999**

	Men	Women	Difference, Women–Men	Ratio, Women/Men
Australia	14.3	41.4	27.1	2.9
Austria	2.8	24.4	21.6	8.7
Belgium	7.3	36.6	29.3	5.0
Canada	10.3	28.0	17.7	2.7
Denmark	8.9	22.7	13.8	2.6
Finland	6.6	13.5	6.9	2.0
France	5.8	24.7	18.9	4.3
Germany	4.8	33.1	28.3	6.9
Greece[a]	5.3	15.4	10.1	2.9
Iceland	9.1	35.2	26.1	3.9
Ireland	7.9	31.9	24.0	4.0
Italy	5.3	23.2	17.9	4.4
Japan	13.4	39.7	26.3	3.0
Luxembourg	1.6	28.3	26.7	17.7
Netherlands	11.9	55.4	43.5	4.7
New Zealand	11.3	37.2	25.9	3.3
Norway	8.2	35.0	26.8	4.3
Portugal	5.0	14.6	9.6	2.9
Spain	2.9	16.8	13.9	5.8
Sweden	7.3	22.3	15.0	3.1
Switzerland	7.7	46.5	38.8	6.0
United Kingdom	8.5	40.6	32.1	4.8
Non-U.S. average (unweighted)	7.6	30.3	22.7	4.0
European Union	6.0	30.3	24.3	5.1
United States	8.1	19.0	10.9	2.3

Source: OECD (2000, table E, 218). Data in table 2.8 © OECD; for full citation see references.

Note: Part-time work is defined as usually working less than thirty hours on one's main job, with the following exceptions: actual hours worked for Australia, Finland, and Japan; hours worked on all jobs for Australia and Switzerland; less than thirty-five hours for Japan. Wage and salary workers for the United States.

[a] 1998 data are used for Greece.

women's labor-force-participation rates across countries, it is important to note that the higher incidence of part-time employment among women in other OECD countries than in the United States is likely to reflect differences in preferences and cultural factors as well as economic conditions. We make no judgment here regard-

TABLE 2.9 **Average Annual Hours Worked per Employed Person**

Country	1979	1990	1999	Difference, 1999 vs. 1979
Australia	1,904	1,869	1,864	−40
Canada	1,836	1,790	1,777	−59
Finland	1,837	1,728	1,727	−110
France	1,806	1,657	1,604	−202
Germany (West)	1,745	1,593	1,535	−210
Iceland	N.A.	N.A.	1,873	N.A.
Japan	2,126	2,031	1,842	−284
New Zealand	N.A.	1,820	1,842	N.A.
Norway	1,514	1,432	1,395	−119
Spain	2,022	1,824	1,827	−195
Sweden	1,516	1,546	1,634	118
Switzerland	N.A.	N.A.	1,579	N.A.
United Kingdom	1,815	1,767	1,720	−95
Non-U.S. average 1979 country sample (unweighted)	1,812	1,724	1,693	−120
Current-year sample (unweighted)	1,812	1,732	1,709	−103
United States	1,905	1,943	1,976	71

Source: OECD (2000, table F, 219). Data in table 2.9 © OECD; for full citation see references.
Note: 1997 is used instead of 1999 for Canada. 1998 is used instead of 1999 for Finland, France, Italy, Japan, and Switzerland.
N.A. = Not available.

ing the consequences for well-being of these differences but simply note their effect on labor input in the United States compared to other OECD countries.

Table 2.9, which provides data on average annual hours worked per employed person in the United States and other OECD countries, reinforces the overall conclusions drawn from our consideration of part-time employment. Although the OECD notes that these data are unsuitable for comparisons across countries at a given point in time (owing to differences in their sources), we can usefully compare changes over time in the United States and other countries. Table 2.9 shows that, among the sample of countries for which there were data for both 1979 and 1999, average work hours fell by 120 (6.6 percent) over this period in the other OECD countries but rose by 71 (3.7 percent) in the United States. Thus, work hours per employed person in the United States were increasing relative to those in other countries at the same time that employment-to-population ratios were rising in the United States relative to those elsewhere. Thus, consideration of work hours reinforces the conclusions that we reached earlier about employment in the United States compared to that in the other countries.

While the data presented in this chapter show a more rapidly rising relative level of labor input among U.S. workers than among workers elsewhere, whether this should be viewed as a favorable indicator of labor-market performance is unclear. On the one hand, if workers generally would prefer more employment opportunities, then the falling work hours in other OECD countries may be perceived as a problem. This would be the case, for example, if people were having trouble finding full-time or full-year work. Or, as in the case of France as of January 1, 2000, shorter work hours could reflect a government-mandated shorter workweek, an attempt to generate more jobs (Jeffreys 2000). On the other hand, to the extent that falling work hours in other countries are due to an expansion of holidays or vacations, they might be viewed as part of total compensation and should be counted as a benefit of employment. It is also possible that a higher incidence of part-time work reflects the choices of workers who want greater flexibility in their daily schedules.

Temporary Employment

Another aspect of employment that may shed light on the effect of institutions is the incidence and growth of temporary employment. While the employment relationship is highly regulated in many OECD countries (as we discuss in detail in chapter 3), new forms of flexibility have emerged that potentially provide more job opportunities than otherwise. For example, in countries like Italy and Spain, there is a large unregulated sector in which taxes, union wages, and other rules can be avoided. In some cases, this takes the form of self-employment, while, in others, the government does not enforce its regulations (Erickson and Ichino 1995;

de la Rica and Lemieux 1994). Perhaps at least as important as the underground economy is the sharply increasing practice in the OECD of allowing fixed-duration employment contracts. For example, the fraction of EC workers with temporary jobs grew from 4 percent in 1983 to 10 percent in 1991 (Bentolila and Dolado 1994).

While it is tempting to view the growth of temporary employment in the OECD as at least in part a response to the rigidity of the regular employment system, it is important to bear in mind that there are a number of demand- and supply-side reasons for the use of such arrangements and that, while data are limited, indications are that the incidence of such employment has been increasing in the United States as well (Houseman 2001). A comparison with the United States would be instructive, indicating whether the other OECD countries have been especially motivated to turn to these arrangements by their less flexible labor-market institutions. Unfortunately, two difficulties limit the usefulness of such a comparison. First, it is not possible to obtain U.S. data for precisely the same time period or for the same definition of temporary work as can be obtained for the other OECD countries. Second, as we discuss in chapter 3, the incidence of such jobs in some OECD countries has been restricted by regulations that ban certain types altogether or heavily regulate the conditions under which other types may be offered (OECD 1999).

Bearing these qualifications in mind, in table 2.10 we show data for 1983 and 1991 for the other OECD countries that are based on a common definition of temporary workers, including those employed by temporary agencies and those with fixed-term contracts, and data for 1995 for the United States that are based on two alternatives that match up as closely as possible with the OECD definition. The first definition includes agency temporaries and short-term hires, that is, workers who said that their jobs were temporary. The second additionally includes on-call workers (that is, workers who are expected to be available for employment on short notice).[8] The table indicates that the incidence of temporary employment in the United States—4.5 to 6.4 percent—tends to be lower than that in many of the other OECD countries and less than the unweighted average for the others of 11.0 percent in 1991. This is especially impressive given that the U.S. data are for

TABLE 2.10 **Temporary Employment as a Percentage of Total Employment in OECD Countries, 1983 and 1991**

	1983	1991
Australia	21.1[a]	19.7
Belgium	5.4	5.1
Denmark	12.5[b]	11.9
Finland	11.1	13.1
France	3.3	10.1
Germany (West)	9.9[b]	9.3
Greece	16.3	14.7
Ireland	6.2	8.3
Japan	10.3	10.5
Italy	6.6	5.4
Luxembourg	3.2	3.3
Netherlands	5.8	7.7
Portugal	16.9[a]	16.5
Spain	11.3[c]	32.2
United Kingdom	5.5	5.3
Non-U.S. average (unweighted)	8.9	11.0

United States
  Agency temporaries and
    short-term hires
	N.A.	4.5[d]

Agency temporaries,
  short-term hires, and
  on-call workers
	N.A.	6.4[d]

Source: For the United States: Houseman (2001) based on CPS data. For other countries: Bentolila and Dolado (1994), based on OECD data.
Note: With the exception of the United States, temporary employment includes those employed by temporary agencies and on direct fixed-term contracts.
N.A. = Not available.
[a]1987.
[b]1984.
[c]1985.
[d]1995.

a later year and temporary employment has been increasing. Moreover, as mentioned earlier, many of the other countries heavily regulate the use of temporary employment, and this is not the case in the United States. The lower actual incidence of temporary employment in the United States in the face of fewer regulations suggests a stronger demand for temporary employment among employers elsewhere in the OECD. This would be expected if the more rigid labor-market institutions covering regular employees outside the United States give employers a greater incentive to seek flexibility by employing temporary workers.

WAGE LEVELS AND WAGE INEQUALITY

While employment is an important aspect of labor-market performance, we also need to take into account the quality of the jobs that people hold. Earnings are the most readily available measure of job quality, and we draw extensively on earnings data in examining this feature of the labor market in a comparative context. In this section, we review current trends in wage levels, wage inequality, productivity, and labor costs to form a picture of the response of the United States and other OECD countries to the changing economic environment of the 1980s and 1990s. We will be especially interested to see whether wage levels and relative wages are more flexible in the United States, as would be expected given the more extensive role of wage-setting institutions in other OECD countries. Ideally, one would like to have data on other aspects of compensation, but this information is less readily available on an international comparative basis. However, we will review BLS figures on unit labor costs, which include both wage and nonwage compensation.

Table 2.11 shows data on median real weekly earnings for full-time workers for the three time periods 1979 to 1981, 1989 to 1990, and 1994 to 1998.[9] The precise years covered for each country vary somewhat within these periods, depending on data availability (see the notes to the table for the years covered). Weekly earnings are expressed in purchasing-power-corrected U.S. dollars. The purchasing-power correction is an attempt to make the wage data comparable by correcting across countries for the differences in the cost of purchasing a fixed market basket of commodities. It tells us how much a median full-time worker could buy with his or her earnings in each country. The real-wage series are obtained by first using the index of purchasing-power parity to convert each country's median wages into current year U.S. dollars. The GDP personal-consumption-expenditures (PCE) deflator is then used to obtain 1998 U.S. dollars.[10]

Before examining the results in table 2.11, it is important to

TABLE 2.11 Median Weekly Earnings, Full-Time Workers, in 1998 U.S. Dollars (Purchasing-Power Corrected)

	Men				Women			
	1979 to 1981	1989 to 1990	1994 to 1998	Percentage Change, 1979 to 1981 through 1994 to 1998	1979 to 1981	1989 to 1990	1994 to 1998	Percentage Change, 1979 to 1981 through 1994 to 1998
Australia	413.39	421.17	497.73	20.4	330.71	343.04	431.82	30.6
Austria	370.70	403.13	449.09	21.1	240.60	271.54	310.66	29.1
Belgium		432.10	481.79			362.80	434.33	
Canada	549.65	595.71	637.43	16.0	347.92	395.17	444.72	27.8
Germany (West)	490.55	517.68	583.69	19.0	351.86	381.71	440.69	25.2
Italy		418.49	420.12			336.97	350.10	
Japan	303.92	363.33	430.60	41.7	178.46	214.23	273.89	53.5
Netherlands		505.62	541.19			379.22	416.30	
Sweden	418.75	444.87	454.11	8.4	350.86	350.70	379.22	8.1
Switzerland		614.95	688.37			452.32	517.48	
United Kingdom	386.13	490.83	543.94	40.9	241.86	332.16	407.58	68.5
Non-U.S. Average								
1979 to 1981 sample	419.01	462.39	513.80	22.6	291.75	326.94	384.08	31.6
Current-year sample	419.01	473.44	520.73		291.75	347.26	400.62	
United States	608.98	594.16	575.75	−5.5	380.87	419.41	439.26	15.3

Source: Unpublished OECD data.

Note: For earnings definitions and exclusions, see table 2A.2. The years covered for each country are as follows: Australia (1979, 1989, 1998); Austria (1980, 1989, 1994); Belgium (1989, 1995); Canada (1981, average of 1988 and 1990, 1994); (West) Germany (1984, 1989, 1995); Italy (1989, 1996); Japan (1979, 1989, 1997); the Netherlands (1990, 1995); Sweden (average of 1978, and 1980, 1989, 1996); Switzerland (1991, 1996); United Kingdom (1979, 1989, 1998); United States (1979, 1989, 1996).

bear in mind some limitations of these data. The data are for weekly earnings rather than the preferred measure of hourly wages. However, the restriction of the OECD database to full-time workers standardizes for hours to a considerable extent and, thus, more closely approximates a measure of the price of labor than would data on weekly earnings for all employed workers, including part-timers. Another limitation is that even the real-wage figures do not account for productivity differences across countries and, therefore, are merely suggestive rather than conclusive indicators of international differences in the labor cost of production. (We look explicitly at productivity and unit-labor-cost differences below.) Bearing these limitations in mind, the wage data remain useful indicators of international differences in labor-market performance in the 1980s and 1990s.

Table 2.11 indicates that, from 1979 to 1981 through 1994 to 1998, real wages grew much more rapidly in the other OECD countries than in the United States. U.S. men's real wages fell 5.5 percent during this period; in contrast, averaging over the sample of OECD countries for which 1979 to 1981 data were available, men's real wages rose 22.6 percent in purchasing-power-corrected terms. And, although U.S. women's real pay rose 15.3 percent in real terms, women's real wages rose 31.6 percent in the other OECD countries.[11]

While, at the beginning of the period, median wages were higher in the United States than in other OECD countries, over the 1980s and 1990s these other nations caught up to and, in a number of cases, surpassed the United States. In purchasing-power-corrected wages, what had been a 45 percent advantage for U.S. men in 1979 to 1981 shrank to 12 percent by 1994 to 1998, and the 31 percent U.S. women's advantage fell to 14 percent over the same period.

While it appears that the real weekly earnings of full-time workers increased faster in the other OECD countries than in the United States, it is also necessary to consider trends in productivity growth before reaching any conclusions about changes in the relative competitiveness of American workers. If productivity also rose faster in these other countries, it is possible that this increase was sufficient to offset the effect of higher wages on labor costs. In this case, we would conclude that median labor costs did not

FIGURE 2.1 **Unit Labor Costs in Manufacturing in U.S. Dollars (Exchange Rates), 1977 = 100**

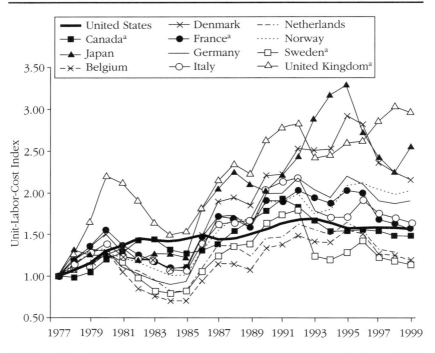

Source: Accessed October 16, 2001 on BLS website at: *www.bls.gov.*
[a]Compensation adjusted to include employment taxes.

play a role in raising unemployment in the other countries, although changes in relative labor costs compared to productivity across skill levels could still have had an effect on employment among particular groups.

A recent paper by Stephen Nickell and Richard Layard (1999) sheds light on these issues by presenting information on productivity levels and increases. BLS data on changes in unit labor costs shown in figure 2.1 will also be useful. Nickell and Layard give various measures of productivity levels for 1992 to 1994 in a number of OECD countries on a purchasing-power-corrected basis. For the first measure, GDP per capita, the United States has a substantially higher level than do any of the other countries, which, on average, have 73 percent of the U.S. level. However, a larger share of the population is employed in the United States than in the other countries. Thus, GDP per employed worker in the other countries averages 82 percent of the U.S. level. Further, American workers work longer hours. This difference contributes importantly to the results. While the other countries had an 18 percentage point shortfall in output per worker, they had only a 5 to 7 percentage point shortfall in GDP per hour worked. And several countries had higher GDP per work hour than did the United States, including Belgium, France, Germany, the Netherlands, and Norway, while only Belgium, with its 3 percent advantage, had higher GDP per worker than did the United States. Overall, the data indicate that American workers are about as productive, on average, as those in other OECD countries.[12]

We now turn to data on changes in productivity from the mid-1970s to the early 1990s from Nickell and Layard (1999). An increase in labor productivity shows the rise in output not accounted for by growth in the quantity of labor employed, and an increase in total factor productivity shows the rise in output not accounted for by growth in the quantity of labor or capital. The latter is an indicator of technological progress. Both measures grew more slowly in the United States during this period. On average, annual labor productivity growth was 1.02 percent lower in the United States than in the other countries, while annual total factor productivity growth was 1.11 percent lower. This may help explain the fall in real-wage levels in the United States relative to those in the other countries. Looking at the countries listed in table 2.11 for which we have wage data for both 1979 to 1981 and 1994 to 1998, we see that real median wages in U.S. purchasing-power-corrected dollars grew 1.3 percent per year faster in these countries than in the United States over this period. The Nickell and Layard data indicate that annual labor-productivity growth was 1.0 percent higher in these countries than in the United States, on average. So differential productivity growth can explain about 80 percent of the slower annual growth in real wages in the United States, leaving a residual of 20 percent that cannot be explained by this factor and could potentially be associated with rising labor costs in the other OECD countries relative to those in the United States.

While economywide productivity data are available only

through the early 1990s, recent data for the manufacturing sector only indicate that, in the 1990s, productivity growth in the United States accelerated relative to that in other countries. The trend for the period when both series are available suggests that changes in manufacturing productivity in the 1990s may give us a representative picture of the whole economy for comparative purposes. For example, BLS data show that, over the period 1977 to 1992, output per hour worked in manufacturing rose an average of 3.2 percent per year across a sample of ten Western countries, compared to a growth rate of 2.6 percent for the United States.[13] This difference is qualitatively similar to the economywide productivity-growth figures discussed earlier. The BLS data indicate that, from 1992 to 1999 (1998 for the Netherlands), manufacturing productivity growth rose in the United States to an annual rate of 4.4 percent but fell slightly to 2.8 percent in the other countries. Overall, the manufacturing data indicate that, between 1977 and 1999, productivity grew at a rate of 3.1 percent in both the other countries and the United States but that, as the 1990s came to a close, American productivity growth showed a sharp absolute and relative improvement.

Taken together, the data considered here suggest that labor costs may have been rising in the other OECD countries compared to those in the United States. Explicit information on trends in labor costs over the period 1977 to 1999 is available from the BLS for the manufacturing sector, the major sector of traded goods. Unit labor costs (ULC) are labor costs per unit of output:

$$ULC \equiv (\text{labor cost})/(\text{output}) = (\text{labor cost per hour})/(\text{output per hour}) \tag{2.2}$$

Equation (2.2) shows that unit-labor-cost data take into account productivity as well as wage- and nonwage-labor costs. They, thus, provide a comprehensive measure of relative competitiveness for this sector.

Figure 2.1 shows data on unit labor costs in U.S. exchange-rate-corrected dollars for twelve countries, including the United States. We use exchange rates to make comparisons across countries on the assumption that this is the most relevant concept affecting the decisions of businesses about where to locate. Labor costs in 1977 have been set equal to 100 for all countries. The figure shows that, from 1977 to about 1992, unit labor costs grew faster in nine of the other eleven countries than in the United States. Since 1992, exchange-rate movements appear to have lowered relative unit labor costs in most of the other countries. But, nonetheless, by 1999, unit labor costs had still risen faster since 1977 in six of the other eleven countries than they had in the United States and by about the same as in the United States in one country (France); labor costs rose by less than they had in the United States in only four countries. American manufacturing, then, appears to have increased its international competitiveness, at least with respect to labor costs, compared to most of the other countries over the 1980s and 1990s.

In addition to a concern about overall wage levels, economists have long been interested in the determinants and consequences of wage inequality. Wage inequality may be an important indicator of the well-being of those at the bottom of the distribution, particularly if perceptions about poverty are related to relative rather than absolute living standards. On the other hand, to the extent that labor-market institutions artificially reduce wage inequality, they may have adverse employment effects for those whose wages are raised the most. Compressing wages may also reduce the economy's ability to respond to price signals in the labor market. For example, reducing the return to skill may decrease individuals' incentives to acquire skills and, thus, lead to a decline in overall economic performance (Edin and Holmlund 1995). We will discuss these possible incentive and resource-allocation effects of wage compression further in chapter 4.

Table 2.12 provides some evidence on wage inequality during the period 1979 to 1998 for several countries. The earnings data come from the same unpublished OECD source as was used to analyze wage levels in table 2.11. Our measures of inequality are the 50–10 weekly wage ratio and the 90–50 weekly wage ratio. The figures *10, 50,* and *90* refer to percentiles of each country's distribution of weekly earnings for full-time workers where we focus on the men's and women's distributions separately. Thus, the 50–10 wage ratio is the ratio of the wages of an individual at the 50th percentile of the distribution to the wages of an individual at the 10th percentile. Similarly, the 90–50 wage ratio is the ratio of the wages of an individual at the 90th percentile to the

TABLE 2.12 50–10 and 90–50 Weekly Earnings Ratios, Full-Time Workers

	50–10				90–50			
Country	1979 to 1981	1989 to 1990	1994 to 1998	Percentage Change, 1979 to 1981 through 1994 to 1998	1979 to 1981	1989 to 1990	1994 to 1998	Percentage Change, 1979 to 1981 through 1994 to 1998
A. Men								
Australia	1.63	1.68	1.63	.0	1.68	1.68	1.87	11.2
Austria	1.63	1.65	1.67	2.6	1.62	1.65		
Belgium		1.41	1.38			1.60		
Canada	2.07	2.25	2.22	7.0	1.67	1.73	1.70	1.3
Finland	1.46	1.51	1.46	-.4	1.67	1.73	1.64	-1.4
France (net earnings)	1.66	1.63	1.60	-3.9	2.04	2.14	2.06	.8
Germany (West)	1.52	1.45	1.46	-4.3	1.68	1.71	1.80	7.2
Ireland			1.99				1.96	
Italy		1.40	1.40			1.62	1.74	
Japan	1.59	1.64	1.61	.8	1.63	1.73	1.73	6.3
Netherlands		1.51	1.57					
New Zealand	1.63	1.75	1.83	11.8	1.66	1.70	1.95	17.1
Spain			1.95				2.07	

Sweden	1.31	1.35	1.40	7.3	1.59	1.60	1.68	6.0
Switzerland		1.44	1.49			1.68	1.73	
United Kingdom	1.63	1.77	1.80	10.5	1.59	1.81	1.90	19.0
Non-U.S. average								
1979 to 1981 sample	1.61	1.67	1.66	3.2	1.68	1.76	1.81	7.7
Current sample	1.61	1.60	1.65	2.4	1.68	1.72	1.83	8.9
United States	1.95	2.14	2.21	13.0	1.82	2.05	2.13	16.7
B. Women								
Australia	1.59	1.64	1.57	−1.4	1.51	1.59	1.34	−10.9
Austria	1.93	1.93	2.03	5.4	1.74	1.79		
Belgium		1.40	1.47			1.56		
Canada	2.12	2.26	2.25	6.3	1.76	1.80	1.78	0.8
Finland	1.40	1.38	1.32	−5.6	1.47	1.57	1.55	5.6
France (net earnings)	1.59	1.65	1.56	−2.0	1.70	1.71	1.71	.4
Germany (West)	1.79	1.75	1.60	−10.6	1.73	1.59	1.64	−5.2
Ireland			1.92				1.94	
Italy		1.32	1.30				1.64	
Japan	1.42	1.42	1.43	0.3	1.54	1.55	1.60	3.5
Netherlands		1.67	1.63			1.65		
New Zealand	1.58	1.69	1.67	6.1	1.54	1.55	1.68	9.3

(Table continues on p. 58.)

TABLE 2.12 *Continued*

Country	50–10				90–50			
	1979 to 1981	1989 to 1990	1994 to 1998	Percentage Change, 1979 to 1981 through 1994 to 1998	1979 to 1981	1989 to 1990	1994 to 1998	Percentage Change, 1979 to 1981 through 1994 to 1998
Spain			2.07				2.07	
Sweden	1.24	1.29	1.34	7.5	1.35	1.38	1.43	5.5
Switzerland		1.69	1.55			1.57	1.56	
United Kingdom	1.50	1.60	1.69	12.8	1.60	1.83	1.83	14.3
Non-U.S. average								
1979 to 1981 sample	1.62	1.66	1.65	1.9	1.59	1.63	1.62	1.9
Current sample	1.62	1.62	1.65	2.1	1.59	1.63	1.67	5.1
United States	1.65	1.87	1.96	18.6	1.76	2.01	2.13	20.8

Source: Unpublished OECD data.

Note: For earnings definitions and exclusions, see table 2A.2. The years covered for each country are as follows: Australia (1979, 1989, 1998); Austria (1980, 1989, 1994); Belgium (1989, 1995); Canada (1981, average of 1988 and 1990, 1994); France (1979, 1989, 1996); Finland (1980, 1989, 1996); (West) Germany (1984, 1989, 1995); Ireland (1994); Italy (1989, 1996); Japan (1979, 1989, 1997); Netherlands (1990, 1995); New Zealand (1984, average of 1988 and 1990, 1997); Spain (1995); Sweden (average of 1978, and 1980, 1989, 1996); Switzerland (1991, 1996); United Kingdom (1979, 1989, 1998; United States (1979, 1989, 1996).

wages of an individual at the 50th percentile. Using the 50–10 and 90–50 wage ratios as our inequality measures, as opposed to other possible summary indicators of inequality such as the standard deviation, allows us to examine different portions of the wage distribution separately. For example, if wage floors are an important influence on a country's labor market, then this is likely to be reflected most strongly in the 50–10 wage ratio.

We examine wage distributions among men and women separately rather than the overall wage distribution because the latter concept is influenced not only by the extent of wage compression, but also by the share of the workforce that is female and by the gender pay gap. As we note later in chapter 7, many factors besides economic opportunities affect the relative representation of women in the labor force. Moreover, women's relative labor-market skills compared to men's may be very different across countries. Thus, focusing on overall wage inequality could potentially obscure the wage-compressing effect of collective bargaining and other institutions that we expect to observe. In fact, however, our findings would be quite similar if we examine overall wage inequality. We, nonetheless, focus on data for men's and women's distributions separately since, for the reasons given, this provides the clearest comparison. In chapter 7, we analyze explicitly and in detail the determinants of international differences in the gender pay gap. We find that one important factor working to reduce a country's gender pay gap is the degree of overall wage compression, as measured by the extent of men's wage inequality.

The data reported in table 2.12 on differences and changes in wage inequality are strongly suggestive of a substantial effect of collective bargaining and other institutions on the wage distribution. First, for both men and women in each period, wage inequality as measured by either the 50–10 or the 90–50 wage ratio is higher in the United States than in the other countries, on average. Second, over the period 1979 to 1998 for both men and women, inequality by either measure rose much faster in the United States than in the other countries. Both these findings are consistent with a greater influence of collective bargaining outside the United States. However, it must be acknowledged that greater or more rapidly growing heterogeneity with respect to the skills of the U.S. labor force could also produce such patterns. In later chapters, we review studies based on micro data that will allow us to determine to what extent the higher level of U.S. wage inequality and its more rapid growth can be attributed to greater variance in worker characteristics per se, such as education, literacy, and experience, as opposed to higher labor market rewards to those characteristics. This distinction between characteristics and rewards is important since the rewards may be viewed as labor-market prices that potentially influence employer decisions to hire and fire workers and worker decisions to acquire skills or to supply labor.[14]

With this caveat in mind, it is, nonetheless, instructive to proceed with a detailed comparison of the levels of and changes in wage inequality in the United States with those of other OECD countries. Looking first at men in panel A of table 2.12, we see that, while both the 90–50 and the 50–10 gaps are higher in the United States, the difference between the U.S. and the non-U.S. average is larger for the 50–10 than for the 90–50 gap. For example, in 1979 to 1981, the wages of a man at the 50th percentile of the wage distribution compared to those of a man at the 10th percentile were 95 percent higher in the United States and 61 percent higher, on average, in the other OECD countries, while the wage advantage of a man at the 90th percentile compared to a man at the 50th percentile was 82 percent in the United States and 68 percent, on average, in the other OECD countries. Thus, the 50–10 ratio was 21.2 percent higher in the United States than elsewhere, but the 90–50 ratio was only 8.3 percent higher.[15] And the 50–10 gap rose slightly more rapidly in the United States relative to the other countries than did the 90–50 gap: the former by 13.0 percent, compared to 3.2 percent (based on the 1979 to 1981 other country sample), and the latter by 16.7 percent, compared to 7.7 percent. The larger international differences for the 50–10 gap suggest the importance of wage floors in countries with centralized wage-setting mechanisms, while the faster increase in this inequality measure in the United States is consistent with a role for wage-setting institutions in these other countries in moderating the negative effect of recent trends in technological change and international trade on low-skilled workers.

A number of the other countries experienced changes in wage

inequality that were comparable in magnitude to those in the United States, and it is instructive to consider what was occurring in these countries as well. For example, as we discuss in detail in later chapters, in New Zealand, Sweden, and the United Kingdom, the legal environment or the structure of collective bargaining was changed in the 1980s or 1990s to reduce the influence of unions or large-scale bargaining units on wage setting. Consistent with our expectations based on these changes in wage-setting institutions, the results reported in table 2.12 show a relatively rapid growth of wage inequality in these countries. Between 1979 and 1998, increases in the 50–10 and 90–50 wage ratios in New Zealand and the United Kingdom were fairly similar to those experienced in the United States, and, while the increase in the 50–10 gap was smaller in Sweden than in the United States, it was nearly twice as large as the increase in the average for the other OECD countries.

Turning to the differences and changes in women's wage inequality shown in panel B of table 2.12, we again find that, overall, wage inequality is higher in the United States than in the other countries, on average, and that it increased much more rapidly, at both the bottom and the top of the wage distribution, over the period 1979 to 1998 in the United States than elsewhere. And, as was the case for men, New Zealand, Sweden, and, especially, the United Kingdom saw substantial increases in women's wage inequality over this period, although these were less than the rise in inequality among U.S. women. However, in contrast to the results obtained for men, those for women indicate that the difference between the United States and the other countries is larger for the 90–50 gap than it is for the 50–10 gap. If wage floors are, indeed, important, we might have expected a pattern for the relative sizes of the 50–10 and 90–50 gaps for women that was similar to the one found for men. One possible explanation of the difference is that, in general, women are much more heterogeneous than men are with respect to their work experience and commitment to the labor force. However, U.S. women appear to be at least as, if not more, committed to the paid labor force than do women in most other countries (Blau and Kahn 1992, 1995, 1996b). Thus, the relatively large 50–10 gaps for Austrian, Canadian, and German women shown in panel B of table 2.12 may reflect, not higher rewards to labor-market skill for women in those countries, but rather greater heterogeneity in their labor-force attachment.

The combination of more rapidly rising wage inequality and more slowly growing or falling median real wages in the United States has meant that workers at the bottom of the distribution have fared particularly poorly in the 1980s and 1990s. At the beginning of the 1980s, U.S. workers at the bottom of the wage distribution substantially outearned their counterparts abroad, but, by the late 1990s, their wages had fallen behind in real terms. For example, for the 1979 to 1981 sample of countries shown in table 2.11, we find that, in 1979 to 1981, U.S. purchasing-power-corrected real wages of U.S. workers at the 10th percentile of the distribution were 20.0 percent higher for men and 27.7 percent higher for women, substantial margins.[16] Between the periods 1979 to 1981 and 1994 to 1998, real wages at the 10th percentile fell 16.3 percent for men in the United States but rose 18.7 percent, on average, for men in the other countries. Women at the 10th percentile experienced a 2.8 percent fall in their real wages in the United States, compared to a 28.2 percent rise in real wages in the other countries. By 1994 to 1998, U.S. workers at the 10th percentile were outearned by their counterparts in other countries by 18.3 percent among men and 3.3 percent among women.

Finally, table 2.13 compares the gender pay gap across countries and over time. This is, of course, an interesting dimension of wage inequality in its own right, but it is also important because it potentially sheds light on the effect of wage-setting institutions. The high wage floors in other countries are expected to have a particularly large effect on people at the bottom of the country's overall wage distribution. These are disproportionately likely to be women. And, indeed, we do find that, during the period 1979 to 1981, the United States had one of the lowest female-to-male wage ratios of the included countries—62.5 percent, compared to a non-U.S. average of 71.2 percent. However, over the period 1979 to 1998, the gender pay gap fell much more rapidly in the United States than in other countries. By 1994 to 1998, the gender pay ratio of 76.3 percent in the United States was almost as large as the average of 77.4 percent in the other countries (for the 1979 to 1981 sample). To the extent that rising wage inequality over the 1980s and 1990s in the United States hurt the low skilled and

TABLE 2.13 **Female-to-Male Median Weekly Earnings Ratio, Full-Time Workers**

Country	1979 to 1981	1989 to 1990	1994 to 1998	Change, 1979 to 1981 Through 1994 to 1998	
				Absolute	Percentage
Australia	80.0	81.4	86.8	6.8	8.4
Austria	64.9	67.4	69.2	4.3	6.6
Belgium		84.0	90.1		
Canada	63.3	66.3	69.8	6.5	10.2
Finland	73.4	76.4	79.9	6.5	8.8
France (net earnings)	79.9	84.7	89.9	10.0	12.5
Germany (West)	71.7	73.7	75.5	3.8	5.3
Ireland			74.5		
Italy		80.5	83.3		
Japan	58.7	59.0	63.6	4.9	8.3
Netherlands		75.0	76.9		
New Zealand	73.4	75.9	81.4	8.0	10.9
Spain			71.1		
Sweden	83.8	78.8	83.5	−.3	−.3
Switzerland		73.6	75.2		
United Kingdom	62.6	67.7	74.9	12.3	19.6
Non-U.S. average					
1979 to 1981 sample	71.2	73.1	77.4	6.3	8.8
Current sample	71.2	74.6	77.8	6.7	9.4
United States	62.5	70.6	76.3	13.8	22.0

Source: Blau and Kahn (2000c, 92).

Note: For earnings definitions and exclusions, see table 2A.2. The years covered for each country are as follows: Australia (1979, 1989, 1998); Austria (1980, 1989, 1994); Belgium (1989, 1995); Canada (1981, average of 1988 and 1990, 1994); France (1979, 1989, 1996); Finland (1980, 1989, 1996); (West) Germany (1984, 1989, 1995); Ireland (1994); Italy (1989, 1996); Japan (1979, 1989, 1997); Netherlands (1990, 1995); New Zealand (1984, average of 1988 and 1990, 1997); Spain (1995); Sweden (average of 1978 and 1980, 1989, 1996); Switzerland (1991, 1996); United Kingdom (1979, 1989, 1998); United States (1979, 1989, 1996).

those in low-paying industries and occupations, the remarkable fall in the U.S. gender pay gap is perhaps surprising. As we show in chapter 7, U.S. women sharply upgraded their labor-market skills during this period, and this improvement was more than enough to outweigh the adverse effects of rising overall wage inequality on their relative wages (see Blau and Kahn 1997). Nonetheless, the gender ratio remains considerably lower in the United

States than in a number of other countries. Given the relatively high skills of U.S. women relative to those of men, it might be argued that even a ratio close to the average for the other countries represents a surprisingly weak showing for the United States. This issue is also investigated in considerable detail in chapter 7.

CONCLUSIONS

In this chapter, we have reviewed international evidence on employment and wages in the United States and other OECD countries from the 1970s to the 1990s. While the United States has experienced relatively favorable performance with respect to unemployment and employment, its real-wage and productivity levels have declined relative to those in other countries, despite some improvement in productivity growth in the United States in the 1990s, and wage inequality has risen much faster in the United States than elsewhere. Some of the faster growth in real wages abroad can be accounted for by higher productivity growth in the other countries; however, on net, we find that unit labor costs rose more slowly in the United States than elsewhere. The combination of more rapidly rising wage inequality and falling relative real-wage levels in the United States has meant that U.S. workers at the bottom of the wage distribution had falling real wages in the 1980s and 1990s and now fare absolutely worse than do those in other countries. The gender pay gap, however, has fallen faster in the United States than in other OECD countries. Whereas the United States once had one of the lowest gender wage ratios (female-to-male wages), by the late 1990s the U.S. gender ratio of 76 percent was close to the average for the other OECD countries. Nonetheless, the gender pay gap remained higher in the United States than in half the other countries, often considerably so.

An overall evaluation of labor-market performance in the United States and elsewhere in the OECD during the 1980s and 1990s must balance out these divergent trends. Real-wage declines and rising inequality in the United States must be seen as negative outcomes there. However, the U.S. record of falling unemployment rates and rising relative employment are outcomes that many Europeans envy (Siebert 1997). Moreover, the more rapidly declining gender pay gap in the United States likely also represents progress to the extent that it reflects a reduction in barriers to women's opportunities to advancement in the labor market. In the remaining chapters of this book, we review evidence from studies that will help us determine the causes of these performance trends. A better understanding of the sources of these trends should put us in a better position to evaluate existing policy approaches to enhancing our labor-market performance and to formulate new strategies as needed.

APPENDIX 2A

TABLE 2A.1 Unemployment Rates and Employment-to-Population (E/P) Ratios by Age, 1979

	Unemployment Rate			E/P Ratio		
	Fifteen to Twenty-Four	Twenty-Five to Fifty-Four	Fifty-Five to Sixty-Four	Fifteen to Twenty-Four	Twenty-Five to Fifty-Four	Fifty-Five to Sixty-Four
A. Men						
Australia	11.0	2.9	3.1	67.0	91.7	67.4
Canada	13.1	4.7	4.5	62.3	90.4	72.9
Finland	11.1	5.4	3.6	56.8	87.3	54.3
France	9.3	3.2	4.1	47.6	93.3	67.0
Germany (West)	2.9	2.0	5.5	60.9	93.0	63.2
Ireland	10.0	6.6	6.5	62.0	88.8	72.8
Italy	21.3	1.9	2.0	38.3	91.5	36.8
Japan	3.6	1.6	4.4	42.3	95.7	81.5
Netherlands	7.3	2.9	3.3	45.6	90.3	63.2
Norway	5.7	0.6	1.0	50.8	92.2	81.1
Portugal	10.2	2.4	0.3	70.3	92.8	75.4
Spain	17.7	5.7	5.0	58.3	90.1	73.8
Sweden	4.7	1.3	1.8	68.4	94.2	77.8
Non-U.S. average (unweighted)	9.8	3.2	3.5	56.2	91.6	68.2
United States	11.4	3.4	2.7	66.5	91.2	70.8

B. Women

Australia	13.6	5.1	2.3	53.5	48.8	19.8
Canada	12.6	7.3	4.9	54.0	54.2	32.3
Finland	10.5	4.3	5.5	47.2	77.8	39.0
France	18.6	5.5	5.1	36.0	59.5	37.0
Germany (West)	5.2	3.8	5.9	54.2	53.3	26.8
Ireland	8.1	4.5	4.4	49.8	26.3	19.3
Italy	30.7	7.1	7.4	27.7	36.2	9.7
Japan	3.2	1.9	1.2	42.9	55.2	44.8
Netherlands	8.9	2.8	2.7	42.2	33.0	14.0
Norway	5.6	1.2	.0	49.1	65.2	49.2
Portugal	27.3	7.3	.7	46.3	50.7	32.2
Spain	22.0	4.6	1.1	38.5	28.9	21.6
Sweden	5.3	1.6	2.2	66.0	79.8	53.3
Non-U.S. average (unweighted)	13.2	4.4	3.3	46.7	51.5	30.7
United States	12.2	5.2	3.2	54.8	59.0	40.4

Source: OECD (1996 table B, 188–9). Data in table 2A.1 © OECD; for full citation see references.

TABLE 2A.2 **Earnings Definitions and Exclusions (OECD Descriptions)**

Country	Earnings Definition	Workers Not Covered
Australia	Gross weekly earnings in main job (all jobs prior to 1988) of full-time employees	No exclusions
Austria	Gross daily earnings, standardized to a monthly basis, taking into account the recorded number of days of insurance contributions (excluding civil servants)	Most civil servants and all apprentices
Belgium	Gross weekly earnings of full-time workers (including civil servants)	No exclusions
Canada	Gross annual earnings of full-time, full-year workers	No exclusions
Finland	Gross annual earnings of full-time, full-year workers.	No exclusions
France	Net annual earnings of full-time, full-year workers	Agricultural and general government workers
Germany (West)	Gross monthly earnings of full-time workers	Apprentices
Ireland	Gross weekly earnings of full-time employees	Not specified
Italy	Gross monthly earnings of full-time employees	Agricultural and general government workers
Japan	Scheduled monthly earnings of regular, full-time employees	Employees in establishments with fewer than ten regular workers and all employees in the public sector, agriculture, forestry and fisheries, private household services, and foreign embassies
Netherlands	Annual earnings of full-time, full-year-equivalent workers	No exclusions
New Zealand	Usual gross weekly earnings of full-time employees	No exclusions

TABLE 2A.2 *Continued*

Country	Earnings Definition	Workers Not Covered
Spain	Gross annual earnings of full-time employees	Workers in enterprises with fewer than ten employees; workers in enterprises of NACE sectors A, B, and L to Q
Sweden	Gross annual earnings of full-year, full-time workers	No exclusions
Switzerland	Annual earnings of full-time, full-year-equivalent workers	No exclusions
United Kingdom (Great Britain only)	Gross weekly earnings of all full-time workers (on adult or junior rates of pay)	No exclusions
United States	Gross usual weekly earnings of full-time workers aged sixteen and over	No exclusions

Source: Unpublished OECD data file.

—— Chapter 3 ——

Labor-Market Institutions: How Do Labor-Market Institutions in the United States Compare to Those in Other Countries?

I N THE PREVIOUS chapter, we presented dramatic evidence that labor markets have performed very differently in the United States than in other advanced countries on a number of important dimensions. Several of the patterns uncovered were seen to be consistent with the overall hypothesis that labor markets are much closer to a laissez-faire model in the United States than elsewhere. A main goal of this book is to determine the extent to which institutional differences and policy interventions are responsible for these differences in performance. In order to achieve this aim, we must see just how institutions and policies differ across countries and, having done that, determine whether these differences affect labor-market outcomes. In this chapter, we take a first step in that direction by providing some detailed evidence on the institutional setting in which employment and wages are determined in the United States and other OECD countries. In later chapters, we focus on the analytic questions related to identifying the effects of institutions on outcomes, given that market forces can also affect employment, wage levels, and the wage distribution.

The data that we present in this chapter—collected from a variety of sources—show that, indeed, both wage-setting institutions and government policies intervene in the labor market much less in the United States than in other advanced industrialized countries. There appears to be much less market influence on wages in these other countries than in the United States. And institutions make it more difficult to lay off workers elsewhere. Further, entitlements to benefit programs appear to offer individuals greater incentives to stay out of work in other OECD countries than in the United States. And the government plays a much less active role in finding jobs for workers and in training them in the United States than elsewhere.

A theme common to the analyses in later chapters is that these institutions affect and interact with each other to influence the labor market (Siebert 1997). For example, high administered wages determined by collective bargaining and contract extension may put many workers' jobs at risk. Restrictions on hiring and firing, a common intervention in continental Europe, may, thus, have an especially large effect, protecting the jobs of those whose wages are raised the most by these interventions. And, to the extent that interventions in wage setting do produce unemployment, benefit entitlements and active labor-market policies help cushion the blow for those without work.

At the same time, employment-protection and benefit-entitlement programs may themselves influence the stance taken by unions in collective bargaining in the first place: unions are likely to be more aggressive in the presence of a generous unemployment-insurance (UI) system that provides income insurance for unemployed workers or employment-protection regulations that make it very difficult for firms to discharge workers. And some benefit programs like UI are also likely to give people incentives to stay out of work, diminishing the moderating effect that the unemployed have on union wage demands.

Thus, interventions in the labor market by unions and the government in many OECD countries may be viewed as forming a package. A conundrum facing these countries is that some of the palliative measures designed to safeguard the well-being of workers in economic downturns may themselves make it more difficult to regain high employment levels after the economy is hit with shocks that raise unemployment levels.

WAGE-SETTING INSTITUTIONS

In considering institutions that directly affect wage setting, we first examine the prevalence of collective bargaining. Table 3.1 provides information on the extent of union membership (density) and collective-bargaining coverage for a number of OECD countries over the period 1980 to 1994. *Union density* refers to the share of workers who are members of unions, while *collective-bargaining coverage* refers to the share of workers who have their wages determined by collective bargaining, whether or not they are union members themselves. Table 3.1 shows dramatically lower levels of both union density and collective-bargaining coverage in the United States than in other Western countries over the entire period.

In considering the extent of union influence on the economy, the distinction between membership and coverage is crucial. While coverage and membership track each other fairly closely in the United States, it is common in many European countries, as well as in Australia, for the terms of collective-bargaining agreements to be routinely extended by the government to workers who are not union members or who are employed by firms that were not initially party to the original contract. This practice implies that the direct influence of unions on wages and wage structure in the economy may extend far beyond their membership, although we would expect levels of union membership to have an important influence as well. An indication of the prevalence of contract extensions is that, while an average of 41 percent of workers in the other OECD countries were union members in 1994, collective-bargaining contracts covered fully 71 percent of employees.

The cases of France and Spain are extreme examples of the contract-extension phenomenon. Only 9 percent of French workers and 19 percent of Spanish workers are union members, but union contracts cover 95 and 78 percent of workers in these two countries, respectively. Many of the other countries of continental Europe and Australia also follow this pattern, although not to such an extreme. Union density in Australia, Austria, Germany, Italy, the Netherlands, and Portugal ranged between 26 and 42 percent

TABLE 3.1 **Union Density and Collective-Bargaining Coverage: 1980, 1990, 1994**

	Union Density			Collective-Bargaining Coverage		
	1980	1990	1994	1980	1990	1994
Australia	48	41	35	88	80	80
Austria	56	46	42		98	98
Belgium	56	51	54		90	90
Canada	36	36	38	37	38	36
Denmark	76	71	76		69	69
Finland	70	72	81	95	95	95
France	18	10	9	85	92	95
Germany	36	33	29	91	90	92
Italy	49	39	39	85	83	82
Japan	31	25	24	28	23	21
Netherlands	35	26	26	76	71	81
New Zealand	56	45	30		67	31
Norway	57	56	58		75	74
Portugal	61	32	32	70	79	71
Spain	9	13	19		76	78
Sweden	80	83	91		86	89
Switzerland	31	27	27		53	50
United Kingdom	50	39	34	70	47	47
Non-U.S. average						
Current sample	48	41	41	73	73	71
1980 sample	48	41	41	73	70	70
United States	22	16	16	26	18	18

Source: OECD (1997, table 3.3, 71). Data in table 3.1 © OECD; for full citation see references.

in 1994, but collective-bargaining coverage ranged between 71 and 98 percent. Interestingly, the Scandinavian countries have very high levels of both union density and collective-bargaining coverage. Thus, the countries of continental Europe and Australia have extremely high levels of collective-bargaining coverage, with nine of the fourteen countries in this group showing at least 80 percent coverage as of 1994. In contrast, Canada, Japan, New Zealand (at least after 1991, as we discuss in detail later in this chapter and in chapter 6), the United Kingdom, and the United States have relatively low levels of both membership and coverage, with the United States falling near the bottom of the union-density rankings and at the bottom in terms of collective-bargaining coverage. Among this group, collective-bargaining coverage ranges from 18 percent in the United States to 47 percent in the United Kingdom.

As may be seen from the table, union density has decreased in most of the countries over the period 1980 to 1994. Union density was lower in 1994 than in 1980 in thirteen of the nineteen countries shown. On average, between 1980 and 1994, union density decreased by 7 percentage points, or 15 percent, in the other OECD countries and by 6 percentage points, or 27 percent, in the United States. These broad declines in the share of workers in unions could indicate that there was some reduction in union influence on the economy in most countries. However, again, the distinction between membership and coverage is important. Changes in collective-bargaining coverage were generally very modest. With the exception of four countries—Japan, New Zealand, the United Kingdom, and the United States—the extent of collective-bargaining coverage was very stable over the period 1980 to 1994. As a result of this divergence in coverage trends between the United States and most other OECD countries, not only is it the case that unions cover a much smaller portion of employment in the United States than elsewhere, but collective-bargaining coverage has also been falling in the United States relative to that in other countries over the 1980s and 1990s. In 1980, 26 percent of U.S. workers had their wages determined by collective bargaining, compared to an average of 73 percent in the other OECD countries; by 1994, this was true of only 18 percent of U.S. workers but of an average of 70 to 71 percent of workers in the other countries.

Apart from the United States, two countries with especially dramatic declines in union density and coverage were the United Kingdom in the 1980s and New Zealand in the 1990s. Collective-bargaining coverage in the United Kingdom decreased from 70 to 47 percent over the 1980s, as union membership fell from 50 to 39 percent, while coverage in New Zealand fell from 67 to 31 percent during the early 1990s, as union membership dropped from 45 to 30 percent. These remarkable changes likely reflect the influence of the major shifts in government policy toward trade unions that preceded them.

The Thatcher reforms in the United Kingdom constituted a

multifaceted program designed to move the economy closer to a laissez-faire ideal (Blanchflower and Freeman 1994) and included a variety of policy shifts, such as abolishing the closed shop and limiting union picketing as well as reducing the generosity of the welfare state by lowering the UI replacement ratio and abolishing wages councils. The Thatcher programs appear to have had a strong negative effect on union coverage in the United Kingdom (Freeman and Pelletier 1990).

In New Zealand, a national government was elected in 1990 that believed that the country's highly structured system of labor relations was too rigid to allow for high levels of employment and income in the face of increasing domestic and foreign competition (Maloney 1994; Harbridge and Moulder 1993). In May 1991, the government enacted the Employment Contracts Act, which made freedom of association and freedom of contract the guiding principles in employment relationships. These goals were to be achieved by abolishing a number of features of the old system, including national arbitration awards, contract extensions to non-union workers, and compulsory union membership. The dramatic fall in union density and coverage in New Zealand since 1991 is strong evidence of the effect of the new law.

The experience of the United Kingdom and New Zealand provides a unique opportunity to examine labor markets before and after radical changes in the collective-bargaining system that can be attributed to government intervention. And, in our consideration of evidence on the effect of unions on wage setting in a later chapter, we will examine these two cases closely.

While union membership and collective-bargaining coverage are important features of wage-setting systems, the level at which wages are negotiated—for example, the plant, the firm, the industry, or the economy—and the degree of coordination among unions, on the one side, and employers, on the other, can also be important in determining the effect of collective bargaining on wage levels and the wage distribution.

At one extreme, wage setting in the union sector may be quite decentralized, as in the United States, where bargaining takes place primarily on a single-firm basis and, in most cases, collective-bargaining contracts cover far less than the company's full workforce (Hendricks and Kahn 1982; Katz 1993). Moreover, in the United States, federations of unions such as the AFL-CIO exert relatively little influence on actual bargaining, and employer associations are also less influential than are those in many European countries (Katz and Kochan 1992). Thus, coordination among the parties on each side—unions and employers—is also low in the United States.

At the other extreme are the Scandinavian countries and Austria, in which the major union federation signs an agreement with the employer association covering a major portion of the labor force (Leion 1985; Thorsrud 1985; OECD 1989, 1997; Tomandl and Fuerboeck 1986; Kahn 1998a). Moreover, in several instances, the government has become closely involved with labor and management in setting wages at the national level as well. This kind of partnership among labor, management, and government in national wage setting has been termed *corporatism* and represents a very high level of both centralization and coordination (Calmfors and Driffill 1988).

In later chapters, we examine evidence on the effect of these different bargaining arrangements on the wage distribution and employment. For now, we discuss theoretical effects of centralization on the level and distribution of wages. First, greater centralization of negotiating structures appears to have opposing effects on union behavior with respect to the average level of wages. On the one hand, in centralized, national-level negotiations, parties are much more likely to take into account the effects of their wage settlements on the health of the economy than they are when bargaining takes place in a more decentralized way (Calmfors and Driffill 1988). In such bargains, unions represent a large portion of the labor force and, to some degree, are bargaining over national wage levels, so it is easy to see a connection between national wage levels and national employment determination. In contrast, under decentralized wage setting, the parties can usually assume that the bargain that they strike will have little effect on the national economy. Very centralized bargaining may, then, lead to some overall wage restraint. On the other hand, larger bargaining units face less labor-market competition than do smaller ones, suggesting greater union bargaining power and more-aggressive union behavior in centralized units.

Second, the effect on the wage distribution of centralized bargains struck at the industry- or economywide level is also likely to differ from that of those struck in a decentralized setting. Since their coverage is so broad, centralized wage agreements must necessarily be very simple and usually call for industrywide or national-level wage floors. Since there is little scope for interfirm or interindustry wage differentials, these contracts will tend to affect the bottom of the wage distribution the most. Thus, compared to the very decentralized wage setting under trade unions that prevails in the United States, centralized wage setting tends to bring up the bottom of the wage distribution (Blau and Kahn 1996a). Of course, if such wage compression had first-order negative macroeconomic effects, then more-centralized units might want to take these effects into account. However, given national-level negotiations, it may be very difficult to do this.

The level of bargaining, then, can potentially affect both average wage levels and the wage distribution, and, with this in mind, we consider evidence drawn from the OECD on centralization and coordination. Table 3.2 presents information on levels of and changes in centralization and coordination of collective bargaining over the 1980s and early 1990s. Each dimension—centralization and coordination—is given a subjective assessment by the OECD, an assessment based on a study of the literature on comparative industrial relations (OECD 1997). Both centralization and coordination are relevant concepts in understanding the nature of wage-setting practices under trade unions. We have seen that the centralization of bargaining may be expected to influence both wage levels and wage inequality. But simply looking at the formal level at which negotiations take place (for example, the plant, the firm, the industry, or the economy) may give an incomplete picture of the union influence on wages.

For example, in Japan, union wages are set at the firm level by enterprisewide unions and companies, suggesting that wage setting is very decentralized there. And, as can be seen in table 3.2, Japan is, in fact, tied with Canada and the United States as having the lowest possible degree of centralization. However, bargaining is very highly coordinated across firms in Japan: Japan receives the highest possible rating for coordination, along with Austria and Germany. That is, even though negotiations in Japan take place at the enterprise level (and, thus, appear to be decentral-

TABLE 3.2 **Characteristics of Wage-Setting Institutions: 1980, 1990, 1994**

	Centralization			Coordination		
	1980	1990	1994	1980	1990	1994
Australia	2+	2+	1.5	2+	2+	1.5
Austria	2+	2+	2+	3	3	3
Belgium	2+	2+	2+	2	2	2
Canada	1	1	1	1	1	1
Denmark	2+	2	2	2.5	2+	2+
Finland	2.5	2+	2+	2+	2+	2+
France	2	2	2	2−	2	2
Germany	2	2	2	3	3	3
Italy	2−	2−	2	1.5	1.5	2.5
Japan	1	1	1	3	3	3
Netherlands	2	2	2	2	2	2
New Zealand	2	1.5	1	1.5	1	1
Norway	2	2+	2+	2.5	2.5	2.5
Portugal	2−	2+	2	2−	2	2
Spain	2+	2	2	2	2	2
Sweden	3	2+	2	2.5	2+	2
Switzerland	2	2	2	2+	2+	2+
United Kingdom	2	2−	1.5	1.5	1+	1
United States	1	1	1	1	1	1

Source: OECD (1997, table 3.3, 71). Data in table 3.2 © OECD; for full citation see references. *Note: Centralization* refers to the prevailing level at which collective bargaining takes place. *Coordination* refers to the degree of coordination among unions and among employers.

ized), there is a strong emphasis on wage patterns, implying a de facto national wage bargain. This high degree of coordination leads to a much higher effective level of centralization than would appear to be the case at first glance (Soskice 1990).

Several conclusions about wage setting can be drawn from table 3.2. First, throughout this period (the 1980s and the early 1990s), the United States had the lowest levels of both centralization and coordination in the OECD. And, of course, during this time, the United States also had the smallest union sector in relation to its employment of any advanced industrialized country (using a coverage measure for the extent of collective bargaining). We may think of individual bargaining between nonunion workers and their employer as the most extreme form of decentralized wage setting (Katz 1993). Therefore, the large nonunion sector in the United States, in conjunction with the low degree of centralization and coordination in the U.S. union sector, strongly indicates that the United States has the least-centralized wage-setting system among its peers.

A second conclusion that can be drawn from table 3.2 is that, while the most common pattern in the data is no change in the centralization or coordination score over the period, the trend among the countries in which change did occur tends toward less-centralized or -coordinated systems by 1994 compared to 1980. However, the decentralizing trend was not by any means universal. Of the nineteen countries included in the table, eight had no change in either their coordination or their centralization score. Five of the remaining countries had declines in both centralization and coordination, and two had a decrease in one but no change in the other, making a total of seven with some tendency toward decreasing centralization or coordination. Two of the remaining countries had increases in both centralization and coordination, and two had an increase in one and no change in the other, making a total of four with some tendency toward increasing centralization or coordination.

Since table 3.2 indicates that more countries seem to be decentralizing than centralizing their wage-setting systems, it is instructive to note briefly which countries have decentralized and what types of institutional changes have been associated with decentralization.[1] In Sweden and Norway, the influence of the central employer-union federation (the LO) was diminished starting in the 1980s, although, by the end of that decade, some recentralization had occurred in Norway. This latter recentralization provides an opportunity to examine wage outcomes in a country in which changes in the bargaining system were taking a direction opposite to that taken by changes in bargaining systems elsewhere, and we discuss the Norwegian case in more detail in a later chapter (see also Kahn 1998a).

Other cases of decentralization can be cited. The passage of the Employment Contracts Act in New Zealand, for example, greatly reduced the influence of unions in wage setting. According to the data presented in table 3.2, this act represented a continuation of a trend toward decentralization that began in the 1980s. In

Australia, tribunal decisions have allowed more interfirm variation in wage settlements in recent years than in the past. In Britain and the United States, multiemployer units continued to crumble in the 1980s and 1990s. Table 3.2 reveals a decrease in both centralization and coordination in Britain. And, while, in the United States, no change in either centralization or coordination—both already at the OECD's minimum score—is seen, the reduction, beginning in the 1980s and continuing into the 1990s, in the incidence of multiemployer units and of pattern bargaining among single-firm units suggests that the absolute level of centralization and coordination represented by this minimum score is falling as well. Some trends toward decentralization were also apparent in Germany, despite the apparent constancy in its wage-setting arrangements in the OECD data, and Italy, despite its overall increases in centralization and coordination as rated by the OECD. In both countries, bargaining shifted in some cases from the industry to the plant level in the late 1980s. In addition, in Italy, the *scala mobile,* a national system of wage indexation established in 1975 that acted as a centralizing mechanism for wage determination, went out of existence in 1992 (Erickson and Ichino 1995).

Finally, we again note that these trends toward decentralization were not universal. In addition to the recentralization that occurred in Norway, Portugal had slightly more centralized arrangements by the mid-1990s than it had had in 1980. And several of the continental European countries, including Austria, Belgium, France, the Netherlands, and Switzerland, appear to have had fairly stable systems over the period (Golden and Wallerstein 1995).

Whether wage setting is decentralizing faster in the United States than elsewhere is an open question. By some indicators, this appears to be the case, and it is certainly true for a number of specific comparisons. Collective-bargaining coverage has been declining in the United States relative to that in other countries, and, as noted above, nonunion pay setting may be considered the most extreme form of decentralized wage setting. Further, as we have seen, within the union sector, bargaining is becoming less centralized in the United States, as it is in several other countries. While wage-setting systems such as those in New Zealand and the United Kingdom may be unraveling as fast as the U.S. system is, wage setting in the United States is highly likely to be relatively less centralized now than it was twenty years ago in comparison to the continental European countries listed earlier that had fairly stable arrangements or increasing centralization. And, regardless of whether the difference between the United States and specific countries has been increasing or decreasing, it is clear that the United States retains its position as having the most decentralized wage setting among the advanced nations.

While a country's collective-bargaining system is, in many respects, the most important institutional influence on its wage setting, statutory minimum wages are another mechanism that can affect the wage structure. Most OECD countries have a national minimum wage, and information on minimum-wage levels in 1997 is presented in table 3.3 for some major OECD countries. On the basis of these data, we conclude that statutory minimum wages tend to have less influence on the labor market than does collective bargaining. To see this, first note that the Scandinavian countries, as well as some major continental European countries, such as Austria and Germany, do not even appear in the table. In these countries, in place of statutory minimum wages, industry- or economywide minimum wages are set in large-scale collective-bargaining agreements. And, even in the countries listed in table 3.3, actual wages are, in most cases, far above the minimum. For example, according to OECD (1998b), in the 1990s the share of workers earning no more than the national minimum wage was only 5.1 percent in the United States (1996), 4.7 percent in Portugal (1997), 3.7 percent in the Netherlands (1994), and 11 percent in France (1996).

Of course, national minimum wages can affect those above the minimum, and the research we survey in chapter 6 indirectly incorporates these potential effects. Moreover, the minimum wage can have a substantial effect on particular subgroups, such as youths, and that is another reason why it is worth considering the influence of statutory minima.[2] While table 3.3 shows that the real value of the U.S. minimum wage in 1997 was slightly higher than the average of the countries listed, it was a smaller fraction of the level of median full-time earnings in the United States (38 percent) than elsewhere (an average of 48 percent). Minimum wages are particularly high in relative terms in Australia, France, Lux-

TABLE 3.3 **Statutory Hourly Adult Minimum Wages in U.S. Dollars, 1997**

	Exchange Rates	Purchasing-Power Parity	Relative to Full-Time Median Earnings (Percentage)
Australia	5.99	7.30	55.5
Belgium	6.77	6.40	50.4
Canada	4.53	5.33	39.6
France	6.58	5.56	57.4
Greece	2.74	3.06	51.4
Japan	4.88	3.38	30.8
Luxembourg	7.23	6.91	53.9
Netherlands	6.42	6.00	49.4
New Zealand	4.07	4.46	45.6
Portugal	1.78	2.32	64.1
Spain	2.53	2.94	32.4
Non-U.S. average	4.87	4.88	48.2
United States	5.15	5.15	38.1

Source: OECD (1998b, table 2.2, 36; table 2.3, 37); Australian Council of Trade Unions (courtesy of Grant Belchamber, senior research officer and advocate). Data in table 3.3 © OECD; for full citation see references.
Note: In countries where the minimum wage is set on a daily, weekly, or monthly basis, the figures have been converted to hourly wages assuming 8 hours per day, 40 hours per week, and 173.3 hours per month. In calculating the value of the minimum relative to overall earnings, mean hourly pay in manufacturing is used for Greece, Luxembourg, and Portugal. The Australian median refers to adult employees, and data are for 1998.

embourg, and Portugal. Moreover, the real value of the minimum wage has been falling in the United States since the late 1970s. For example, using the GDP personal-consumption-expenditures deflator, the 1979 U.S. minimum wage, which was $2.90 in 1979 dollars, had a real value in 1998 dollars of $5.91; this is about 15 percent above the actual value of the 1998 minimum wage of $5.15.[3] We lack information on changes in the real value of the minimum wage in other countries. However, the low current value of the U.S. minimum wage and the substantial decrease since the 1970s in its real value suggest not only that the minimum wage has a smaller current effect on the labor market in the United States than in the other countries, but also that this fall in the minimum wage's real value likely represents a reduction in its influence compared to other countries since the 1970s.

Taken together, the evidence presented in tables 3.1 to 3.3 indicates much less intervention by unions and minimum wages in the United States than in other countries. Further, these forces have been receding in the United States absolutely and most likely relative to many of the other countries as well.

An additional potentially important source of institutional influence on wages is the size of the public sector. The government is less constrained than most private-sector firms by the need to show a profit. Because wages in the public sector are set through the political process, we view the extent of public-sector employment as a further indicator of the nature of wage-setting institutions. Indeed, Robert Gregory and Jeff Borland (1999) review a number of studies that indicate that public-sector wages show less variation than do those in the private sector, even after controlling for the demographic composition of the employees in each sector. And Freeman (1988) suggests that public-sector employers have less incentive than do those in the private sector to resist trade unions, implying an interaction between the political aspects of public-sector wage determination and collective bargaining.

Gregory and Borland (1999) present data on levels and changes in the extent of public-sector employment relative to total employment across OECD countries between 1975 and 1995. In 1995, the U.S. incidence of public-sector employment was, at 14 percent, considerably lower than the average for the other OECD countries of 19 percent. Public-sector employment was particularly high relative to that in the United States in a number of the Scandinavian countries, including Denmark, Norway, and Sweden, which had shares of over 30 percent, and in Austria, Finland, and France, which had shares of 23 percent or more. In contrast, in 1975, the United States actually had, at 17.8 percent of the total, a somewhat higher incidence of government employment than the average elsewhere in the OECD of 15.6 percent. These positions had reversed by 1985, as the incidence of public-sector employment rose, on average, in the other countries and fell in the United States. These trends continued in the 1990s. Overall, between 1975 and 1995, the share of public-sector employment fell 21 percent in the United States, compared to a rise of 22 percent elsewhere. Fourteen of the twenty countries with complete data for the period 1975 to 1995 had increases in the share of public-sector employment, with only the six remaining countries, Australia, Canada, Japan, the Netherlands, the United Kingdom, and the United States, seeing a decrease.

Thus, not only did the United States have a lower share of public-sector employment in 1995, but the extent of public-sector employment there had declined compared to the average for the other OECD countries and especially to the experience in continental Europe. Considering the public sector, then, gives us another reason to believe that, relative to other OECD countries, the United States was moving closer to a laissez-faire model.

The observed trends in the size of the public sector may or may not represent conscious policy-making decisions to change the size of the government. For example, if the private sector expands, then the relative size of the government sector will fall even if government policies do not change. However, it is quite possible that the expansion in the relative size of the government—or at least some portion of it—does in many OECD countries represent the effect of an increased demand for public services perhaps driven in part by worsening employment problems. For example, as discussed later in this chapter and in more detail in later chapters, governments often use public-sector employment as part of a policy to provide work for the unemployed. And it is quite possible that the secular increase in unemployment has increased the demand for other government services as well. Most important from our perspective is that, regardless of the reasons for the changes we have summarized here, their consequences are similar. Thus, changes in the size of the government sector should be thought of as constituting an aspect of institutional intervention in labor markets.

RESTRICTIONS ON CHANGES IN LABOR UTILIZATION: EMPLOYMENT PROTECTION, TEMPORARY EMPLOYMENT, AND FIXED-TERM EMPLOYMENT CONTRACTS

The data considered so far in this chapter indicate far less intervention by unions and government in the market process of wage determination in the United States than elsewhere. Further, the differences between the United States and other countries appear to have been increasing over the 1980s and 1990s. As we show in the rest of this chapter, other OECD countries also have much more regulation along a variety of other dimensions in addition to wage determination than the United States does. Like those governing public-sector employment, many of these laws and rules may be seen as attempts to deal with the adverse employment consequences of union wage setting.

One of the most direct of these interventions concerns restrictions on the employer's right to hire and fire workers. While such interventions by the government are fairly modest in the United States, the countries of continental Europe, and, to a lesser extent, other OECD nations, impose major restrictions on these employment decisions. These constraints can be seen as a mechanism for protecting the jobs of those whose employment is at risk owing to the high levels of wages and benefits that unions have been able to win at the bargaining table. One implication of this difference in the strength of employment protection, discussed at greater length in later chapters, is that, if it is more difficult to discharge workers, they may become more aggressive when bargaining with their employers. Employment protection may in many countries of continental Europe interact with widespread trade unionism to make union wage demands less responsive to high unemployment there than in the less regulated United States.

Countries in the OECD have enacted a variety of laws that regulate firms' choices about changing the level of labor input, either through hiring or through discharging workers. Among other things, these laws require that certain procedures be followed before employees can be discharged, mandate severance pay when companies discharge workers, impose restrictions on the use of temporary employees who are not entitled to full benefits or the full protection of job security, and regulate the procedures for collective dismissals such as those that are a consequence of plant closings. Table 3.4 contains overall country ratings by the OECD of the strictness of these laws in the late 1980s and the late 1990s. Tables 3.5 and 3.6 contain information about specific provisions in two important areas: mandated severance pay and the regulation of fixed-term employment contracts.

While the scores reported in table 3.4 are influenced by the weights attached to different types of regulations by the OECD and might, thus, appear to be somewhat arbitrary, the comparisons between the United States and other countries are, nonetheless, instructive. In both the late 1980s and the late 1990s, the United States had the weakest regulations in the OECD with respect to protection of regular employees against dismissal as well as the use of temporary employees. On the other hand, legislation requiring sixty days' warning for workers in the case of mass layoffs places the United States at about the OECD average with respect to procedures in the event of collective dismissals. Nonetheless, the OECD considered the U.S. laws on employment protection, taken as a whole, to be the weakest among all its member countries in both the late 1980s and the late 1990s (OECD 1999, 66).

While there was little change over the 1990s in the strictness of the rules governing regular employment in the other OECD countries, there was a trend toward liberalization in the regulations governing temporary employment. Of twenty countries with data on legislation concerning regular employment for both the late 1980s and the late 1990s, fifteen, including the United States, had no overall change in the strictness of their laws, one country (Germany) stiffened its regulations, and four made them less strict. Overall, the non-U.S. average score for this category dropped only slightly, from 2.3 to 2.2. In contrast, eight of nineteen countries with data reduced the strictness of their temporary-employment regulations between the late 1980s and the late 1990s, ten, including the United States, kept the degree of restraint the same, and only one (France) increased it. The non-U.S. average for this category declined more substantially, from 2.6 to 2.0. Combining all forms of employment protection into one index, the OECD found that, of nineteen countries with this information, ten liberalized their laws, eight kept them the same, and one (France) made them more restrictive. Overall, the countries of Southern Europe (Greece, Italy, Portugal, and Spain) had the strictest laws regulating employment protection.

Table 3.5 provides some detail on a particularly important regulation in the area of job protection: mandated severance pay. The table shows the number of months of salary to which workers

TABLE 3.4 **Summary Indicators of the Strictness of Employment-Protection Legislation**

	Regular Employment		Temporary Employment		Collective Dismissals, Late 1990s
	Late 1980s	Late 1990s	Late 1980s	Late 1990s	
Central and Western Europe					
Austria	2.6	2.6	1.8	1.8	3.3
Belgium	1.5	1.5	4.6	2.8	4.1
France	2.3	2.3	3.1	3.6	2.1
Germany	2.7	2.8	3.8	2.3	3.1
Ireland	1.6	1.6	.3	.3	2.1
Netherlands	3.1	3.1	2.4	1.2	2.8
Switzerland	1.2	1.2	.9	.9	3.9
United Kingdom	.8	.8	.3	.3	2.9
Southern Europe					
Greece	2.5	2.4	4.8	4.8	3.3
Italy	2.8	2.8	5.4	3.8	4.1
Portugal	4.8	4.3	3.4	3.0	3.6
Spain	3.9	2.6	3.5	3.5	3.1
Nordic countries					
Denmark	1.6	1.6	2.6	.9	3.1
Finland	2.7	2.1	1.9	1.9	2.4
Norway	2.4	2.4	3.5	2.8	2.8
Sweden	2.8	2.8	4.1	1.6	4.5
North America					
Canada	.9	.9	.3	.3	3.4
United States	.2	.2	.3	.3	2.9
Asia and Oceania					
Australia	1.0	1.0	.9	.9	2.6
Japan	2.7	2.7		2.1	1.5
New Zealand		1.7		.4	.4
Non-U.S. average					
Current sample	2.3	2.2	2.6	2.0	3.0
Late 1980s sample	2.3	2.2	2.6	2.0	3.0

Source: OECD (1999, table 2.5, 66). Data in table 3.4 © OECD; for full citation see references.

Note: Scores range from 0 to 6, with higher numbers indicating greater strictness of regulation.

TABLE 3.5 **Months of Mandated Severance Pay for No-Fault Dismissals by Tenure Category**

	Nine Months		Four Years		Twenty Years	
	Late 1980s	Late 1990s	Late 1980s	Late 1990s	Late 1980s	Late 1990s
Central and Western Europe						
Austria	.0	.0	2.0	2.0	9.0	9.0
Belgium	.0	.0	.0	.0	.0	.0
France	.0	.0	.4	.4	2.7	2.7
Germany	.0	.0	.0	.0	.0	.0
Ireland	.0	.0	.2	.2	2.2	2.2
Netherlands	.0	.0	.0	.0	.0	.0
Switzerland	.0	.0	.0	.0	2.0	2.0
United Kingdom	.0	.0	.5	.5	2.4	2.4
Southern Europe						
Greece	.3	.3	.9	1.0	4.6	5.8
Italy	.7	.7	3.5	3.5	18.0	18.0
Portugal	3.0	3.0	4.0	4.0	20.0	20.0
Spain	.5	.5	2.6	2.6	12.0	12.0
Nordic countries						
Denmark	.0	.0	.0	.0	1.5	1.5
Finland	.0	.0	.0	.0	.0	.0
Norway	.0	.0	.0	.0	.0	.0
Sweden	.0	.0	.0	.0	.0	.0
North America						
Canada	.0	.0	.2	.2	1.3	1.3
United States	.0	.0	.0	.0	.0	.0
Asia and Oceania						
Australia	.0	.0	1.0	1.0	1.0	1.0
Japan	.0	.0	1.5	1.5	4.0	4.0
New Zealand		.0		1.5		5.0
Non-U.S. average						
Current sample	.2	.2	.9	.9	4.2	4.3
Late 1980s sample	.2	.2	.9	.9	4.2	4.3

Source: OECD (1999, table 2.2, 55). Data in table 3.5 © OECD; for full citation see references.

who are dismissed through no fault of their own are entitled, according to their seniority levels. Throughout this period, the United States had no mandated severance pay at any level of seniority, although many companies voluntarily choose to pay severance. For example, in a sample of 129 companies in Connecticut in which large firms were disproportionately represented (relative to the United States as a whole), Truman Bewley (1999) found that 63 (49 percent) provided severance benefits for their hourly workers. Since larger firms are more likely to provide severance benefits than are smaller firms, it is likely that the incidence of severance pay in the United States overall is less than 49 percent. In contrast, table 3.5 shows that governments in many other countries mandate severance pay for certain categories of workers. For example, while only the Southern European countries required severance pay for discharged workers with nine months of seniority, as of the late 1990s eleven of twenty-one countries required severance pay for workers with four years of seniority, and fourteen countries required severance pay for workers with twenty years of seniority. Moreover, the number of months of required severance pay tended to increase with seniority. The theme of different benefit entitlements at different age levels is a common one, and we will return to it shortly.

At every level of seniority, the Southern European countries had the most generous mandated severance pay. Other countries mandating especially generous severance pay, particularly at higher seniority levels, were Austria, France, Ireland, Japan, New Zealand, Switzerland, and the United Kingdom. The incidence and generosity of mandated severance pay were virtually identical in the late 1990s and the late 1980s. This constancy is consistent with the stability of the OECD's overall assessment of the strictness of protection for regular employment over the 1990s (table 3.4).

Table 3.6 gives data for a number of OECD countries on the regulation of fixed-term contracts offered to temporary employees in the late 1980s and the late 1990s. The first two columns indicate, for each period, whether there are any restrictions on the circumstances under which a firm can use fixed-term contracts, with 0 indicating the most restrictive laws and 3 signifying that there are no such restrictions. The United States, of course, places

TABLE 3.6 **Regulation of Fixed-Term Contracts**

	Contractual Freedom Indicator (1 to 3)		Maximum Number of Successive Contracts		Maximum Cumulated Duration (Months)	
	Late 1980s	Late 1990s	Late 1980s	Late 1990s	Late 1980s	Late 1990s
Central and Western Europe						
Austria	2.5	2.5	1.5	1.5	No limit	No limit
Belgium	.0	2.0	1.0	4.0	24.0	30.0
France	1.0	1.0	3.0	2.0	24.0	18.0
Germany	2.0	2.5	1.0	4.0	18.0	24.0
Ireland	3.0	3.0	No limit	No limit	No limit	No limit
Netherlands	3.0	3.0	1.0	3.0	No limit	No limit
Switzerland	3.0	3.0	1.5	1.5	No limit	No limit
United Kingdom	3.0	3.0	No limit	No limit	No limit	No limit
Southern Europe						
Greece	.0	.0	2.5	2.5	No limit	No limit
Italy	.5	1.0	1.5	2.0	9.0	15.0
Portugal	2.0	2.0	3.0	3.0	30.0	30.0
Spain	2.0	1.0	6.0	3.0	36.0	36.0
Nordic countries						
Denmark	3.0	3.0	1.5	1.5	No limit	No limit
Finland	1.0	1.0	1.5	1.5	No limit	No limit
Norway	1.0	1.0	1.5	1.5	No limit	No limit
Sweden	2.0	2.5	2.0	No limit		12.0
North America						
Canada	3.0	3.0	No limit	No limit	No limit	No limit
United States	3.0	3.0	No limit	No limit	No limit	No limit
Asia and Oceania						
Australia	3.0	3.0	1.5	1.5	No limit	No limit
Japan		2.5	2.5	2.5		No limit
New Zealand		3.0		5.0		No limit
Non-U.S. average						
Current sample	1.9	2.2				
Late-1980s sample	1.9	2.1				

Source: OECD (1999, table 2.3, 62). Data in table 3.6 © OECD; for full citation see references.
Note: The contractual-freedom indicator is defined as follows: 0 = allowed only for material reasons (that is, task requires only fixed duration); 1 = specific exemptions exist in case of employer need (for example, launching a new venture) or employee need (for example, searching for a first job); 2 = when specific exemptions exist on both employee and employer sides; 3 = no restrictions other than duration and number of successive contracts.

no restrictions on these contracts, while, as of the late 1990s, twelve of the remaining twenty countries placed some restrictions on the situation under which an employer can use these contracts. Over the 1990s, there was some indication of a trend toward easing these restrictions in that four countries (Belgium, Germany, Italy, and Sweden) expanded the list of situations in which a fixed-term contract may be offered while only one (Spain) made its regulations more restrictive.

The last four columns of table 3.6 show the limitations on the number and total duration of fixed-term contracts that a firm is permitted to offer a worker before the firm is required to treat that worker as a regular employee. As of the late 1990s, the United States was one of only five countries that did not restrict the successive number of such contracts and one of fourteen nations that placed no restrictions on the cumulated duration of fixed-term contracts. Here, again, we see some trend toward relaxing these restrictions. Of twenty countries with information on the maximum number of contracts for both the late 1980s and the late 1990s, five increased the maximum, two reduced it, and thirteen kept it the same. Of eighteen nations with data on maximum duration, three increased the maximum, one decreased it, and fourteen left it the same.

To summarize our overall findings on restrictions in utilizing labor, we find that, as in the case of the other interventions that we have examined, the regulation of hiring and firing is far stricter in the rest of the OECD than it is in the United States.[4] However, unlike a number of other interventions that we have examined, such regulations—particularly those regarding temporary employment—appear on average to have been liberalized during the 1990s in these other countries relative to those in the United States.

Nonetheless, in light of the greater prevalence of restrictions on temporary employment in the other OECD countries, our finding in chapter 2 that there was a considerably *lower* incidence of temporary employment in the United States than in the other countries is especially striking. This suggests that there is greater demand for temporary employment by either employers or employees outside the United States, a demand that is sufficiently strong to override the negative effects of these other countries' more-restrictive laws. It seems most likely that these contracts are a way for employers in many OECD countries, particularly the countries of Southern Europe, to escape the mandated benefits that they are required to provide to regular employees, including seniority-related severance pay.

Of course, in a competitive labor market with completely flexible wages, even if the employer is permitted to offer temporary contracts, the lack of protections in such agreements will require the firm to pay a compensating wage differential for these jobs that leaves workers as well off as they would be as regular employees. A similar argument applies to mandated severance pay: with flexible wages, such laws will merely result in lower wages than otherwise. In such a world, the right to offer temporary contracts or the requirement to give severance pay will make no difference for total labor input or the present value of total compensation.[5] However, to the extent that wage-setting institutions prevent compensating differentials from being realized, these laws can, in fact, influence employment. Moreover, if it is expensive to fire workers, then, even if lower wages compensate for firing costs, the fixed costs of employment have risen relative to the variable costs. Some of these fixed costs would likely involve more-intensive screening of applicants. In such a case, even with a fixed labor input (fixed because the total hourly labor cost remained the same), there will be fewer jobs and more hours per worker. In later chapters, we discuss evidence on these issues.

MANDATED BENEFITS

Social-insurance systems tend to be far more generous in other OECD countries than in the United States. These differences have several important implications for the operation of labor markets. First, because of the more extensive safety nets in place in these other countries, being out of work there has, in most cases, less-severe consequences for family income than it does in the United States. The existence of these programs may, thus, reduce the resolve of the electorate to pursue policies that lower unemployment. Second, since most social-insurance programs stop paying benefits when recipients return to work, there is often a strong incentive to remain unemployed. On the other hand, many programs require initial employment for eligibility. It is, thus, possible that employment, or at least labor-force participation, is enhanced through the availability of these employment-related benefits (Blank and Freeman 1994). Finally, as emphasized in many analyses of European unemployment, relatively high benefit levels place a floor under wages and, thus, can affect the wage distribution as well as the stance that unions take in bargaining with employers (Blau and Kahn 1999). In this respect, then, generous systems of social insurance can have the same qualitative effect on union wage demands as do systems of employment protection.

Table 3.7 provides some evidence on the generosity of UI systems as well as on the extent of government spending on active labor-market policies such as training and subsidized employment. The information on replacement ratios indicates the fraction of the average worker's wages that is replaced during a three-month spell of unemployment. The UI systems in the United States (one for each state) had relatively low benefit levels in 1971, with an average replacement ratio of 32 percent, in comparison to the non-U.S. average of 39 percent. Over the 1970s, UI systems in the OECD, including the U.S. system, became more generous. But the increase was larger outside the United States, and, by 1981, the gap in replacement ratios had increased from 7 to 14 percentage points. The trends in generosity for the United States and the other OECD countries diverged in the 1980s, UI systems in other countries becoming marginally more generous and replacement ratios in the United States falling. By 1991, there was a 20 percentage point gap between the United States and other countries in replacement ratios, with a replacement ratio of 31 percent in the United States and an average ratio of 51 percent in the other OECD countries.

The growing gap in replacement ratios between the United States and other OECD countries raises the possibility that changing UI-benefit levels are a possible explanation for the diverging unemployment experience of the United States and these other countries. However, it is important to recognize that rising benefit levels in other OECD countries may themselves have been a response to higher levels of unemployment there. As the probability of unemployment rose and remained at high levels, support may

TABLE 3.7 **Characteristics of Unemployment-Insurance (UI) Systems and Active Labor-Market Policies**

	UI System				Spending on Active Labor-Market Policies, 1991
	Replacement Ratio			Maximum Duration (Years), 1989 to 1994	
	1971	1981	1991		
Australia	19	33	38	Indefinite	3.2
Austria	29	42	44	2	8.3
Belgium	35	45	43	Indefinite	14.6
Canada	36	44	51	1	5.9
Denmark	63	67	61	2.5	10.3
Finland	63	34	53	2	16.4
France	58	55	57	3	8.8
Germany (West)	42	40	40	Indefinite	25.7
Greece	50	50	50	1	
Ireland	32	56	41	Indefinite	9.1
Italy	10	4	15	.5	10.3
Japan	45	47	46	.5	4.3
Netherlands	80	80	70	2	6.9
New Zealand	38	37	33	Indefinite	6.8
Norway	36	60	60	1.5	14.7
Portugal	0	44	65	.8	18.8
Spain	36	74	66	3.5	4.7
Sweden	38	64	83	1.2	59.3
Switzerland	26	68	77	1	8.2
United Kingdom	47	39	24	Indefinite	6.4
Non-U.S. average (unweighted)	39	49	51		13.3
United States	32	35	31	.5	3.0

Sources: Nickell and Layard (1999, 3045); Blöndal and Pearson (1995, 141–42).
Notes: UI replacement ratios are for the first three months of unemployment for the average worker. Active-labor-market-policy spending per unemployed worker as a percentage of GDP per member of the labor force. Benefit duration for Greece is measured as of 1991.

have built for increasing the income adequacy of the benefits that unemployed workers receive.

In addition to having relatively low replacement ratios, the UI systems in the United States have the shortest maximum duration of benefits: in most cases, an individual can collect UI benefits for at most six months, although, in some exceptional circumstances, benefits can be extended for another three months. In contrast, in every other OECD country, with the exception of Italy, Japan, and Portugal, benefits can last at least a year, and, in six countries, benefits may be received indefinitely.[6] The contrast in benefit generosity and duration between UI systems in the United States and elsewhere may be one important reason why we found in chapter 2 that the incidence of long-term unemployment was so much higher in the other OECD countries.

Finally, table 3.7 shows government spending on active labor-market policies across the OECD countries. These programs involve activities such as training, employment subsidies, or direct job creation through public-sector employment (OECD 1999). The table gives spending per unemployed worker as a percentage of GDP per member of the labor force. As may be seen in the table, such spending is much more extensive in other OECD countries than in the United States, which ranks last of all the OECD countries surveyed. By this measure, per unemployed worker, the United States spent 3 percent of GDP per member of the labor force on active labor-market policies, compared to an average of 13.3 percent spent by the other OECD countries. Expenditures were especially high in Sweden and West Germany.

Active labor-market policies are likely to be a response to employment problems, representing government attempts to cope with increased joblessness. But, like job-protection mandates and UI systems, active labor-market programs may also have perverse effects, exacerbating employment problems. In particular, if there are generous government programs of subsidized employment awaiting unemployed workers, unions may be more aggressive in wage bargaining (Calmfors and Forslund 1991). And, while these programs may reduce the extent of joblessness, they may also crowd out some private-sector employment and, thus, have a smaller net effect than expected given the expenditure figures (Forslund and Krueger 1997).

Data presented by Stephen Nickell and Richard Layard (1999, 3040) for 1992 indicate that government-mandated vacation entitlements are also far more generous in other countries than in the United States. There is no mandated paid vacation in the United States. In comparison, in nineteen other OECD countries for which data were available, an average of 3.5 weeks of vacation time (seventeen to eighteen days) is the minimum mandated level even beyond public holidays. However, while vacation time is likely to be higher in other countries than in the United States, the contrast is less sharp than these figures imply. The vast majority of private-sector, full-time workers in the United States (91 percent in 1996 to 1997) are eligible for paid vacation time voluntarily provided by their employers (Foster 2000). Paid vacation time increases with the employee's length of service, averaging nine days after one year of service, fifteen days after ten years, and eventually topping out at eighteen days after twenty years. Since average current job tenure in the United States is on the order of three to five years (Ehrenberg and Smith 2000), the average American worker is entitled to fewer than fifteen days of paid vacation. This is less than the seventeen- to eighteen-day average minimum in the other countries. The contrast is particularly sharp for new employees, who would get only nine days on average in the United States.

Like vacation time, mandated parental leave is far more generous outside the United States as well. In the United States, as of 1993, workers were granted twelve weeks of unpaid family leave. The voluntary provision of paid family leave is extremely rare in the United States, with only 2 percent of American workers eligible for such leave (Foster 2000). In contrast, in 1995, average mandated leave time in nineteen other OECD countries was sixty-five weeks, and, in many cases, this was paid leave (Nickell and Layard 1999, 3040).

It is possible that these entitlements to vacation and parental leave are at least partly responsible for the shorter annual work hours in other countries that were seen in the previous chapter (table 2.5). Moreover, as we discuss in detail in later chapters, family-leave entitlements can affect the gender pay gap as well.

We noted in the last chapter that, while the incidence of employment among older individuals (those aged fifty-five to sixty-four) was lower than that of prime-age adults (those aged twenty-five to fifty-four) in every country, it was comparatively high in the United States. Table 3.8 presents some information on one possible cause of such differences: the nature of the retirement system. In 1992, U.S. men had a higher normal retirement age (that is, the age at which one becomes eligible for full social secu-

TABLE 3.8 **Retirement-System Characteristics, 1992**

	Age Eligible for Normal Retirement Benefits		Integration of UI and Pension Systems?	Reduced Benefits Available for Early Retirees Without Long Service?	Full Benefits Available for Early Retirees with Long Service?
	Men	Women			
Australia	65	60	Yes	No	No
Germany	65	65	Yes	No	Yes
United Kingdom	65	60	Yes	No	No
Austria	65	60	Yes	No	Yes
Italy	60	55	No	No	Yes
Switzerland	65	62	No	No	No
Netherlands	65	65	Yes	No	No
Norway	67	67	No	No	No
New Zealand	61	61	No	No	No
Canada	65	65	No	Yes	No
Japan	60	58	No	No	No
Spain	65	65	No	Yes	No
Ireland	66	66	Yes	No	No
Sweden	65	65	No	Yes	No
United States	65	65	No	Yes	No

Source: OECD (1995 table 4.1, 72; table 4.3, 74). Data in table 3.8 © OECD; for full citation see references.

rity benefits) than did men in three other countries, a lower retirement age than in two countries, and the same retirement age as in nine countries. However, the retirement age for women was higher in the United States than in seven of the other countries, the same in the United States as in five countries, and lower in the United States than in two countries. Moreover, six countries integrate their retirement and UI systems by allowing unemployed older workers to collect UI benefits until they become eligible for retirement pay, while the United States does not. On the other hand, the United States was one of four countries to allow workers to collect reduced benefits and retire early, while three countries (but not the United States) allow full benefits for early retirees with long service. Overall, the retirement systems of these other OECD countries appear to make labor-force withdrawal more attractive than does the U.S. retirement system—with the exception of the U.S. reduced-benefits entitlement.

The final benefit programs that we survey are those that provide sickness and disability benefits. These benefits are paid to workers who become sick or disabled, and they typically end when the individual returns to work. They are, thus, similar on their face to unemployment benefits in that they provide financial incentives to stay out of work. Data on sickness and disability benefits are provided by Sveinbjörn Blöndal and Mark Pearson (1995, 157–58). The data indicate that while the United States has no mandated sickness benefits, all other OECD countries except Switzerland have such a program, and the average replacement ratio among countries with such programs was 54.3 percent in 1974 and 47.4 percent in 1993. Similarly, while all OECD countries had disability programs, those outside the United States were considerably more generous than was the American program. The U.S. replacement ratio was 26 percent in 1974 and 30 percent in 1993, while replacement ratios outside the United States averaged 45.8 percent in 1974 and 47.7 percent in 1993. While both sickness and disability programs were more generous outside the United States, on average, replacement ratios for both types of programs were coming down over the 1980s and early 1990s in these other countries, compared to those in the United States. Again, the high level of sickness and disability benefits is a further possible reason for lower annual work hours and lower relative employment among the elderly in other OECD countries than in the United States.

Mandated benefits must, of course, be paid for. And higher benefit levels require higher tax revenues. Nickell and Layard (1999, 3038) report that the rate of total taxes on labor—including payroll, income, and sales taxes—was modestly higher, on average, in other countries (48.4 percent) than in the United States (43.8 percent). The difference was larger for marginal tax rates for average production workers: 58.4 percent, on average, in the other countries and 38.5 percent in the United States. These differences in tax rates are intriguing and could be a factor contributing to the differences in labor-market performance documented in chapter 2.

Of course, taxes and mandated benefits may be passed back to workers in the form of lower wages and, thus, may not affect the quantity of labor demanded by very much (Gruber 1994; Gruber and Krueger 1990). However, in analyzing their potential effects on employment, it is important to recognize that taxes and subsidies may impose a wedge between labor costs to the employer and the worker's gain to working. The greater this difference, the lower employment will be, on the assumption that the after-tax wage affects labor supply and the before-tax wage affects labor demand. To the extent that the tax wedge lowers the value of after-tax wages relative to after-tax unemployment benefits, the greater the wedge, the higher the unemployment rate is expected to be. Of course, if all taxes pay for benefits that raise the value of working, then the after-tax wage could be the same as the before-tax wage, and there would be no reason for the total tax rate to be correlated with employment. Whether taxes affect employment, then, is an empirical question, and, in later chapters, we survey evidence on the degree to which this is the case.

Related to the issue of taxes is the phenomenon of industrial subsidies. Jonathan Leonard and Marc Van Audenrode (1993) find that these amount to 3 to 6 percent of GDP in the European Community but only 0.5 percent of GDP in the United States. Moreover, Leonard and Van Audenrode argue that, not only are industrial subsidies much more extensive in Europe than in the United States, but they are also given disproportionately to declining firms and industries. Thus, in effect, declining firms are kept going by taxing expanding firms. According to Leonard and Van Audenrode, an important indirect effect of such policies is to make European unions more aggressive when bargaining since they know that any extreme disemployment effects of their wage bargains will be reduced through subsidies. The same caveat about the shifting of taxes applies to subsidies as well. Nonetheless, we must consider the greater likelihood of subsidies for failing firms as part of the institutional environment that distinguishes much of the OECD from the United States.

CONCLUSIONS

In this chapter, we have shown that there is far greater intervention by labor-market institutions in wage setting and the allocation of labor in many other OECD countries than there is in the United

States. Moreover, mandated benefits are much more extensive and tax rates higher in these countries as well. The juxtaposition of this information about labor-market institutions and regulations and our description of employment, wage levels, and wage inequality in chapter 2 suggests a strong role of institutions in explaining these outcomes. The United States has less union and government intervention as well as less unemployment and more wage inequality than is found elsewhere. Moreover, in the 1980s and 1990s, unemployment worsened elsewhere relative to that in the United States, while real-wage levels fell and wage inequality rose in the United States compared to those in these other countries. Thus, it is possible that the interventionist policies and institutions in these other countries have kept wages from adjusting to changing economic circumstances, producing these wage and employment outcomes. In the remainder of this book, we carefully consider the evidence bearing on this conclusion.

Chapter 4

Detecting the Effect of Institutions on Labor-Market Performance: Conceptual Issues

I N THE LAST two chapters, we documented the considerable differences between labor-market performance and labor-market institutions in the United States and other OECD countries. The data reported there are consistent with the view that institutions are an important part of the story explaining why the United States has had greater success in lowering unemployment than have other OECD countries but has also experienced lower real-wage growth and higher and more rapidly rising wage inequality. But this juxtaposition of data on outcomes and differences in institutions is not sufficient to establish a fully convincing case for the importance of institutions. An important first step is to consider the anticipated effect of institutional intervention on these outcomes from the perspective of economic theory.

We must also probe empirical evidence in greater detail, making full use of micro data on individuals, which allow us to adjust for international differences in the composition of the population that may also affect employment and wage outcomes, as well as of sophisticated statistical analyses of these data. This is important because there are other factors besides institutions, such as macroeconomic shocks, that can influence wage and employment outcomes, and it is essential to account for their effects before reaching conclusions about the effect of institutions. Moreover, the employment problems created by these other factors may then cause a country to alter the character of its institutions. For example, high unemployment may lead some countries to increase the generosity of the unemployment-insurance (UI) system, as appears to have occurred in Switzerland between 1990 and 1995 (see Sheldon 1997, 72–73). In this case, the greater generosity of the UI system is a response to a country's employment problems rather than the cause of them, although it may, in turn, contribute to the persistence of these problems.

In this chapter, we present the economic analyses that provide a theoretical framework for studying the effect of institutions on labor markets. We first discuss the role that institutions can play in creating desirable or undesirable wage, productivity, and employment outcomes. Under some circumstances, institutional intervention may correct market failures and, thus, produce superior economic outcomes. And, while there are circumstances under which institutional interventions will contribute to overall unemployment or exacerbate relative-employment problems for particular groups, economic theory does not unambiguously predict that wage interventions, employment protection, mandated benefits, or high taxes will produce such employment problems. Thus, empirical evidence is especially crucial in determining what the effect of these labor-market institutions has actually been. We then address the difficult issues of research design that can potentially allow us to separate out cause and effect and to account for other influences on labor-market outcomes besides institutional intervention. With this framework in hand, we turn in subsequent chapters to an evaluation of the available evidence on the effect of institutions on labor-market performance.

WHY ARE THERE LABOR-MARKET INSTITUTIONS?

Before analyzing the effect of institutions on the labor market, it is worth considering the reasons for their existence in the first place. This issue is of interest in its own right since an understanding of where the demand for institutions comes from will help us predict likely institutional responses to economic developments. For example, a large increase in inflation uncertainty is likely to raise the demand for wage indexation on the part of risk-averse workers

(Ehrenberg, Danziger, and San 1983). Similarly, declines in inflation uncertainty are expected to reduce workers' resistance to limiting systems of indexation, as appears to have occurred in Italy the mid-1980s (Erickson and Ichino 1995).

A second important motivation for considering the reasons for the emergence of institutions is related to economic methodology. An observed empirical association between institutions and outcomes, such as unemployment rates or wage inequality, may, indeed, reflect a true causal relationship. However, as we have just seen, it is also possible that the causation runs from the outcomes to the establishment of the institutional arrangements or that the same set of underlying factors led to both the institutions and the observed economic outcomes. In these latter cases, we would overestimate the effect of institutions on economic outcomes by attributing the observed association between institutions and outcomes entirely to the causal effect of the former on the latter. For example, declining unionization has been credited by some authors with causing a portion of the observed increase in wage inequality in such countries as the United Kingdom and the United States. However, if such underlying factors as international trade and technological change contributed to the reduction in unionization and the rise in inequality, then these authors may be attributing too much of the increase in inequality to deunionization.

Even granting that institutions themselves may be endogenous, we still expect them to play an important role in moderating the effect of economic forces. Indeed, as our indexation example suggests, this is one source of the demand for institutions in the first place. Of course, it is also the case that market forces may reassert themselves even after an institutional arrangement is implemented or modified. For example, in the United States, the minimum wage may be viewed as an institution that has relatively little effect on the labor market. This is because it is set at such a low level that most workers would earn more than the minimum in any case. Thus, it is important to bear in mind that the mere presence of an institution does not mean that it has a significant effect on the labor market. The extent to which market forces do or do not override the effect of institutions in particular cases is an empirical question.

Two approaches to the question of the emergence of institutions have been proposed in recent years. First, it has been argued by some that labor-market regulations can correct market failures, chiefly several of those related to imperfect information. Such institutional interventions may, thus, increase economic efficiency by changing the outcome that would have resulted from the unfettered operation of market forces. Second, others have taken an explicit political-economy approach. This entails identifying politically powerful groups and attempting to understand what is in their economic self-interest. In contrast to the case in which institutions are initiated to correct market failures, institutional interventions that arise to meet the interests of particular groups will not necessarily promote economic efficiency. We now provide some examples of these two kinds of explanations.

The types of labor-market failures that figure most prominently in the literature on the emergence of institutions involve job security, wage setting, or job search. First, it has been argued that firms can benefit from offering workers job security because such an arrangement is likely to make workers more willing to undertake firm-specific training investments for which the returns would otherwise be uncertain (Hashimoto 1990). On-the-job training involves the acquisition of new skills, such as learning new production methods, for which the returns will come in the future. When training is firm specific, these skills increase the workers' skills only at the particular firm that provides the training and, hence, will not be rewarded elsewhere. Workers are, thus, expected to be more willing to undertake such investments if their jobs are secure.

However, problems may arise if only one firm in a labor market offers job security (implicitly or explicitly). Workers who would have otherwise expected to be discharged from their jobs will be among those most attracted to that firm. If there is also asymmetric information, for example, if workers have better information about their likely performance on the job than firms do, firms will be unable to screen out undesirable workers. The resulting adverse-selection problem is likely to reduce the willingness of firms to offer job security. Just as in insurance markets, we may get a suboptimal level of job security. Laws mandating job security or raising the cost of discharging workers can help solve the adverse-selection problem and, thereby raise economic efficiency (Levine and Tyson 1990). The same reasoning has been applied to government-mandated parental-leave policies. Without such mandates, individual firms offering leave will attract the workers most likely to take leave (Ruhm and Teague 1997).

A second insurance-related motivation for institutions has been used to provide an efficiency rationale for wage-equalizing mechanisms, such as highly centralized collective-bargaining structures, that impose a low level of wage inequality on major portions of the labor market. If, before entering the labor market, risk-averse individuals are uncertain about how the market is going to reward their human capital, they may have a demand for income insurance. However, private insurance markets will not supply such a product for the usual reasons of adverse selection, moral hazard, and correlated risks. That is, if there were privately provided income insurance, people who expect income problems would be among those most attracted to it (the adverse-selection problem). And, once individuals had such an insurance policy, they might very well behave in ways that raise the likelihood of needing the insurance, for example, by quitting their jobs or taking jobs with a high layoff probability (the moral-hazard problem). Finally, if such privately provided income insurance existed, it is likely that many people would need it at the same time since recessions would affect many policyholders all at once (the correlated-risks problem). Thus, the financial solvency of income-insurance providers would be severely tested during recessions.

For all these reasons, we do not expect private markets to offer income insurance, even though the public undoubtedly has a demand for such protection. Lars Ljungqvist (1995) and Jonas Agell and Kjell Lommerud (1992) interpret wage leveling as a form of income insurance, implying that institutions leading to such an outcome may raise economic welfare and, thus, enhance economic efficiency in the sense of providing positive net benefits to society. And, of course, the same reasoning applies to the public provision of UI (Gruber 1997a). While long-term employment relationships may partially insure workers' incomes (Rosen 1985), the adverse-selection, moral-hazard, and correlated-risks problems discussed here suggest that this insurance may be less complete than the public desires.

An additional potentially welfare enhancing effect of wage equalization could be realized if large industry wage differentials would exist in the absence of wage-setting intervention. There is considerable evidence that different industries pay different wage levels for similarly qualified labor, although there is some controversy over whether unmeasured productivity could explain these differentials (see Krueger and Summers 1988; Murphy and Topel 1990; and Gibbons and Katz 1992). To the extent that such industry differentials are not due to differences in worker productivity or to compensating non-wage factors, they may reflect the decision of some firms to pay above-market wages. It has been argued that it may be profitable for these firms to do so because it results in better work performance, lower turnover, and a larger supply of qualified applicants (Shapiro and Stiglitz 1984; Stiglitz 1974; Bulow and Summers 1986). These above-market wage levels have been termed *efficiency wages* since they enhance the economic efficiency (that is, the profitability) of the firm.

While the payment of above-market wages may be beneficial from the perspective of the individual firm, when some industries pay such efficiency wages and others do not, labor may be misallocated from the economy's point of view. In particular, the marginal-revenue product of labor for identical workers will be higher in the industries paying efficiency wages. The total value of output, given the level of labor and capital inputs, could be increased if we could shift some labor from low-wage, low-productivity industries to high-wage, high-productivity industries (Bulow and Summers 1986). An encompassing union policy of wage equalization across industries can eliminate this source of inefficiency by causing the shrinkage of the low-wage sector and the expansion of the high-wage sector. Coen Teulings and Joop Hartog (1998) argue that this reasoning characterizes economies in which wages are set at a highly centralized level, such as in the Scandinavian countries, and Douglas Hibbs and Håkan Locking (2000) present some evidence that reducing interindustry wage differentials in Sweden in the period 1968 to 1984 raised overall labor productivity. However, to the extent that there are other sources of interindustry differentials, such policies can also create inefficiencies by eliminating wage differentials that would otherwise encourage people to move to sectors in which labor is scarce or to invest in on-the-job training.

Other types of institutional interventions that, it might be argued, enhance efficiency relate to job search. For example, active labor-market policies such as training or relocation allowances may help correct possible market failures in matching workers and employers that result from incomplete information in the labor market. UI can also be viewed in the same light to the extent that it helps workers find better job matches.

While these theories remind us that institutional interventions can potentially increase economic welfare on efficiency, as well as on equity, grounds, they do not yield sharp predictions about where and when particular institutions are most likely to emerge. For example, we might expect government intervention regulating job-security provisions to be more likely the worse the adverse-selection problem facing private firms in the absence of government action. In general, such problems are more severe the greater the heterogeneity of the labor force with respect to productivity and the more difficult it is for firms to learn about the productivity of individual workers prior to hiring them. Thus, we might expect greater demand for job-security-enhancing policies on efficiency grounds in countries with more heterogeneous workers and with poorer labor-market information about those workers' ability. However, there is likely to be less consensus in favor of job-security policies in such settings than there is in settings where the electorate is more homogeneous. Similarly, controlling for risk aversion, the demand for wage leveling should be greater the larger is the ex ante uncertainty regarding market wages for an individual. But finding a coalition in support of such policies in economies with widely divergent labor-market outcomes for seemingly similar individuals may be difficult.

These examples imply that issues of political economy can soften the predictions of efficiency-based models for the formation of institutions. A political-economy approach can, given some reasonable assumptions, help us understand the growth and demise of certain labor-market rules and laws. Gilles Saint-Paul (1996) uses such a framework to analyze what he claims to be the European resistance to reforming the traditional labor-market institutions of generous UI, high minimum wages, and high firing costs, even in the face of persistent high unemployment.

Saint-Paul's basic approach to studying laws and institutions is to focus on the "decisive voter" in the democratic systems of the European OECD countries. For example, to the extent that the employed are more numerous and better organized than the non-employed, policies benefiting the former are likely to be adopted even if they result in persistent high unemployment. High mandated firing costs are an example of a law that protects incumbents ("insiders") at the expense of those without jobs ("outsiders"). More generally, insiders may push for very high wage levels, as long as their own jobs are protected. On the other hand, Saint-Paul predicts that, the larger the group of outsiders, the more likely labor-market reforms increasing firm flexibility will be enacted. For example, in the early 1990s in Spain, about 20 percent of the labor force was unemployed, and 33 percent of the employed were on fixed-duration contracts (Bentolila and Dolado 1994). Since nearly half the labor force could be considered outsiders, one might suppose that this country was ripe for labor-market reforms benefiting these groups.

Like the economic-efficiency framework, the political-economy approach may also not yield airtight predictions. This is due in part to problems of aggregating preferences and to the changing makeup of the groups (today's outsiders may anticipate being tomorrow's insiders). And many of the features characterizing European insiders also characterize Americans employed at high wages, implying that something more is needed if we are to explain why the United States has so much more labor-market flexibility than do other OECD countries. Yet the political-economy analysis forces us to focus on who gains and who loses from specific policies, and it can, in many instances, yield interesting insights about why governments make the decisions they do.

Ultimately, the U.S.-European differences in labor-market flexibility likely reflect the same factors that have resulted in such a low rate of unionization in the United States. The origins of this difference date back to the nineteenth century, when, it has been argued, individuals perceived much greater opportunity for upward social mobility and wealth accumulation in the United States than in Europe (Pelling 1960). If these perceptions were, in fact, generally held, then it is easy to see why collectivist policies of social-democratic trade unionism and welfare capitalism caught on to a lesser extent in the United States than in Europe.

THE ECONOMIC EFFECTS OF
WAGE-SETTING INSTITUTIONS

In this section, we review economic theories on the employment effects of wage-setting institutions. We will see that, under some circumstances, economic theory predicts that raising wages above market levels will cause employment problems and that, under others, institutional interventions in wage setting can actually increase employment. Moreover, there are likely to be economic effects of institutional intervention that go beyond the effect on employment, and we discuss these as well.

There is a considerable literature examining the tendency of unemployment in many parts of Europe to remain high even long after an initial economic shock raised unemployment in the first place. This inertia in the unemployment rate is termed *hysteresis*.[1] An example of a mechanism that has been proposed as causing hysteresis is a deterioration of workers' skills as their duration of unemployment increases; this lowers their probability of leaving unemployment (Ljungqvist and Sargent 1998). In a similar vein, it is sometimes claimed that the long-term unemployed exert little downward pressure on wages since they do not search hard for jobs (Nickell 1987). Thus, an initial increase in unemployment can become difficult to undo as unemployment duration increases. And generous systems of UI benefits with unlimited potential duration of benefit collection can clearly contribute to the long duration of unemployment.

Hysteresis may also arise as a result of the behavior of unions. For example, it is claimed that, at any given unemployment rate, unions will be more aggressive the higher unemployment was in the previous period since insiders' jobs are less threatened when unemployment is falling than when it is rising. Thus, in principle, union wage bargaining can slow down the decline in unemployment during a recovery (Layard, Nickell, and Jackman 1991), although, as we explain later in this chapter, more aggressive unions do not necessarily cause higher unemployment in the first place.

Monopoly Unions Versus Efficient Bargains

Virtually all empirical research on the effect of union wage-setting mechanisms on employment makes the assumption that, although unions influence wage and benefit levels through bargaining, employers determine the level of employment through their hiring decisions. This framework has been termed the *monopoly-union model* to reflect the idea that unions attempt to take wages out of competition (one wage for the labor market) and let firms make hiring decisions.[2]

An immediate implication of the monopoly-union framework is that, other things equal, higher union wage levels will cause a reduction in employment levels. In deciding on their wage demands, unions must balance the gains of higher wages for employed members against the additional job losses that these higher wages will cause. In this framework, anything that reduces the costs associated with being unemployed will make the union more aggressive.

This way of thinking about union behavior is reflected in the observations that economists have made about the effect on union wage demands of UI, active labor-market policies, job protection, and employment subsidies. Since each of these government policies reduces the losses associated with unemployment, each is expected to raise union wage demands. This, then, produces further employment problems.[3]

Considering the effects of UI, employment protection, and the like on union behavior implies that labor-market institutions interact. Thus, for instance, changing one institution—for example, reducing the extent of collective bargaining in New Zealand or the United Kingdom—will have different effects depending on the other types of institutional interventions that are left in place. Moreover, if unions disproportionately raise the wages of those at the bottom, then the ensuing employment problems are expected to be greater for them. The reasoning is analogous to the expected effect of minimum wages on employment. If firms are on their labor-demand curves and take wages as given, then higher minimum wages will lower employment, with especially large effects on those whose wages are raised the most.

The monopoly-union framework provides an explanation for why, when bargaining proceeds in a decentralized fashion, as it does in the United States, some unions bargain for much higher wage premiums than do others. For example, in the 1970s in the United States, the union relative-wage effect was considerably higher in the construction industry than elsewhere (Lewis 1986, 127). The monopoly-union model predicts that, all else equal, the lower the elasticity of demand for labor, the higher the union wage demand will be since a given wage increase will have a smaller negative effect on employment. In industries like construction where workers are highly skilled and there are, thus, few substitutes available, the demand for labor is less elastic, and, on the basis of the monopoly-union model, we expect union wage demands to be higher. While some portion of high construction wages undoubtedly compensates workers for their variable work schedules, union wage premiums on top of these already high wages have historically been very large as well (Lewis 1986).

While the monopoly-union model provides an intuitively appealing framework for analyzing the effect of collective bargaining on labor-market performance, it has long been recognized by economists that labor and management can do better for themselves by jointly setting pay and employment levels.[4] To see this, consider that, under monopoly unionism, the firm is free to adjust employment to maximize profits given the wage level that has been imposed on the firm through collective bargaining. This means that the effect of a small increase in employment on the firm's profits will be very small because the firm has already adjusted hiring to maximize profits. However, the marginal value of additional employment to the union can be quite high if some of its members are unemployed, which is likely to be the case if the union has raised wages above the competitive level. Near the employment level corresponding to maximum profit, then, the marginal value of additional employment to the union is likely to be greater than the marginal cost of additional employment to the firm. This means that both sides can be made better off if the union accepts a lower wage and the firm allows employment to grow to a higher level than it would have chosen on its own. Such a contract has been termed an *efficient bargain* since it has been set with the goal of jointly maximizing the welfare of both parties, although it may not necessarily be efficient from society's point of view. As will be seen shortly, while such contracts raise worker pay over the competitive level, they need not result in any fall in employment.

A hypothetical example can make the idea of efficient bargains more concrete. Suppose that we begin with a relatively small firm hiring labor in a competitive labor market. The result will be a competitively established level of wages and benefits, which we call w_c. If the firm maximizes profits, it will hire labor up to the point at which the marginal-revenue product of labor is just equal to w_c.

Now suppose that the firm becomes unionized and that the union goal is to maximize the total surplus income of its members over what they could earn in other jobs, namely, w_c.[5] Under the monopoly-union model, the union will negotiate a wage, say w_m, such that

$$w_m > w_c \qquad (4.1)$$

since there will be no gain over the competitive outcome if the union does not negotiate a raise for its members.

As we have seen, the union wage demand is determined by balancing the gains to its members of a higher wage against the employment losses expected to result from the higher wage since, by assumption, the union allows the firm to determine hiring. This means that

$$\mathrm{MRP}_u = w_m > w_c = \mathrm{MRP}_c, \qquad (4.2)$$

where MRP_u is the marginal-revenue product of labor in this firm, and MRP_c is the marginal-revenue product of labor elsewhere in the labor market. Marginal-revenue product is the increase in the firm's revenue associated with hiring an additional worker. Under competitive conditions in the product market, the marginal-revenue product of labor is equal to the increase in output associated with adding an additional worker, the marginal product of labor (MP), multiplied by the price at which that output can be sold (P);

that is, MRP $=$ MP $\times$ P. Since, under competition in the product market, the firm is a price taker, P is constant at the price determined in the market where the firm sells its output. This means that the firm's marginal-revenue product of labor is closely related to how productive its workers are.[6] If the firm has product-market power, then MRP $=$ MP $\times$ MR, where MR (marginal revenue) is the change in revenue when one more unit of output is sold. Marginal revenue will fall as output increases if the firm faces a downward-sloping product-demand schedule.

Under this type of contract, there will be some union members who lose their jobs and must look for work, presumably in the competitive sector. However, according to equation 4.2, the marginal-revenue product of these disemployed union members will necessarily be lower in other firms than it would be in the union firm. This means that the total surplus to be divided by labor and management, that is, the sum of firm profits and the union's total income surplus over the competitive level, could be increased by adding employment beyond the monopoly-union level. In fact, this total labor and management surplus can be maximized by keeping employment in the firm at its original, non-union level. At any employment level less than this, labor will have a higher marginal-revenue product in the union firm than at other competitive firms.

In order to get management to go along with a so-called efficient bargain, the union will have to accept a wage that is below the monopoly-union level. In order to get the union to go along with the efficient bargain, the firm will need to pay wages above the competitive level. Where wages are set depends on the relative bargaining strength of the two sides, which will be affected by the economic resources available to labor and management in the event of a strike. But the upshot is clear: management must hire more workers than it would have chosen to hire at the negotiated wage. And, under these conditions, union wage bargaining has no effect on employment. Rather, it merely redistributes income from the firm to the workers. While we have assumed that the union members are risk neutral, Ian McDonald and Robert Solow (1981) show that, when union members are risk averse, employment in an efficient bargain is likely to be even higher than it is at the competitive level.[7]

From the standpoint of economic performance, the efficient-bargaining framework has the remarkable implication that strong unions might not cost their members jobs and could even increase employment if union members are risk averse. Moreover, as the example presented earlier suggests, compared to the monopoly-union outcome, both labor and management can be made better off under efficient bargaining. This suggests that there are incentives for both sides to set wages and employment jointly. However, it may be much more difficult to monitor and enforce efficient bargains than monopoly-union contracts. This conclusion is based on the idea that, since the firm is forced off its demand curve in the efficient-bargaining model, it will have incentives to try to shed labor. The union must continually attempt to monitor the firm's employment, and it may not have the resources to do so successfully. On the other hand, under the monopoly-union model, the firm is allowed to be on its demand curve for labor, so there is no enforcement problem as long as the firm pays the level of wages and benefits called for in the contract. And this can be monitored simply by reading one's paycheck! Thus, although there may be some incentives for labor and management to set wages and employment jointly, there may be additional enforcement costs as well. Therefore, whether we even have efficient contracts and off-the-demand-curve outcomes becomes an empirical question.

Labor-Market Monopsony

The example discussed dealt with a situation in which, before it became unionized, the firm operated in a competitive labor market in which it took the level of pay and benefits as given. Suppose, however, that, prior to unionization, a firm has some degree of labor-market power in the sense that it faces an upward-sloping labor-supply schedule: if it cuts wages, it will lose some, but not all, of its workers. This contrasts with the situation of a competitive firm, which will lose all its workers if it pays below-market wages. The most extreme case of labor-market power is monopsony, where the firm is literally the only buyer of labor in the market. This is analogous to monopoly in the product market where the firm is the only seller of the particular product. Pure monopsony is probably very rare in a modern urban economy since it is likely to be limited to isolated, single-company towns. However, any time a firm's workers must expend resources, lose some income, or experience psychic discomfort as a result of changing jobs, the firm potentially has some degree of market power over its current employees (which we will term *monopsony power*). Since changing jobs is not costless, monopsony power has the potential to be widespread, even in a modern urban economy (Card and Krueger 1995; Manning 1996).

If a firm does have monopsony power over its workers, it is expected that it will use some of its market power to pay workers less than they would have received in a competitive labor market. Since the firm faces an upward-sloping labor schedule, this will result in less employment at the firm than would have prevailed in a competitive labor market, this lower wage driving some workers into other activities or other areas of the economy. If we then confront the firm with a union-negotiated wage increase or a minimum-wage mandate that raises wages to what they would have been under competition, then employment at the firm may actually *increase*. In effect, such wage interventions, which constrain the firm from paying wages below a particular level—in this case, the union pay scale or the legislated minimum—take away the firm's monopsony power and force it to behave as a competitor in the labor market. Of course, employment could still fall if a union or a minimum-wage law pushed wages considerably above the competitive level. However, the interesting implication from considering the monopsony model is that, where the firm has some degree of monopsony power, it is quite possible for wage interventions to cause an increase, or at least no decrease, in employment.

The Centralization and Coordination of Collective Bargaining

While collective bargaining itself is expected to have an important influence on wages and possibly on employment as well, the nature of union-management bargaining structures is also believed to be potentially quite important in affecting these outcomes. Specifically, it has increasingly been recognized that structures that are very centralized or in which the strategies of labor and management groups are highly coordinated have very different outcomes than less-centralized structures do. Formal examination of the effect of wage centralization began in 1988 with the publication of a highly influential paper by Lars Calmfors and John Driffill that was primarily concerned with macroeconomic performance. Calmfors and Driffill attempted to explain why some collective-bargaining systems led to wage restraint and high employment levels but others yielded high real wages and low employment levels. This work and the extensions that followed used the monopoly-union framework, in which employment is determined unilaterally by firms after wage bargains have been struck—hence the presumed negative relation between real-wage levels and employment.

The key insight of the Calmfors and Driffill approach was to note that the level at which negotiations take place will greatly influence the wage-bargaining stance taken by unions and management. *Centralization* refers to the degree to which coalitions are created across unions and across firms or industries. At one extreme, consider the most decentralized form of collective bargaining—enterprise bargaining between one union and part or all of one firm. This type of bargaining characterizes the United States more than other countries, with the possible exception of Canada. (Of course, individual, nonunion wage setting is even more decentralized than is enterprise unionism, and the United States, with its low union coverage, is highly decentralized along this dimension as well.) If the industry in question is competitive, there will be almost no scope for a union to raise its members' relative wages, so we will, of necessity, observe wage restraint and high employment levels.

Making negotiations more centralized has two opposing effects on union wage policy. On the one hand, bringing more firms into the bargaining unit lowers the effective elasticity of demand for labor since union firms will face less competition from nonunion firms. For example, if, instead of organizing only one firm in the industry, the union is able to induce all firms to join the bargaining unit, then union wage policy is likely to become more aggressive as the employment losses caused by a given wage increase are reduced. On the other hand, the more workers included in the bargaining unit, the better able the union is to internalize what would have been externalities had bargaining been less centralized. For example, a union in a single-firm bargaining unit is unlikely to take into account the effects of higher union-negotiated wages on other workers (or even its own members) through higher product prices or higher taxes to finance larger UI payouts. In contrast, when an encompassing union signs a contract with a large employer federation that covers all workers economywide, the price effects of higher wages directly lower the real wages of union members, and the taxes that pay for higher UI benefits will come out of the incomes of union members.[8] The union will practice wage restraint in this situation because the response of prices and taxes to high wages hurts its own members.

An additional example in the same spirit concerns whether the union leadership anticipates a response of the central bank to their wage bargains. The central bank's likely response to rapid increases in overall wage levels is monetary restraint. Unions are much more likely to take this response into account when negotiations are conducted at the national level and the anticipated monetary response will have a more substantial effect on wage levels than when negotiations are locally based (Hall and Franzese 1998; Flanagan 1999).

Calmfors and Driffill's (1988) model, thus, predicts wage restraint for encompassing unions as well as for completely decentralized union-management bargaining pairs. The intermediate case is the worst from a macroeconomic point of view: enough centralization to assure the union's ability to raise wages without much job loss, but not enough centralization to induce the union to take into account the price and tax consequences of its wage bargaining.

This basic framework has been extended to include analyses of such issues as monopolistic competition and international trade (for a summary, see Calmfors 1993). These considerations may modify the inverted U-shaped relation between wage restraint and centralization. For example, under monopolistic competition, even unions bargaining at the level of the individual firm can raise wages, but the arguments for higher wage bargains under industry-level bargaining than under firm-level bargaining remain: consumers find it more difficult to substitute across industries than among firms within an industry (Layard, Nickell, and Jackman

1991). Trade can counterbalance the postulated effects of central-ization. With an open economy, foreign competition will restrain even industrywide monopoly unions (Danthine and Hunt 1994). In the limit, in a small, open economy with world markets for each good produced, centralization will make no difference at all (Calmfors 1993).

A final implication of centralized wage-setting processes concerns the origins of welfare-state programs. According to Lawrence Summers, Jonathan Gruber, and Rodrigo Vergara (1993), in corporatist societies, such as Sweden, wage-setting and labor-allocation decisions are determined by groups rather than by individuals.[9] Labor representatives will be less averse to high taxes than individuals will be because unions recognize the link between taxes and welfare-state benefits. If centralized unions can control the total labor supplied (a controversial assumption), the negative effect of higher taxes on labor supply is likely to be greater where labor-supply levels are set by individuals, as in the United States, than in a corporatist society. This is the case because, in corporatist societies, the connection between taxes and benefits in the minds of those determining the total labor supply (that is, the central union federation) is much more direct than it is in the minds of individual workers. Since it is possible to raise taxes in corporatist economies with fewer adverse effects, public support for an extensive welfare state is likely to be greater in such societies. This reasoning implies that causality runs from wage-setting institutions to welfare-state characteristics rather than vice versa.

As evidence for this view, Summers, Gruber, and Vergara point out that Sweden did not embark on a policy of truly centralized bargaining until roughly 1956. At that time, taxes were only a slightly higher fraction of GNP than they were in the United States. However, after 1956, Sweden's tax rates took off relative to those in the United States. Since the Social Democrats were in power both before and after the shift in wage-setting regimes, a change in the governing party cannot account for the increase in tax rates.

If the mechanism outlined by Summers, Gruber, and Vergara (1993) is correct, then the centralization of wage setting is a fundamental cause of more-generous social-benefit programs that themselves may then affect the wage distribution. However, a weakness of this argument is that, even in countries such as Sweden, it may be difficult for union federations to control the labor supply of individual members. Moreover, this reasoning runs counter to that of Calmfors and Driffill (1988) discussed earlier that it is precisely the greater sensitivity of encompassing unions to the negative effects on their members of higher taxes (and prices) due to higher negotiated wage bargains that leads them to practice greater wage restraint. Nonetheless, the takeoff of social spending in Sweden after the centralization of wage bargaining is intriguing evidence in support of a causal ordering. An alternative explanation of the correlation of wage-setting structures and social benefits to that offered by Summers, Gruber, and Vergara is that encompassing unions support generous social benefits to deal with the disemployment that results from high wage floors and that would otherwise generate pressure to lower these floors. Under either interpretation, however, the prime mover is the wage-setting system.

Collective Bargaining and Wage Inequality

In virtually every study of collective bargaining, unions are found to reduce the degree of wage inequality within their jurisdictions. Moreover, more-centralized collective-bargaining arrangements tend to produce less wage inequality than occurs under less-centralized arrangements. In later chapters, we summarize this literature and present some further data on these issues as well. We are concerned now, however, with understanding such effects from an economic point of view. Why should a union negotiate a contract that leads to a lower degree of wage dispersion than we would have seen without a union? There are two levels on which one can understand such behavior—an accounting level and a deeper behavioral level.

First, on an accounting level, union pay setting and especially highly centralized bargaining units at the industry- or economywide level leave less room than otherwise for pay differentials across workers to emerge. For example, unions typically negotiate pay rates by the job rather than by the person (Freeman 1982). People in similar jobs are more likely to be paid similarly since the contract constrains the variation in pay within a job category (why it does this is a behavioral issue that we will discuss shortly). Further, contracts covering entire industries or groups of industries are likely to be much simpler than agreements that are negotiated at the plant level because it would be very expensive and time consuming to lay out specific wages by firm and by job. This simplicity usually takes the form of industrywide or economywide wage minima (Blau and Kahn 1996a). An implication of this is that there is less room under highly coordinated wage-setting regimes than under more decentralized negotiations and individual pay determination for interfirm or interindustry wage differentials to emerge. Such differentials are an important source of wage differentials generally in countries like the United States where wage setting is highly decentralized (see, for example, Blau 1977; Groshen 1991; Davis and Haltiwanger 1991; Krueger and Summers 1988).

Second, on a behavioral level, several reasons have been offered to explain why unions tend to reduce wage dispersion among their members. One factor is a desire to decrease the power of supervisors over the rewards received by individual workers. There is clearly less scope for supervisors to influence the wages of individual workers when pay is set according to negotiated scales. This resonates with many union members since perceived favoritism under nonunion conditions is one factor that leads people to desire union representation in the first place (Katz and Kochan 1992).

Moreover, if each individual's pay depends only on the negotiated pay scale, the only way in which workers can make more money, other than through promotions, which are typically heavily influenced by seniority (Abraham and Medoff 1985), is for the entire pay scale to rise. This means that union solidarity is likely to be much greater under this scenario than when a union allows individual workers to get ahead through merit pay and performance-based promotions. This is important because unions face a potential free-rider problem among their members to the extent that all those covered by the collective-bargaining agreement benefit from the negotiated wage increase, regardless of how much they have contributed in terms of, for example, attending union meetings, contributing time to work on union mailings, going out on strike, or showing up on the picket line. Pay leveling is a way of ameliorating this potential free-rider problem by limiting workers' options for economic advancement to one based on building the strength of the union.

The same reasoning applies to union movements that opt for economywide wage bargains. These are likely to produce more solidarity across unions than if separate industry or occupation agreements are permitted. For example, the highly centralized negotiating structure in Sweden resulted in part from the desire of other unions (and firms as well) to restrain the metalworkers' union (Flanagan 1999).

Finally, unions may seek to narrow pay differentials if a majority of their potential members earn less than the average wage. This is a situation that could present itself if, in typical nonunion workplaces, the distribution of pay is skewed to the right (Freeman 1980). This essentially means that the wage distribution has a large mass of workers at wage rates below the mean and fewer workers at wage rates above the mean whose higher wages pull up the overall mean. This would be the case if, for example, the bulk of workers were young or unskilled but some of the remainder were highly skilled and relatively well paid. Under these circumstances, union contracts that bring up the bottom may, in fact, raise the income of a majority of union members by more than an alternative policy of equal percentage raises for everyone.

Employment Protection and Unemployment

As we have seen in chapter 3, employment-protection laws and regulations are much weaker in the United States than elsewhere, and we would like to know whether this difference helps explain lower U.S. unemployment rates. Research on this question posits direct and indirect mechanisms by which protection can affect unemployment. The direct effects operate via the incentives that firms face to hire and fire workers, all else equal, while the indirect effects are due to the effect of firing costs on union wage-bargaining behavior.

We expect more stringent laws and regulations governing employment protection to affect employer behavior directly, by increasing firing costs. An interesting insight offered by Edward Lazear (1990) is that, in principle, these costs can be completely offset by the establishment of an appropriate entry fee charged by firms to newly employed workers or, equivalently, by lower starting wages. If firms were able to follow such a policy, the allocation of labor under a system with, for example, mandated severance pay would be the same as one without severance pay. However, there may be constraints on the ability of the firm to charge an entry fee (or offer a reduced starting wage). For example, workers may be liquidity constrained and unable to pay these costs (or accept lower starting wages).[10] In that case, mandated severance pay can have allocative effects. Specifically, we expect severance pay to reduce both layoffs during recessions and new hiring during expansions. The negative effect on layoffs in recessions is straightforward since layoffs are now more costly to the firm. The negative effect on hiring in expansions results from the anticipated added costs of letting these workers go in a future downturn. Thus, firing costs are unambiguously expected to lower fluctuations in the quantity of labor demanded over the business cycle.

The effect of firing costs on overall employment levels, the issue of primary interest to those concerned with persistently high European unemployment, is less clear. A "first-order" approach would suggest that, if entry fees or lowered starting wages do not completely compensate for mandated firing costs, then total labor costs will have risen. We would, thus, expect lower employment levels as a consequence (Hamermesh 1993a, 1993b). However, analyses of the effect of firing costs on the average quantity of labor demanded suggest that this effect is theoretically ambiguous and will depend on several factors (Lazear 1990; Bertola 1992). In particular, Bertola (1992) suggests that the effect of firing costs at given wages (that is, assuming no offset in pay induced by mandated firing costs) depends on the shape of the marginal product of labor (MRP_L) curve and on the presence of discounting and voluntary turnover.

To see this, recall that firing costs will deter both hiring and firing. Thus, their *net effect* on average employment will depend on the size of their effect on hiring relative to the size of their effect on firing. If the number of new job offers deterred by firing costs is larger than the number of jobs saved by the reduction in layoffs, firing costs will lower average employment. Alternatively, if the number of new hires deterred by firing costs is smaller than the number of jobs saved by the reduction in layoffs, firing costs will raise average employment. In the simplest case, with no discounting or turnover, Bertola shows that the outcome is uncertain and will depend on the steepness of the MRP_L curve at lower employment levels (that is, during a recession) compared to higher employment levels (that is, during a boom).

Consideration of discounting and voluntary turnover raises the positive effects or reduces the negative effects of mandated firing costs on average employment levels. First, with discounting, the negative effect of firing costs on discharges is increased relative to the negative effect on hiring. This is the case because firing costs must be paid immediately when workers are discharged while the deterrence to hiring is related to future firing costs. Second, with voluntary turnover, there is some probability that current hires will not need to be discharged; this also raises the negative effect of firing costs on discharges relative to their effect on hiring. If these two effects are large enough, firing costs can actually raise average employment levels even when the shape of the MRP_L curve alone would not indicate such an outcome.

Firing costs can affect employment indirectly through their effect on wage setting. For example, Assar Lindbeck and Dennis Snower (1986) argue that the bargaining position of insiders is enhanced by higher firing costs. Insiders can, thus, extract more rents, and, in a monopoly-union model, this will tend to lower future employment. This is a theme that, as we have seen, is quite common in analyses of institutional interventions in highly unionized economies. Olivier Blanchard and Pedro Portugal (2000) build a theoretical model of the effect of firing costs that assumes that they will raise union bargaining power. As in Bertola's (1992) model, which took wages as fixed, the effects of high firing costs on overall average unemployment are theoretically uncertain, but Blanchard and Portugal's model predicts that they will result in fewer layoffs, longer unemployment durations, and higher union wages. These predictions are, in fact, borne out in Blanchard and Portugal's analyses of OECD data, which show a positive correlation between the strictness of a country's employment protection and its unemployment duration, a negative correlation between strictness and unemployment incidence (which is dominated by layoffs), and no correlation between strictness and overall unemployment.

Employment Effects of Mandated Benefits, Taxes, and Subsidies

As we saw in chapter 3, mandated benefits, taxes, and industrial subsidies are more extensive in other countries than in the United States. We can consider several levels at which these programs can affect employment. Coverage by benefits programs has costs and benefits to firms and is valued by workers. Thus, such programs may affect the overall supply and demand of labor for recipients and nonrecipients alike. Moreover, some of these programs have specific incentive effects on recipients and may, thus, influence unemployment through the behavior of the participants in the benefit programs. Finally, as was the case for employment protection, some benefit programs and other government policies may influence union bargaining power.

Systems of mandated benefits and taxes need not by themselves lead to higher unemployment since we expect them to be paid for indirectly out of wages, through a mechanism similar to mandated severance pay (discussed earlier). Consider UI as an example of a mandated benefit that is paid for by payroll taxes. The taxes, borne nominally by the employer, cause the demand for labor to shift down by the extent of the taxes. If labor-supply schedules are upward sloping, this shift will cause some, but not all, of the tax to be shifted to labor in the form of lower wages, at least if labor markets are competitive. If, at lower wages, people choose to supply less labor to the market, employment and wages will both fall. The payroll tax can be said to cause lower employment through this mechanism, although unemployment need not increase. However, the tax revenue is spent on a benefit that workers value. If, in fact, the insurance value to workers of UI coverage is exactly the same as the cost to the government of providing it, the labor-supply curve will shift down by the amount of the tax, as the demand curve did. In this case, wages will fall by the full amount of the tax, and neither labor costs, from the employer's point of view, nor the total value of working, from the employee's point of view, will be affected by the UI program. This scenario is reasonable when the government mandate or provision corrects a market failure. It is, then, possible for the value of the benefit to be at least as high as its cost.

This reasoning assumes that wages are flexible and are, thus, able to compensate for mandated benefits. If, however, there are wage floors, or if the union bargaining process does not allow wages to adjust fully in response to either mandated benefits or employer payroll taxes, then benefits or taxes can, in conjunction with these rigidities, lead to unemployment. This interdependence provides a further example of the interaction between different labor-market institutions.

In addition to the possible effects of programs like UI on overall labor costs, the behavior of recipients may influence unemployment. Specifically, UI raises workers' reservation wages, as do disability and sick benefits, thus theoretically prolonging each spell of unemployment.

Finally, as noted earlier, if unions know that their members will be covered by generous UI benefits in the event of unemployment, they are likely to be more aggressive than otherwise in demanding wage increases. Under monopoly-union conditions, these demands will cause higher unemployment. On the other hand, if there is efficient bargaining and no jobs are expected to be lost, the effect of more generous UI benefits on overall employment may be minimal. Similar reasoning applies to the possible effect on union bargaining demands of active labor-market policies or industrial subsidies granted to firms in the event of low profits (Calmfors and Forslund 1991; Leonard and Van Audenrode 1993).

Economic Effects of Institutional Intervention Beyond the Effect on Wages and Employment

We have concentrated our discussion on the effects of labor-market institutions on wages and employment in part because these are of central concern to policy makers and the general public and in part because data are most readily available to assess these effects. However, it is important to note that there are several additional predicted effects of institutions on economic performance. We briefly consider them here, although, unfortunately, a limited amount of evidence on these possible effects is available.

First, in countries with extreme wage compression and high

marginal tax rates, labor-supply incentives may be impaired, particularly among highly skilled workers. Similarly, the incentives of workers with the requisite skills to enter higher-productivity occupations and industries may be reduced. While these effects may not produce unemployment, they may reduce economic efficiency.

Second, wage compression may reduce individuals' incentives to invest in their own human capital, at least as long as jobs are plentiful. For example, in Sweden during the 1970s, the government believed that, owing to the low wage returns to a college education, too few people were going to college; as a consequence, it increased subsidies to higher education (Edin and Holmlund 1995). Of course, when jobs are scarce, going to school may be a way of becoming employable, as is suggested in a theoretical model developed by Agell and Lommerud (1997).

Third, as mentioned above, the output mix and factor allocation across industries may be affected by wage compression. Whether this will harm or enhance economic efficiency is an empirical question. The answer depends in part on whether labor was efficiently allocated prior to the wage compression. Evidence for Sweden during the period 1968 to 1984 indicates that equalizing wages across industries (that is, compressing industry wage differentials within occupations) raised overall productivity while equalizing wages within industries (that is, compressing occupation wage differentials within industries) reduced productivity (Hibbs and Locking 2000).

Fourth, as previously noted, job-protection mandates are likely to result in lower levels of worker flows into and out of employment. Even if overall unemployment is not affected, this may reduce the economy's long-term productivity growth by limiting the transfer of resources across plants with differing productivity levels (Davis and Haltiwanger 1999). This negative effect is likely to be stronger the more rapidly consumer demands and technology are changing.

Finally, as noted in chapter 3, public-sector employment as a fraction of total employment has grown in other countries relative to that in the United States. While the government may be able to reduce unemployment by being the employer of last resort, overall productivity and innovation may suffer as a result.

RESEARCH-DESIGN ISSUES IN DETECTING THE EFFECTS OF INSTITUTIONS ON LABOR-MARKET OUTCOMES

We have already seen in chapters 2 and 3 that, in a general sense, the combination of U.S.–other-country differences in labor-market outcomes and in measures of labor-market institutions produces evidence that is consistent with the idea that institutions have an important influence on wage and employment outcomes. However, in order convincingly to answer the question of whether institutions do, in fact, play an important causal role, we need a research design that can account for other possible explanations for this apparent correlation between institutions and outcomes besides the theories discussed in this chapter.

As an example of the kind of alternative explanations that we mean, the duration of unemployment may be longer in countries with more-generous UI programs, not because of any behavioral effect of UI benefits on the recipients, but because countries hit with high unemployment involving long periods of joblessness are, possibly, more likely to enact protective measures to ensure the living standards of their citizens. A similar story may apply to systems of generous employment protection: countries with high layoff rates and, therefore, high unemployment rates may generate the largest demand for employment protection. We call this phenomenon *reverse causality.*

A related possibility concerns the negative correlation that we observed in the descriptive data between collective bargaining and wage inequality. It is possible that high levels of collective-bargaining coverage reflect national norms about fairness in wage setting. Thus, a negative correlation between wage inequality and collective-bargaining coverage could merely reflect the consequences for the wage structure of having strong national norms for fairness. Collective bargaining may merely be the forum in which wages are set, having little independent substantive effect on the wage structure. Under these circumstances, it is possible that encouraging collective bargaining in countries without such norms will have no effect on the wage structure. Moreover, highly unionized countries also generally have more-generous social programs, such as UI systems. If we observe a negative correlation between unionization and wage inequality, how do we know that this is due to union negotiating behavior rather than to generous benefit programs like UI acting as a floor for wages? Various labor-market institutions often form a package, and it may be very difficult to disentangle the effects of one specific institution from those of another.

We call this problem *omitted-variables* bias. In the case of unions and wages, there may be other factors, like national norms for fairness or the generosity of UI systems, correlated with the explanatory variable of interest. The omission of these factors from the analysis could lead us to a possibly spurious conclusion that collective-bargaining institutions play a role. Or, as another example, countries plagued by health problems may enact generous sick-leave and disability-leave policies. There may, then, be a correlation between low employment levels and generous sick- and disability-leave policies that reflects the underlying health problems of the population rather than any behavioral effect of the leave policies. The tendency of centralized wage-setting institutions and generous social benefits to be correlated illustrates another potential omitted-variables problem that may arise in studying any one institution. If other institutions like generous benefit programs arise for reasons independent of the degree of centralization and union coverage, then we must be careful to control for them in assessing the effect of unionization. Of course, if Summers, Gruber, and Vergara's (1993) reasoning holds true, then unions and the centralization of wage setting are the prime movers, and controlling for the effect of other institutions would not be necessary.

Omitted-variables problems may also arise with a research design that uses only the type of aggregate data that we presented in chapter 2. In this case, it is possible that the *composition* of the population or the labor force can explain outcomes like wage inequality or employment. For example, the United States may have higher wage inequality because its labor force is more heterogeneous in terms of characteristics like education and age that influence wages, not because of its wage-setting institutions. To take another example, it is possible that, in one country, the young have relatively high employment rates because they are more highly educated rather than because of low minimum wages.

These hypothetical examples illustrate the point that, in order to obtain convincing evidence on the effect of institutions, we need a research design that takes account of the problems of reverse causality and omitted variables, including composition effects. We now consider some general approaches to these problems that represent the type of evidence on which we will draw in later chapters.

First, one research strategy that potentially addresses both the reverse-causality and omitted-variables problems is to examine particular countries that abruptly changed the nature of their institutional intervention and where possible to compare them to other countries that did not. For example, as we discuss in some detail in chapter 6, in 1991 New Zealand enacted the Employment Contracts Act (ECA), severely curtailing the power of trade unions. And union coverage plummeted thereafter. By comparing wage inequality changes before and after 1991 in New Zealand with those in other countries, we may be able to observe the true effects of the legislation. Of course, one would have to account for other differences in economic climate between New Zealand and other nations. But the fact that wage or employment outcomes changed in an abrupt way around 1991 in New Zealand relative to those in other countries would be strong evidence that the institutional intervention had some effect.

In this case, we would be using the 1991 ECA as a natural experiment and other countries that did not change their institutional setup as a control group.[11] The reverse-causality issue would be addressed by comparing the *changes* in wages and employment in New Zealand before and after 1991 with those in the control group of countries, thus controlling for any initial differences in wage or employment levels that may have induced New Zealand to pass this legislation. Moreover, by examining these changes, we control, in effect, for long-standing national norms of fairness that may be expected to change relatively slowly in comparison to any abrupt changes in wage inequality around 1991. In this way, one can at least partially control for differences in norms of fairness. While it might be argued that the passage of the legislation itself may have reflected changing norms in New Zealand, it is still likely that, in the months after the passage of the ECA, the legal environment changed much more dramatically than did the norms. Thus, using the legislation as a natural experiment is likely to be a valid research design.

A related research-design strategy is to use a priori expectations about subgroups that may be more affected by a particular policy than other groups would be. For example, suppose that one country increases its minimum wage and that another country does not. Since we expect young people to be more affected by minimum wages than prime-age adults will be, an interesting research design is to compare *changes* in the employment of youths relative to that of adults in the two countries. This strategy addresses the reverse-causality issue by controlling, in effect, for the initial relative employment of youths. Moreover, by comparing changes in the relative employment of youths in the two countries, the problem of omitted variables is also addressed, as long as we can be sure that basic supply and demand factors changed similarly in both countries.

While the natural-experiment approach may, under some conditions, be quite informative about the effect of a particular institutional intervention, it may be difficult to generalize from the results of one study. For example, a careful study may allow us to conclude with confidence that the passage of the ECA in New Zealand affected that country's wage structure; however, such a result would not tell us whether, in general, collective bargaining affects the wage distribution. To arrive at such a conclusion, we need a large sample of countries and time periods.

The desire to answer more-general questions relating to a number of countries provides the motivation for a second research design in which a larger sample of countries and time periods is analyzed to establish patterns of relationships between labor-market outcomes and labor-market institutions. Studies based on a comparison of wages and employment across a broad range of countries and time periods preserve our ability to generalize, but, in such analyses, it may be more difficult to establish causation or control for all relevant variables. In such a sample, there may be relatively few events like the passage of the ECA that would allow for very sharp tests of the effect of collective bargaining. Nonetheless, broader patterns can yield important evidence confirming the effect of wage-setting institutions, especially when care is taken to adjust for the effect of important explanatory variables.

In formulating a research project based on a broad range of countries, it will be essential to have micro data on individual wage and employment outcomes if many questions of interest are to be addressed. Only micro data allow researchers to deal adequately with the composition problems that we discussed earlier. For example, using micro data, one can control for the measured heterogeneity of population characteristics, such as age or education, before reaching conclusions about the effect of wage-setting institutions on wage and employment outcomes. Micro data can also be very useful in the natural-experiment approach in that such information can allow us to isolate the groups that we anticipate will be most affected by a particular institutional intervention.

Given the limitations of each type of approach—the case-study-oriented natural experiment and the broader cross-national comparison—it is helpful to examine each type of evidence. So, for example, the results of broader comparisons may be more convincing when employed in conjunction with case-study, natural-experiment evidence. This also points to the usefulness of using a variety of research designs and approaches to data collection when studying a particular issue.

CONCLUSIONS

In this chapter, we have surveyed economic theories on the expected effect of labor-market institutions on wage and employment outcomes. We have shown that economic theory cannot make unambiguous predictions about the effect of labor-market institutions like wage-setting interventions on employment levels. This makes the careful empirical investigation of these effects all the more important, both from the practical perspective of public policy and from the more academic perspective of better understanding how the labor market works. Evaluating the economic effects of policy interventions can help us decide what are appropriate policies in the first place. And empirical findings can help us discriminate among economic models with conflicting predictions—for example, monopoly-union, efficient-bargaining, and employer-monopsony models. For instance, if collectively bargained wage hikes were consistently found to raise employment or, at least, not to lower it, this would suggest that either efficient bargaining or employer monopsony is the appropriate characterization of the labor market. This finding may, in turn, have policy implications. In the case of employer monopsony, economic analysis has strong implications about the welfare effects of this type of labor-market structure—employment and wage levels under monopsony are "too low" relative to a competitive ideal, and the value of national output could be raised by moving toward more competitive labor markets.

An additional goal of this chapter has been to consider some of the difficult issues of research design that arise when attempting to determine the effect of labor-market institutions on labor-market performance. There is a kind of tension in this discussion. On the one hand, some of our most basic questions involve international differences in overall unemployment or wage inequality. We want to know, for example, why the United States has, in recent years, had low unemployment, compared to most other advanced countries, but considerably higher levels of wage inequality. On the other hand, from a scientific point of view, some of the most convincing evidence on the effect of institutions involves very specific comparisons that may not provide a direct answer to these questions. For example, did New Zealand's 1991 labor legislation change the path of its wage structure relative to that in other countries? This suggests that, while evidence from fortuitously arising natural experiments is of considerable interest, it will not be sufficient if we are fully to address the questions that motivated this study. In our opinion, the most sensible way in which to proceed is to examine several types of research and evidence, including careful analyses of long-run, basic differences in outcomes across countries, in an attempt to gain a picture of the importance of institutions.

—— Chapter 5 ——

Labor-Market Institutions and Unemployment: Macroeconomic Evidence

W E BEGIN OUR discussion of evidence on the effect of labor-market institutions on labor-market performance with one of the most basic and fundamental questions that one can ask: What influence do institutions have on a country's overall unemployment rate? This question is motivated both by the importance of unemployment as a negative indicator of labor-market performance and by the striking differences in unemployment across countries that we noted in chapter 2. Economists are concerned about unemployment in part because of the great importance of labor income to individual families' well-being. In addition, nations that have persistently high levels of unemployment are, over a long period of time, forgoing the opportunity to produce more goods and services for current consumption as well as a larger stock of investment goods for enhancing the living standards of future generations.

The diversity in the unemployment experience of OECD countries is readily apparent from table 2.1. For example, in 1999, unemployment in several countries, including Japan, the Netherlands, Norway, and the United States, averaged just 3.9 percent, considerably below the rate in a number of other continental European countries, for example, France, Germany, Italy, and Spain, where it averaged 11.8 percent. Can labor-market institutions explain these sharp differences?

A second macroeconomic question suggested by the overall unemployment data is, Why has unemployment grown faster

133

since the 1970s in some countries than in others? Table 2.1 indicates that the United States had an unemployment rate nearly double that of other OECD countries in 1973 but that, by 1999, the U.S. rate was only about half the level in the other countries. Moreover, some countries, such as Japan and Norway, saw only modest increases in unemployment between the 1970s and the 1990s, while others, such as France, Germany, and Spain, saw massive increases. Can institutions explain these time patterns?

This chapter examines macroeconomic evidence on these questions. Many of the research-design problems that we discussed in the last chapter, such as reverse causality, omitted variables, and composition effects, are present in the macroeconomic studies that we discuss here. And we will point out the possible implications of these difficulties for the validity of the results of these studies. However, these macro-level questions are among the most fundamental ones that we can ask about economic performance. If we want to confront these large issues, we must look at macroeconomic data.

THE CENTRALIZATION OF WAGE-SETTING INSTITUTIONS AND UNEMPLOYMENT

As we saw in our discussion in the previous chapter, the opposing effects of bargaining centralization on wage restraint may imply an inverted U-shaped relation between centralization and unemployment: we expect wages to be most restrained and, assuming that employment is demand determined, unemployment rates to be lowest in decentralized and in completely centralized systems. Empirical research on this issue has taken the form of small-scale international comparisons of up to roughly twenty countries, sometimes in a regression framework.

A problem in this literature is difficulty operationalizing the concept of centralization. At the two extremes, it is clear that the bargaining regimes of the Scandinavian countries involve more coordination across firms, sectors, and unions than does the U.S. system of firm- or plant-level bargaining units in the context of a predominantly nonunion labor market. However, it may be problematic to decide on a ranking for intermediate countries such as

Australia, France, Germany, or the Netherlands (Calmfors and Driffill 1988; Soskice 1990). Nonetheless, such a ranking has been devised by Calmfors and Driffill (1988), a ranking based on the degree of cooperation in wage bargaining among unions and among employers. The Calmfors and Driffill ranking has been further refined by the OECD to take account of centralization and coordination separately. These OECD measures were presented in chapter 3.

The Calmfors and Driffill approach to measuring centralization has been employed in several comparative studies analyzing macroeconomic outcomes, including the unemployment rate. The long-run differences across countries in unemployment rates identified by cross-sectional regressions may be viewed in the context of "natural-rate" theories. These theories assert that the economy will settle on an equilibrium unemployment rate when inflationary expectations are realized (Blanchard and Katz 1999). In effect, we are attempting to determine whether labor-market institutions affect the unemployment rate associated with an economy's macroeconomic steady state.

In simple regressions involving under twenty countries, Calmfors and Driffill (1988) and R. E. Rowthorn (1992) both found that unemployment did, indeed, have the expected inverted U-shaped relation with centralization in the 1980s. However, the estimated shape of this relation has been found to be very sensitive to how certain countries are classified with respect to centralization, a troubling weakness in this body of research. For example, David Soskice (1990) makes the case that Japan and Switzerland are examples, not of decentralized bargaining, as claimed by Calmfors and Driffill (1988), but of a high level of centralization, caused by a high degree of employer coordination in wage setting. When the data are reanalyzed given this assumption, the relationship between centralization and unemployment becomes monotonically negative. Whatever the merits of this argument, Soskice's findings demonstrate that the results of studies in this area can be extremely sensitive to classification errors. In addition, the inverted U-shaped relationship has been found not to be robust with respect to the time period examined (Flanagan 1999).

Other work using this approach also tends to find either a negative or an inverted U-shaped relation between centralization and unemployment (Calmfors 1993). But the estimated relation is also sensitive to whether one separately distinguishes between employer and union coordination (Layard, Nickell, and Jackman 1991) or between decentralized collective bargaining and non-union wage setting (Nickell 1997). For example, Richard Layard, Stephen Nickell, and R. Jackman's (1991) aggregate cross-national data show that, all else equal, employer coordination leads to greater restraint (that is, lower unemployment) than does union coordination; and Nickell (1997) finds that union density is positively associated with unemployment, other things equal.

This macroeconomic research has also been criticized for paying insufficient attention to more-traditional macroeconomic variables such as fiscal and monetary policy that can also influence unemployment (Flanagan 1999). Of course, empirical models excluding these variables could be seen as reduced forms in which the researcher allows bargaining structure to affect central-bank policy (a link investigated by Iversen, Pontusson, and Soskice 1998 and Cukierman and Lippi 1999). But, to the extent that central-bank policies are caused by some of the same underlying factors that influence bargaining structure (perhaps openness to international trade or supply shocks), excluding these underlying causes from econometric models may exacerbate any biases in estimates of the effects of institutions. We would, thus, like to ascertain the effect of bargaining structure both controlling and not controlling for monetary policy, in order to place some bounds on the true effect of wage-setting institutions. In what follows, we discuss some research that does, in fact, control for such policies.

Some of the comparative work on macroeconomic outcomes has explicitly examined the process through which centralization appears to influence unemployment. One mechanism is the rigidity of real wages in the face of macro shocks such as the oil-price increases of the 1970s and early 1980s. Layard, Nickell, and Jackman (1991) find that, in the 1970s and 1980s, centralized wage-setting institutions were associated with more real-wage flexibility with respect to the unemployment rate. This likely reflects the fact that wage negotiators at the national level take into account the negative macroeconomic effects of keeping real wages too high in the face of negative demand shocks. And unemployment rose faster in countries with rigid real wages. On the other hand, Fred

Heylen (1993) found evidence of an inverted U shape in this relation, in contrast to Layard, Nickell, and Jackman's monotonic positive effect of centralization on aggregate real-wage flexibility. Again, the sensitivity of the basic results in the face of such a small number of observations is evident.

BRINGING IN FACTORS OTHER THAN CENTRALIZATION TO EXPLAIN OVERALL UNEMPLOYMENT

As noted earlier, much of the literature on the effect of centralization of wage setting on wage outcomes pays insufficient attention to macroeconomic policies and other factors that may influence macroeconomic performance. Not controlling for these other factors may be justified under Summers, Gruber, and Vergara's (1993) theoretical model, which places primary causal importance on wage-setting institutions. However, if there are other independent causes of these other factors influencing macroeconomic performance that are correlated with wage-setting institutions, then failure to consider them may lead to a biased estimate of the effect of wage-setting mechanisms. Although controlling for these other factors may not allow us to estimate the full effect of wage-setting institutions, such a research strategy does address the question of what would happen if we changed the wage-setting process but held other policies constant. In this vein, recent research by Nickell (1997, 1998) and Nickell and Layard (1999) examines the macroeconomic effect of institutions, including extensive controls for other influences on these outcomes.

We focus our attention on the work of Nickell and Layard (1999). This research pools cross sections of data on the same twenty OECD countries over two time periods: 1983 to 1988 and 1989 to 1994. The aim is to explain average levels of unemployment during these two periods. By using six-year averages, Nickell and Layard focus their attention on medium-term differences in unemployment and, thus, average out some year-to-year fluctuations. The key advance of this work over the research on wage-setting centralization that we have already discussed is that the authors control for a variety of other institutional factors and policy variables in estimating the effect of coordination on unemployment. Results for these other variables are of considerable interest in themselves, and their inclusion in the regressions sharpens the interpretation of the coordination measure.

Nickell and Layard included the following explanatory variables as potential determinants of the log of the unemployment rate (they employ the log of the unemployment rate, rather than its actual level, in light of a large body of theoretical and empirical research that suggests that wages are related to the log rather than to the level of unemployment):

- *The total tax "wedge," defined as the sum of the payroll tax, the income tax, and the consumption tax.* As we discussed in chapter 3, to the extent that the tax wedge lowers the value of after-tax wages relative to after-tax unemployment benefits, the greater the wedge, the higher the unemployment rate is expected to be. However, as we also noted in chapter 3, if all taxes pay for benefits that raise the value of working, there would be no reason for the total tax rate to be correlated with employment. Several studies have examined whether labor taxes affect unemployment, with conflicting results. On the one hand, some studies, such as Gruber (1997b) and OECD (1990), find that labor taxes have no long-run effects on labor costs and, therefore, should not affect the quantity of labor demanded, although, as we have seen, taxes could still affect unemployment if they influence the value of working relative to the value of unemployment-insurance (UI) benefits. On the other hand, a number of others, including Francesco Daveri and Guido Tabellini (2000), Anthonie Knoester and Nico Van de Windt (1987), Timo Tyrväinen (1995), and Stefano Scarpetta (1996) as well as Nickell and Layard (1999), find that taxes raise labor costs or unemployment. While we follow Nickell and Layard in including the tax wedge as an explanatory variable in evaluating explanations for the relatively low U.S. unemployment of the 1980s and 1990s, one must be cautious about making strong conclusions about the effect of taxes in light of the conflicting international evidence.
- *Three measures of union influence on wage setting—union density, union coverage, and coordination.* Nickell and Layard

hypothesized that density and coverage would raise unemployment by raising wages above equilibrium levels and that coordination would lower unemployment in light of the Calmfors and Driffill (1988) argument about internalizing the externalities. In light of the U-shaped hypothesis discussed earlier, they also experimented with nonlinear forms of a centralization-rank variable.

- *Two important aspects of the UI system—the replacement ratio and the maximum duration of benefits.* As discussed earlier, these variables should positively affect unemployment both through longer unemployment durations and through more-aggressive union wage-setting behavior.

- *The share of households that were owner occupied.* The idea here is that homeowners are less mobile than renters are and that unemployment will persist longer in economies where labor is relatively immobile. Andrew Oswald (1996) has found that this factor is quite important in explaining differences in unemployment.

- *The extent of active-labor-market-policy spending per unemployed worker.* The reasoning here is that these initiatives can lower the unemployment rate.[1]

- *The average change in the inflation rate.* This variable is included to control for macroeconomic policies during the period. Countries with more-expansionary monetary policies will experience more-rapid growth in inflation and lower average unemployment rates. To understand this prediction, note that Nickell and Layard's specification assumes a "natural-unemployment-rate" framework. In this view, there is an equilibrium unemployment rate that is consistent with any sustained level of inflation. That is, if inflation is fully anticipated by everyone, there is no reason for unemployment to be any different when unit labor costs and prices are both rising by, say, 5 percent per year than when they are both rising by 10 percent. In each case, all participants in the economy correctly perceive the same real level of unit labor costs. However, unemployment can fall in the short run if the central bank abruptly increases the rate at which the money supply grows. If workers' expectations about prices lag behind those of businesses, the inflation rate will rise, but wage levels will not respond as quickly.[2] Businesses will perceive lower real wages, but workers will not. Therefore, the quantity of labor demanded will rise, workers will accept the resulting job offers, and a lower unemployment rate will result. However, workers' expectations will eventually catch up to reality, and workers will demand wage increases to match the higher inflation rate. Ultimately, real wages and employment will return to their initial levels. But, during the period immediately after inflation has, in this example, increased, unemployment will temporarily be below its equilibrium or natural rate. To capture such effects, Nickell and Layard include the average change in the rate of price inflation over the six-year period (1983 to 1988 or 1989 to 1994) as an explanatory variable. Note that, if one uses the regression coefficients to predict the unemployment rate corresponding to particular values of the explanatory variables, one can construct a predicted equilibrium unemployment rate by setting the inflation-change variable to 0 to reflect a sustained, constant level of inflation.

Table 5.1 contains empirical results from Nickell and Layard's study. Each regression coefficient gives the estimated effect of the indicated explanatory variable on the log of the unemployment rate controlling for the other explanatory variables in the regression. Since the dependent variable is in log terms, these are the approximate percentage effects of a unit change in the explanatory variable. So, for example, the coefficient of 0.01 on union density (the percentage of workers who are union members) implies that an increase of 1 percentage point in union density raises the unemployment rate by 1 percent. In the third and fourth columns, we have shown the means of the unemployment rate and the explanatory variables for the United States and the average values for the other countries during the period 1989 to 1994. During this period, the average unemployment rate in the United States was 6.2 percent, compared to an average of 8.1 percent for the other countries, or about 2 percentage points lower. As we saw in chapter 2, the U.S.–other-country difference in unemployment grew larger over the 1990s, so this gap would be larger if it were computed later in the decade.

The coefficients have the predicted sign and are statistically significant in every case. While many of the concerns raised in the last chapter are potentially relevant here—for example, unemployment levels may themselves affect several of the policies, and there may also be labor-force-composition effects on unemployment that are not captured in the regression model—the results are very suggestive. High taxes, high levels of union membership and collective-bargaining coverage, decentralized wage setting, more-generous UI systems, low levels of spending on active labor-market policies, high levels of home ownership, and slower growth in inflation are each associated with higher unemployment, other things equal.

Note that employment protection does not appear in the list of explanatory variables in table 5.1. Nickell and Layard tried models with employment protection included, but found that it did not affect overall unemployment; similar findings are reported by Blanchard and Portugal (2000). Perhaps this result reflects the theoretical ambiguity of the effect of protection mandates on average unemployment: as discussed in chapter 4, we expect such mandates to reduce layoffs (thereby reducing unemployment) but also to reduce hiring (thereby raising unemployment). Indeed, when Nickell and Layard separately examined the determinants of short-term (under a year's duration) and long-term unemployment rates, employment protection was positively (although not significantly) associated with long-term unemployment and significantly negatively associated with short-term unemployment, other things equal. This is what one might expect if job protection insulates workers from becoming unemployed in the first place, but, if they should become unemployed, the lack of hiring leads to long unemployment durations. Evidently, these positive and negative effects cancel out in the determination of the overall unemployment rate.[3]

The parameter estimates reported in table 5.1 suggest that differences in institutions and policies between the United States and the other countries have contributed to the lower U.S. unemployment rate. For example, the United States has lower taxes, less union coverage and lower union density, less-generous UI programs, slightly more slowly declining inflation, and, of course, lower unemployment than the other countries. In the final column of table 5.1, we use the results from the Nickell and Layard study to compute the contribution of differences in the levels of each of the explanatory variables to the difference in unemployment rates

TABLE 5.1 Explaining U.S.–Other-Country Differences in Average Log Unemployment, 1989 to 1994

Variable	Regression Coefficient	t-Statistic	U.S.-Average-Variable Values	Non-U.S.-Average-Variable Values	Contribution to U.S.–Other-Country Log Unemployment Difference
Unemployment rate	. . .	. . .	6.2	8.1	. . .
Log (unemployment rate)	. . .	. . .	1.825	1.953	−.128
Total tax wedge (percentage)	.027	4.0	43.8	48.379	−.124
Union density (percentage)	.010	2.3	15.6	41.626	−.260
Union-coverage index (1 to 3)	.380	2.7	1.0	2.737	−.660
Coordination (2 to 6)	−.430	−6.1	2.0	4.0	.860
UI replacement ratio (percentage)	.013	3.4	50.0	57.0	−.091
UI maximum duration (years)	.100	2.2	0.5	2.395	−.190
Active labor-market policies	−.023	−3.3	3.0	12.774	.225
Owner-occupation rate (percentage)	.013	2.6	64	61.158	.037
Change in inflation (percentage)	−.210	−2.2	−0.440	−0.467	−.006
Total explained by U.S.–other-country differences in the explanatory variables					−.208

Source: Nickell and Layard (1999), with additional calculations by the authors.

Note: The countries are Australia, Austria, Belgium, Canada, Denmark, Finland, France, West Germany, Ireland, Italy, Japan, the Netherlands, New Zealand, Norway, Portugal, Spain, Sweden, Switzerland, the United Kingdom, and the United States. Based on regression results presented in Nickell and Layard (1999).

With the exception of the change in inflation, variable means are available in Nickell and Layard (1999); variables are defined as follows: *total tax wedge* = sum of payroll-tax rate, income-tax rate, and consumption-tax rate; *union density* = percentage of wage and salary workers who were union members; *union-coverage index* ranges from a low of 1 to a high of 3; *coordination* combines labor and management coordination indexes and ranges from 2 to 6; *UI replacement ratio* = percentage of the average worker's wages replaced by the UI system; *UI maximum duration* = maximum number of years of UI benefits (4 = indefinite); *active labor-market policies* = spending per unemployed worker as a percentage GDP per member of the labor force; *owner-occupation rate* = percentage of households that were owner occupied (1990); *change in inflation* = average annual change in the inflation rate (1988 to 1994), taken from the BLS website (*www.bls.gov*); the non-U.S. average includes all countries except Finland, Ireland, Portugal, and New Zealand.

between the United States and the average for the other countries in the log of the unemployment rate during the period 1989 to 1994. The log of the U.S. unemployment rate is 1.825, which corresponds to a U.S. unemployment rate of 6.2 percent, while the average of the logs of the unemployment rates of the other countries is 1.953, which corresponds to an unemployment rate of 7.0 percent. Note that the latter figure is lower than the arithmetic average unemployment rate for the other countries of 8.1 percent because it is based on the geometric average, which tends to put a lower weight on extreme values.

The difference between the log of the U.S. unemployment rate and the average of the logs of the unemployment rates of the other countries is −0.128, or about 13 percent.[4] Table 5.1 shows that, in accounting for this difference, several of the explanatory variables have offsetting effects on the U.S.–other-country difference. For example, union-density and union-coverage differences reduce the U.S. unemployment rate by 0.92 log points, but its co-ordination rank raises the unemployment rate in the United States by 0.86 log points. The net effect of union wage-setting institutions is to lower the U.S. unemployment rate by 0.06 log points, or about half the U.S.–other-country difference. Lower taxes and a less-generous UI system also reduce the U.S. unemployment rate and, in fact, have larger negative effects than unionization: taxes lower U.S. unemployment by 0.124 log points, while the two UI variables together reduce the U.S. unemployment rate by 0.281 log points. These are very large effects relative to the average unemployment difference to be explained of 0.128 log points. A final factor that very slightly reduces the U.S. unemployment rate is its more slowly declining inflation rate, presumably reflecting a less-contractionary monetary policy.

Offsetting these effects that reduce the U.S. unemployment rate are two factors that, according to Nickell and Layard's parameter estimates, raise the U.S. rate relative to that in other countries: the United States has a higher rate of owner-occupied housing, which raises the U.S. rate by 0.037 log points, and, more important, the United States spends far less on active labor-market policies, contributing to an increase in the U.S. rate of 0.225 log points.[5] This latter effect is quantitatively very important and suggests that high-unemployment countries use active labor-market policies to undo some of the unemployment that would otherwise be caused by labor-market institutions such as high taxes, union wage setting, and generous UI benefits. The regression results reported in table 5.1 imply that, without these active labor-market policies, unemployment in the other countries would have been considerably higher than it actually was.

Specifically, at the U.S. level of active-labor-market-policy spending, but holding all the other explanatory variables at their actual levels, the average of the other countries' log unemployment rates would have been 2.178 log points, corresponding to an unemployment rate of 8.8 percent, instead of its actual value of 1.953 log points, corresponding to a 7.0 percent unemployment rate. Thus, more-aggressive active labor-market policies in other OECD countries besides the United States serve to lower those other countries' relative-unemployment rates by nearly 2 percentage points, on average.[6] This finding suggests a theme to which we will return when we consider evidence on the effect of labor-market institutions in particular countries: government policies may be used to counter some of the adverse employment effects that would otherwise result from the effect of wage-setting institutions. Whether active labor-market policies are the most economically efficient way of lowering unemployment is, of course, open to debate.

A final point to note about this comparison of unemployment in the United States and other OECD countries is that the U.S.–other-country differences in the explanatory variables are predicted to explain more (−0.208 log points) than the actual average difference in unemployment (−0.128 log points). In other words, on the basis of the variables in the regression equation, the U.S. unemployment rate should actually be even lower relative to the other-country average than it actually is. This implies that there are one or more variables omitted from the regression equation that would serve to raise U.S. unemployment rates. It could be that the U.S. labor force has a demographic composition that leaves it more prone to unemployment. Later in this chapter, we attempt to assess the effect of demographics in explaining U.S. unemployment relative to that elsewhere. While there may be some omitted factors that would have raised the U.S. unemployment rate in the late 1980s and early 1990s, Nickell and Layard's estimates suggest that a number of institutions, particularly union wage setting, taxes, and UI benefits, did substantially raise unemployment in other OECD countries relative to that in the United States. The results also suggest that these countries then implemented policies to counteract some of these adverse unemployment effects.[7]

While unemployment in the United States was higher than predicted in the late 1980s and early 1990s, the next section shows that, by the late 1990s, unemployment in the United States fell below the levels that one would have predicted from statistical analyses. As we will see, by the end of the 1990s, the U.S. labor market was in the midst of an expansion for which there are several contending explanations.

EXPLAINING CHANGES IN UNEMPLOYMENT: WHY DID THE UNITED STATES GO FROM BEING A HIGH-UNEMPLOYMENT TO BEING A LOW-UNEMPLOYMENT COUNTRY?

The essentially cross-sectional evidence presented in Nickell and Layard's (1999) study shows very striking patterns linking labor-market policies and institutions to overall unemployment in the 1980s and 1990s. However, as noted in earlier chapters, in contrast to the 1980s and 1990s, the United States had relatively high unemployment in the 1960s and 1970s even though its labor-market institutions were less intrusive than were those in other OECD countries then, just as they are now. The behavior of unemployment rates over time suggests that our explanation for international differences in unemployment needs to explain the change in the relative position of the U.S. unemployment rate as well as its lower current level. The so-called unified theory, introduced in chapter 1, can provide such an explanation. Namely, in the 1970s, 1980s, and 1990s, the OECD countries were hit with similar shocks relating to oil crises, the productivity slowdown, technological change, increasing international trade, and changes in monetary policy. The more-flexible labor-market institutions in the United States allowed these shocks to affect primarily real wages, while the more interventionist labor-market institutions elsewhere in the OECD did not allow real wages to respond, producing the remarkable increase in unemployment that we observe in many of these countries today. Of course, some of the other OECD countries did not experience high unemployment in the 1980s and 1990s, notably Austria, Japan, Norway, and Switzerland. Any explanation of the evolution of unemployment in the OECD must be able to account for these success stories as well.[8]

The unified theory has recently been put to the test by Blanchard and Wolfers (2000), whose goal was to explain the evolution of unemployment rates over the period 1960 to 1996 for the same sample of twenty OECD countries studied by Nickell and Layard (1999). Blanchard and Wolfers hypothesized that macroeconomic shocks over this period interacted with labor-market institutions to produce the observed changes in each country's unemployment rate. By averaging unemployment over mostly five-year intervals (1960 to 1965, 1965 to 1970, 1970 to 1975, 1975 to 1980, 1980 to 1985, 1985 to 1990, 1990 to 1995, and 1995 to 1996), they abstracted from short-term fluctuations and focused on long-term trends. According to Blanchard and Wolfers, the major macroeconomic shocks affecting each country over this period included changes in productivity growth, changes in the real interest rate, shifts in the demand for labor, and changes in inflation.

In recent work with Giuseppe Bertola (Bertola, Blau, and Kahn 2002), we extended the Blanchard and Wolfers framework by taking into account demographic shocks. We hypothesized that changes in the demographic composition of the population, specifically the share of the population that is young (aged fifteen to twenty-four), will also influence unemployment. In addition, our model departs somewhat from that of Blanchard and Wolfers in that we have included the change in inflation as an explanatory variable. Blanchard and Wolfers exclude inflation from their model but instead create an equilibrium unemployment rate that is based on the actual unemployment rate, the change in the inflation rate, and a priori assumptions about how these two are related. We chose to include the change in the inflation rate in the regression equations because this specification allows the data to determine the relation between changes in inflation and the observed unemployment rate (rather than a priori assumptions) and sheds greater light on the effects of inflation on observed unemployment and how these effects interact with institutions. We based our empirical analysis on an augmented version of the Blanchard and Wolfers data[9] and focused on the implications of the findings for explaining the unemployment trends in the United States relative to those in the other OECD countries.

We focus here on results from the Bertola, Blau, and Kahn paper. We begin by briefly considering each of the factors that are expected to influence unemployment trends.

First, productivity growth has substantially slowed across the OECD since the 1960s. Blanchard and Wolfers measure productivity growth using the concept of total-factor-productivity (TFP) growth, which is the growth in output (expressed on a per work hour basis) after controlling for changes in the quantities of the inputs of the factors of production. This is essentially a measure of technological progress. Across a sample of European countries, Blanchard and Wolfers find that TFP growth fell from roughly 5 percent per year in 1960 to under 2 percent per year by 1995. The corresponding figures for the United States were 6 percent in 1960 and 0.1 percent in 1995. Blanchard and Wolfers argue that reduced TFP growth can result in higher unemployment for several years if labor-market institutions keep real wages rising at their customary pace. As we saw in chapter 2, unit labor costs have been rising faster in other countries than in the United States, suggesting a slower real-wage response in the former.[10] While, in the long run, there is no reason for unemployment to be affected by the particular level of TFP growth on which a country has settled, since we do not know how many years it takes for real-wage growth to decelerate to its new equilibrium level, higher unemployment in the face of slower TFP growth can persist for some time. Our empirical analysis can tell us how important such effects are.

The second factor is the real long-term interest rate, which Blanchard and Wolfers take to be a summary measure of the cost of capital. Across a sample of European countries, they show that the real interest rate fell from about 2 percent in 1965 to about −1 percent in 1975 and then rose steadily to 5 percent by the 1990s. For the United States, these movements were from 3 percent in 1965 to 1 percent in 1975 and then to 4 percent in the 1990s.

Higher real interest rates restrain economic activity and, therefore, contribute to higher unemployment. Overall, real interest rates were higher in the 1990s than in the 1960s and 1970s, potentially helping to explain the rise in unemployment in general. As was the case for the productivity-growth slowdown, rising real interest rates are expected to cause larger increases in unemployment the more rigid are real wages.

Third, Blanchard and Wolfers note that there may be shifts in labor demand over time that affect unemployment. They measure these shifts by changes in the log of labor's share in national income (relative to 1960).[11] By this measure, labor demand was relatively stable in Europe between 1960 and 1970, then rose over the 1970s, but fell steadily after 1980 to well below its 1960 level. Labor's share fell steadily in the United States over the same period. Blanchard and Wolfers suggest that this reduction in labor's share could have been the result of downsizing and leaner production methods. The downward shift in labor demand could raise unemployment, particularly in Europe, with its relatively rigid real wages.

Fourth, Blanchard and Wolfers note that inflation was increasing in the 1970s but decreasing in the 1980s and 1990s. Using similar logic to that employed by Nickell and Layard (1999), they assume that there is an "equilibrium rate" of unemployment.[12] This is the unemployment rate that corresponds to a constant inflation rate. The observed pattern of inflation rates over the 1970s to the 1990s implies that unemployment was below its equilibrium level in the 1970s and above it in the 1980s and 1990s, at least on average. Thus, OECD unemployment may have been high in the 1980s and 1990s in part because it was above its equilibrium level. Of course, it may also have been high because European labor-market institutions did not allow the other macroeconomic shocks to affect wages sufficiently to generate adequate employment.

Finally, turning to the youth-population-share variable that we have added to the analyses, there are several, possibly opposing, routes through which it can affect the overall unemployment rate. On the one hand, in an accounting sense, a larger youth share is expected to raise unemployment since youths are a high-unemployment group. In this vein, Katz and Krueger (1999) have credited a falling youth share for explaining a portion of the decrease in the U.S. unemployment rate in the 1990s. On the other hand, in contrast to this accounting mechanism, Robert Shimer (1999) argues that a greater youth share may actually lower unemployment by reducing employer search costs. In this framework, business formation and business expansion depend on the ability of employers to find workers who are willing to relocate. A higher youth-population share implies a higher share of such mobile workers and may, thus, contribute to higher employment among both youths and complementary adults.

Shimer (1999) finds evidence in favor of this hypothesis within the United States: states with larger increases in the youth share (defined as the share of fifteen- to twenty-four-year-olds in the total population fifteen years and older) had larger reductions in unemployment, even taking into account the endogeneity of the youth share (more on this later in this chapter). However, across countries, there was no effect of the youth share on unemployment. Shimer (1999) suggested that the difference between the within-U.S. and the cross-country findings was due to the far-greater mobility of capital across states in the United States than across countries in the OECD. Sanders Korenman and David Neumark (2000), however, do find cross-country evidence that a higher youth share is associated with higher *relative* unemployment among young people, suggesting labor-market-substitution effects on the demand side.

In light of the possibility that the current youth share can be affected by the unemployment rate through migration, in Bertola, Blau, and Kahn (2002) we also use births divided by the population fifteen to twenty-four years prior to the current period as a demographic indicator in some of our models. This variable is much less likely than is *current* youth share to be affected by current economic activity (Korenman and Neumark 2000). Later in this chapter, we report on results using the births/population variable because it is less subject to bias due to reverse causation. However, results were qualitatively similar for the more straightforward measure, the youth share of the population.

Having set out the major macroeconomic and demographic forces potentially affecting the OECD countries, we now attempt to explain the remarkable turnaround in U.S. unemployment compared to that in other OECD countries since the 1970s. Following

Blanchard and Wolfers's methodology, we contrast two regression models. The first model includes as explanatory variables country dummies, the macroeconomic shocks, and the youth share of the population. However, this simple model forces the macro shocks and the youth share to have the same effect for each country. In contrast, the unified theory holds that the same shocks will have different effects depending on a country's labor-market institutions because the institutions imply different responses of real wages to the macroeconomic shocks.

In light of this reasoning, we estimate a second, augmented model, one including, in addition to the country dummy variables, the macro shocks, and the youth share, interactions between a linear combination of the shocks (macro shocks and the youth share) and each of the following eight institutional variables: union coverage; union density; coordination; the UI replacement ratio; UI benefit duration; active-labor-market-policy spending; employment-protection-policy rank; and the total tax rate on labor.[13] The institutional variables were taken from Nickell (1997) and Nickell and Layard (1999); we have discussed the definition of and rationale for each in the context of our presentation of results from Nickell and Layard (1999). The variables refer to the average of the periods 1983 to 1988 and 1989 to 1994, except for collective-bargaining coverage, which was taken from OECD (1994a) and refers to 1990.

The augmented model is based on the reasoning that informs the unified theory: while the macroeconomic environment has changed dramatically, these changes will have different effects on unemployment depending on the nature of the institutions. The institutions are assumed to be relatively stable within each country. For example, Sweden is far more unionized than the United States and has been so for a very long time. Therefore, we initially take the institutions to be fixed and interact these fixed values for the institutional variables with the shocks, which, of course, do change over time. But we also acknowledge that, as we saw in chapter 3, some institutions have changed over time. Thus, in supplementary analyses discussed below, we include time-varying measures of several institutions for which we were able to obtain data.[14]

For the purposes of comparison, table 5.2 shows data on the

United States and a subset of nine other OECD countries for which data were available on all dependent and explanatory variables for the periods 1970 to 1975 and 1995 to 1996.[15] In the regressions used in our analyses of U.S. and other-country differences in unemployment changes, however, we include all eighteen OECD countries for which data on the full set of explanatory variables were available for any period.[16] The table shows that, during the period 1970 to 1975, the average unemployment rate in the nine non-U.S. countries was 2.9 percent, compared to 5.4 percent in the United States. By 1995 to 1996, the unemployment rate in the non-U.S. sample had risen to 11.2 percent, while it was only 5.5 percent in the United States, barely changed from its 1970 to 1975 level.

Some of the macroeconomic shocks changed in ways that could help explain the larger increase in the unemployment rate in the other countries compared to the United States. TFP growth slowed more, real interest rates rose more rapidly, and inflation declined by more in the other countries than in the United States. On the other hand, labor's share declined by more in the United States than elsewhere, indicating that the demand curve for labor was shifting inward faster in the United States than in other countries. This trend would increase the U.S. unemployment rate relative to that elsewhere, all else equal. Finally, youth share and prior births declined everywhere as the baby boomers aged, but the decline was greater in the United States than elsewhere. If a higher share of youths raises the unemployment rate (as argued by Katz and Krueger 1999), then these demographic developments could help explain the falling U.S. relative-unemployment rate.

We report results from two regression specifications in appendix table 5A.1. In the first specification, the "shocks-only" model, unemployment is assumed to be a function only of macroeconomic and demographic shocks and country and period dummy variables. The shocks are TFP growth, real long-term interest rates, the labor-demand indicator based on labor's share, the change in the inflation rate, and births divided by the population fifteen to twenty-four years earlier. The second specification, the "shocks-interacted-with-institutions" (or "shocks-interactions") model, includes, in addition to the shock variables and country and period

TABLE 5.2 Data on Institutions, Unemployment Rates, and Macroeconomic Shocks from 1970 to 1975 Through 1995 to 1996, Ten OECD Countries

Variable	1970 to 1975		1995 to 1996		Change, 1970 to 1975 Through 1995 to 1996	
	Non-U.S. Average	U.S.	Non-U.S. Average	U.S.	Non-U.S. Average	U.S.
Unemployment rate	.029	.054	.112	.055	.082	.001
Labor demand	−.011	−.005	−.057	−.070	−.046	−.065
Real long-term interest rate	.018	.020	.054	.039	.036	.019
Total-factor-productivity growth	.030	.009	.015	.002	−.016	−.007
Annual change in inflation	.005	.004	−.002	−.001	−.007	−.005
Youth-population share	.225	.243	.170	.171	−.054	−.071
Births/population fifteen to twenty-four years ago	.021	.025	.016	.015	−.005	−.009
UI replacement ratio	54.000	50.000	54.000	50.000	...	...
UI benefit duration	2.314	.500	2.3145	.500	...	...
Collective bargaining coverage	67.667	18.000	67.667	18.000	...	...

Employment-protection rank	10.889	1.000	10.889	1.000	. . .	. . .
Active-labor-market-policy spending	13.758	2.590	13.758	2.590	. . .	. . .
Union density	40.911	17.300	40.911	17.300	. . .	. . .
Labor tax rate	50.606	43.200	50.606	43.200	. . .	. . .
Coordination index	3.667	2.000	3.667	2.000	. . .	. . .

Source: Blanchard and Wolfers (2000); Bertola, Blau, and Kahn (2002).

Notes: The non-U.S. countries in the table are Australia, Canada, Finland, France, Italy, Japan, Spain, Sweden, and the United Kingdom, which were the countries for which data were available in 1970 to 1975 and 1995 to 1996. Regressions for the determinants of average unemployment over the periods 1960 to 1965 and 1995 to 1996 included these countries as well as Belgium, Denmark, Ireland, the Netherlands, New Zealand, Norway, Portugal, and West Germany. (Each country is included for the periods for which data are available.)

The variables derived from Blanchard and Wolfers (2000) are defined as follows (for further details, see the data appendix to Blanchard and Wolfers [2000]): The *real long-term interest rate* is the nominal interest on long-term government securities minus the annual rate of GDP price inflation over the last five years. *Total-factor-productivity growth* is $[\Delta y - \alpha \Delta L - (1 - \alpha) \Delta K]/\alpha$, where y, L, and K are real measures of output, total labor input, and total capital input in the business sector, and α is labor's share of national income; essentially, this is the change in output that cannot be accounted for by changes in labor or capital inputs, scaled by labor's share of income. Log labor's share is a modified version of the log of labor's share of national income, indexed to equal to zero in 1960. As discussed in more detail by Blanchard and Wolfers in their Data Appendix, the modification to labor's share takes a weighted average of current and lagged real wages, in order to allow for gradual adjustment of factor proportions to demand shifts. The *change in inflation* is the change in the average annualized rate of inflation for the GDP deflator.

The variables on youth share of the population and birth/population fifteen to twenty-four years earlier are from Bertola, Blau, and Kahn (2002) and were constructed using International Labor Organization data.

The institutional variables are from Nickell (1997) and Nickell and Layard (1999) and are averages of the 1983 to 1988 and 1989 to 1994 values; for variable descriptions, see the notes to table 5.1. In the regression analyses, the variables are defined as deviations from their all-country means, where the full eighteen-country sample is used to compute the means.

dummy variables, interactions between a linear combination of the shocks and each of the institutional variables shown in table 5.2.[17] Following Blanchard and Wolfers, in the regression analyses, all variables have been signed so as to lead us to predict a positive effect of each on unemployment. This means that the following variables were multiplied by -1: change in inflation, TFP growth, labor-demand shift, active labor-market policies, and union coordination. This transformation is performed to facilitate the interpretation of the interaction model.

Both sets of regressions include period effects to control for omitted factors that were changing over time and had a similar effect on unemployment across countries. However, to the extent that there were common macroeconomic or demographic shocks such as worldwide productivity trends, then including period effects will cause us to understate the effects of the shocks. We, therefore, present models with period effects included but also note how the results differ in models with period effects excluded. While some specific coefficients are sensitive to the inclusion of period effects, our conclusions regarding the importance of macroeconomic and demographic shocks and institutions on U.S.–other-country differences in unemployment trends are not affected by the inclusion of period effects.

The shocks-only model, reported in table 5A.1, shows that the decrease in labor demand, declining inflation, and the higher youth share (proxied by the birth/population variable) significantly raise the unemployment rate; higher real interest rates also have the expected positive effect, although the coefficient is not significant. While the coefficient on TFP growth is incorrectly signed (negative) and insignificant, when period effects are excluded, the coefficient is positive and highly significant.[18]

The shocks-interactions model, also reported in table 5A.1, shows positive interactions between seven of the eight institutions and the linear combination of the shocks, with five of these at or close to statistical significance. (Note too that the shock-variable main effects are now all correctly signed.) The largely positive interactions mean that, when there are shocks that are expected to raise unemployment, these have larger effects in countries with institutions that are expected to raise unemployment. So, for example, a decrease in inflation or an increase in the youth share has a larger positive effect on unemployment in countries with higher union density, more-generous UI systems, stricter employment-protection laws, weaker active labor-market policies, higher labor taxes, and less-coordinated wage-setting systems.[19] In interpreting the insignificantly positive coefficient on the interaction with union density and the significantly negative coefficient estimated for the interaction with union coverage, it should be recalled that the three variables measuring wage-setting institutions (that is, union coverage, the union-density index, and the coordination index) are highly collinear.

The regression results are used in table 5.3 to explain the difference between unemployment changes over the period 1970 to 1975 through 1995 to 1996 in the United States and elsewhere. Looking first at the model that excludes any information about institutions, we see that, for the non-U.S. countries, changes in macroeconomic variables and the youth share would have predicted a 7.7 percentage point increase in the unemployment rate, in comparison to the actual increase of 8.3 percentage points. For the United States, we would predict a 5.5 percentage point rise in unemployment, while unemployment actually rose by only 0.1 percentage point. Therefore, U.S.–other-country differences in macroeconomic and demographic shocks can explain only a 2.1 percentage point difference in the change in unemployment (roughly equal to 7.7 − 5.5, after rounding), or about 26 percent of the actual difference (8.3 − 0.1 = 8.2). These findings suggest that macro shocks and demographic developments have favored the United States relative to other countries, on net, but they can explain only a modest portion of the observed decrease in the U.S. relative-unemployment rate. The full explanation must be more complicated than a simple comparison of macro shocks and demographic trends for the United States and the other countries.

When we allow shocks to interact with institutions, the model does much better at explaining the U.S.–other-country difference in the change in unemployment. The last row of table 5.3 shows that the interaction model predicts an 8.0 percentage point rise in unemployment outside the United States and a 2.9 percentage point increase in the United States.[20] The model, therefore, explains 5.1 percentage points of the 8.2 percentage point difference in the change in unemployment rates between the United States

TABLE 5.3 **Explaining U.S.–Other-Country Differences in the Change in the Unemployment Rate from 1970 to 1975 through 1995 to 1996**

	Change in Non-U.S. Average (1)	Change in U.S. Average (2)	Difference, Other-Country– U.S. (1)–(2)	Percentage of Total Difference Explained
Actual unemployment rate	.083	.001	.082	N.A.
Predicted unemployment: model includes only shocks and country dummies	.077	.055	.021	26.3
Predicted unemployment: model includes country dummies, shocks, and interactions between shocks and institutions	.080	.029	.051	62.7

Source: Bertola, Blau, and Kahn (2002).
Note: For the regressions on which the simulations are based, see table 5A.1.

and the other countries, or 63 percent of the actual difference.[21] Compared to the shocks-only model, the shocks-interactions model improves our predictions of unemployment changes for both the United States and the other countries, with an especially large improvement in our predictions for the United States.[22] In particular, if we estimate the model ignoring institutions (the second row of table 5.3), we substantially overpredict the increase in U.S. unemployment (an estimated increase of 5.5 percentage points as opposed to an actual increase of 0.1 percentage points). But, when we allow for shocks and institutions to interact, we predict only a 2.9 percentage point increase in U.S. unemployment. The corresponding predictions for the non-U.S. countries are 7.7 percentage points controlling only for shocks and 8.0 percentage points additionally allowing for interactions between shocks and institutions, compared to the 8.1 percentage point actual average increase in unemployment in these countries.

Even when the shocks are interacted with institutions, however, the U.S. unemployment rate remained unexpectedly low in the 1990s. This conclusion was reinforced when we used recently obtained OECD data for the United States to make out-of-sample predictions of U.S. unemployment for the period 1995 to 1999 (Bertola, Blau, and Kahn 2002). We found that, for this latter period, when the U.S. unemployment rate averaged about 4.9 percent, our shocks-interactions regression models overpredicted the U.S. unemployment rate by about 2 percentage points. This means that, given the variables in the regression equation, the U.S. unemployment rate should have fallen less relative to the other-country average than it actually did. This suggests that factors omitted from the regression analysis favored the United States compared to other Western countries. Such factors could include more-favorable shifts in labor-force composition (from the perspective of lowering unemployment), a more-favorable change in the macroeconomic-policy environment than is captured by the regression variables, and the effect of other labor-market institutions not included in the model. For example, it is possible that the late-1990s rise in productivity growth in the United States that we documented in chapter 2 was, in fact, larger than published data indicate.

As Blanchard and Wolfers (2000) acknowledge, their unemployment rates (which we use in our analysis as well) are not standardized. This allows them to go back to 1960 for several countries. However, Blanchard and Wolfers stated that, when they used a subset of countries and years for which standardized unemployment rates were available, they obtained similar results. We have obtained a recently constructed set of standardized unemployment rates and corrected macroeconomic-shock data from the OECD, also for a subset of countries and years, which we used in Bertola, Blau, and Kahn (2002) to see whether the use of standardized-unemployment-rate data would affect our findings.[23] When aggregated over five-year periods, this unemployment series is available for a total of seventy-six observations merged with the OECD-corrected macro and demographic information, covering 1965 to 1969 through 1995 to 1996.

Over the period 1980 to 1984 through 1995 to 1996, the standardized unemployment rate in the United States fell from 8.32 to 5.50 percent, while, in a sample of twelve other OECD countries

(Belgium, Canada, Denmark, Finland, France, Germany, Italy, Japan, the Netherlands, Norway, Spain, and Sweden), it rose from 7.52 to 10.00 percent. When this unemployment measure is regressed on macro shocks, prior birthrates, country dummies, and period dummies, the model explains 21.1 percent of the decrease in the U.S. unemployment rate between 1980 to 1984 and 1995 to 1996 relative to the available comparison group. Including institutional interactions increases the portion explained to 58.3 percent.

These results are qualitatively similar to those obtained, on the same sample and the same specification, for the unemployment measure used by Blanchard and Wolfers (2000) and in our parallel analyses in this chapter. We chose to use the unstandardized-unemployment-rate measure in the basic models summarized in table 5.3 and appendix table 5A.1 because it allowed for a much larger sample size. One reason why the results may be similar for the unstandardized measure is that the use of country dummies in our models corrects for any differences that can be attributed to the lack of standardization in the unemployment rate.

Our basic econometric framework for understanding U.S. unemployment in an international perspective assumes that labor-market institutions do not change over time and emphasizes differences between U.S. and non-U.S. institutions. This may well be a reasonable first approximation. And it may well be that, for the purposes of comparing the United States with the rest of the world, the long-run differences in institutional arrangements are more important than any recent changes. However, institutions do evolve over time, in the United States as well as in the rest of the world. And it is instructive to consider the nature of these changes when attempting to understand developments in the United States. In chapter 6, we provide some detailed evaluation of the effect of these changes on labor-market outcomes, but we consider the magnitude of these changes now in light of the fixed-institutions framework that we have used in this chapter.

In Bertola, Blau, and Kahn (2002), we were able to construct time-varying measures of five of the eight institutions considered earlier. We obtained two of these measures from Blanchard and Wolfers (2000). First, we used their time-varying measure of one-year UI replacement ratios, which they constructed from OECD annual data covering the entire period, 1961 to 1995. Second, we used Blanchard and Wolfers's time-varying employment-protection index, which they constructed from a variety of sources. When there were missing years from their measures, Blanchard and Wolfers either interpolated or assumed no change. We then added three additional time-varying measures not used by Blanchard and Wolfers. These included union density, taken primarily from Visser (1996), and collective-bargaining coverage and coordination, taken from OECD (1997).[24] Visser's (1996) union-density measures were usually available annually from 1970 to 1993. We assigned the 1970 value to periods before 1970 and the 1993 value to 1995. When there were missing data, we interpolated. The collective-bargaining-coverage and coordination variables were generally available for 1980, 1990, and 1994. Again, we assigned the 1980 values to periods before 1980 and the 1994 values to 1995; we used interpolation for missing data. These instances of imputation illustrate some of the difficulties encountered in accounting for institutional change in a regression context.

Table 5.4 illustrates the changes in these institutions for the United States and the average for the nine other countries included in tables 5.2 and 5.3 between 1970 and 1995. The data indicate that institutions have changed in ways that might reasonably be expected to lower the U.S. unemployment rate relative to those in the other countries.[25] First, UI replacement ratios rose both in the United States and elsewhere, but by far more outside the United States (16.89 percentage points versus 3.18). Second, despite recent reductions in the strength of employment protection in several non-U.S. countries (OECD 1999), the employment-protection index was constant in the United States but rose slightly on average from 1970 to 1995 outside the United States. Third, collective-bargaining coverage fell in the United States and elsewhere, with a larger fall in the United States. Fourth, union density was roughly constant outside the United States but fell by 11.17 percentage points in the United States. Finally, coordination fell slightly outside the United States and stayed the same in the United States.[26]

After estimating regression models analogous to those used to construct table 5.3 (see appendix table 5A.2), we used these new models to examine the degree to which they could account for the divergence of unemployment in the United States and other coun-

TABLE 5.4 **Mean Values for Time-Varying Institutions**

	Non-U.S.			U.S.		
	1970	1995	Difference, 1995 to 1970	1970	1995	Difference, 1995 to 1970
UI replacement ratio (one year)	32.41	49.30	16.89	23.74	26.92	3.18
Employment-protection index	2.06	2.13	.07	.20	.20	.00
Collective-bargaining coverage	72.22	69.22	−3.00	26.00	18.00	−8.00
Union density	40.65	40.58	−.07	26.45	15.28	−11.17
Coordination	1.97	1.92	−.06	1.00	1.00	.00

Sources: UI replacement ratio and employment-protection index: Blanchard and Wolfers (2000). Collective-bargaining coverage and coordination: OECD (1997) (original data included only 1980, 1990, and 1994; 1980 values [or earliest available] assigned to 1970, 1994 values to 1995). Union density: Visser (1996) (original data spanned 1970 to 1994; the earliest values were assigned to 1970, the latest to 1995).
Note: Non-U.S. countries include Australia, Canada, Finland, France, Italy, Japan, Spain, Sweden, and the United Kingdom.

tries over the period 1970 to 1996.[27] The model without interactions was found to account for 29.8 percent of the rise in relative unemployment in the other countries, compared to that in the United States. Of this 29.8 percent, 12.4 percentage points were associated with the less-favorable macro shocks and demographics in these other countries, and the remaining 17.4 percentage points were attributed to the less-employment-favorable institutional changes in the other countries. Thus, it appears that institutional changes have raised unemployment outside the United States relative to that in the United States by a modest amount, one that is slightly larger than the combined effect of macroeconomic and demographics shocks. Nonetheless, as was the case in models that assumed time-invariant institutions, the interaction between labor-market institutions and macroeconomic and demographic shocks remains very important in accounting for the divergence in unemployment between the United States and the other countries since 1970. When we allow shocks and institutions to interact, the model explains 63.0 percent of the divergence.

The foregoing evidence suggests that macroeconomic forces such as changes in inflation and real interest rates as well as demographic and institutional changes are all part of the reason why unemployment rates in other Western countries have risen on average relative to that in the United States. However, the interaction of these shocks with labor-market institutions provides the lion's share of the explanation.

While most economists consider changes in inflation to have only temporary effects on unemployment, Ball (1997, 1999) has argued that changes in aggregate demand (experienced as a change in the inflation rate) can have permanent effects on unemployment through mechanisms of hysteresis. One mechanism through which hysteresis may occur is that the long-term unemployed may not search very hard for jobs, and this is the mechanism emphasized by Ball. When unemployment becomes long term, it takes higher and higher levels of overall unemployment to establish the downward real-wage pressure needed to induce firms to hire more labor. If this is true, not only will a falling inflation rate raise the current unemployment rate, but it can also lead to a higher ultimate unemployment rate—even after the decline in the inflation rate has ceased—if the disinflation is severe and long-lived enough. In this view, we will understate the effects of aggregate demand on unemployment if we look only at its effect on current unemployment, as we have done following Blanchard and Wolfers.

However, in the same spirit as Blanchard and Wolfers, Ball hypothesizes that institutions play a role. Specifically, he argues that the unemployment effects of disinflation become more severe the longer the potential duration of UI benefits. Longer potential duration raises the chances that any initial increase in unemployment becomes long term—the kind of unemployment that is very difficult to reduce.

Ball uses this reasoning to suggest that the favorable performance in the United States of the natural unemployment rate over the 1980s and 1990s is tied to that country's shorter deflationary period in the 1980s and its more expansionary monetary policy in the 1990s. His reasoning further implies that any given disinflation rate will have a smaller effect on unemployment in the United States owing to that country's shorter duration of UI benefits.

What is especially unique about Ball's (1997, 1999) analysis is that he examines the effect of aggregate demand on the natural rate, whereas earlier work in macroeconomics assumed that aggregate demand could cause only temporary deviations from the natural rate. For example, in Ball (1997), he constructed a measure of the natural rate and then examined how inflation and UI duration affect the 1980 to 1990 change in the natural-rate measures across twenty countries.[28] While these results were somewhat fragile in light of the fact that there were only twenty observations, Ball did find that the length and the strength of disinflation over this period were positively related to the rise in the natural rate. Further, in several models, he found interaction effects between the macroeconomic forces and the duration of UI benefits, suggesting that the effect of a longer or deeper disinflation on the natural rate was larger the longer the UI-benefit duration. While Ball did not perform an explicit accounting of U.S.–other-country differences in the changes in the natural unemployment rate, his paper did include all the data used, allowing us to implement this accounting now.

According to Ball's (1997) data, the natural unemployment rate in the United States fell by 1.4 percentage points over the period 1980 to 1990. In contrast, across the other nineteen countries in the sample, the natural rate increased by an average of 2.32 percentage points. Thus, the natural rate rose by 3.72 percentage points more in other countries than in the United States. The United States had, somewhat surprisingly, a larger fall in inflation than the other countries did (8.1 percentage points as opposed to 6.41 in the other countries), suggesting that the depth of the disinflation cannot explain the U.S.–other-country unemployment comparison even if, in general, a larger fall in inflation is associated with a larger increase in the natural unemployment rate. However, the longest period of disinflation in the United States was only three years, in comparison to an average of 4.32 years elsewhere. Thus, the U.S. disinflation allowed less time for hysteresis to set in. And, of course, as we have seen, the United States had a shorter duration of UI benefits (0.5 years as opposed to an average of 2.71 years elsewhere), again suggesting a smaller hysteresis response to disinflation in the United States.

When we use Ball's estimates of a regression model for the 1980 to 1990 change in the natural rate as a function of only the two inflation variables (the 1980 to 1990 fall in the inflation rate and the square of the length of the longest period of disinflation), the regression coefficients predict a rise of 1.30 percentage points in the U.S. natural rate and a rise of 2.18 percentage points in the rate elsewhere.[29] Thus, the model without UI effects can explain only 24 percent of the U.S.–other-country difference in the change in the natural rate. However, when we estimated a slightly expanded version of one of Ball's models by including UI duration and its interactions with the two inflation variables,[30] we predicted a fall of 1.21 percentage points in the U.S. natural rate and a rise of 2.31 for the other countries. These predictions are remarkably close to the actual changes of − 1.4 for the United States and 2.32 for the other countries. This shocks-institutions model explains 95 percent of the U.S.–other-country difference.[31] Thus, following Ball in using an alternative measure of unemployment and a different specification of its determinants, we continue to find that, while macroeconomic shocks can explain part of the difference in unemployment experience between the United States and other countries, far deeper insight is obtained when we take into account the shocks' interactions with labor-market institutions (in this case, UI duration).

CONCLUSIONS

In this chapter, we have examined macroeconomic evidence on the effect of labor-market institutions on unemployment, paying particular attention to the remarkable reversal in the U.S. position relative to that of other countries since the early 1970s. We noted that early research on this issue reached somewhat mixed conclusions about the effect of centralized wage-setting institutions on unemployment. Some early studies found that there was a U-shaped relation between centralization and unemployment in the 1970s and 1980s: we observe low unemployment for very decentralized and very centralized wage-setting institutions, with high unemployment for countries with moderate degrees of centralization. Other researchers found a monotonic negative relation between the centralization of wage setting and unemployment. However, all these conclusions were found to be fragile with respect to the classification of countries according to their degree of centralization of wage setting. Moreover, this research, by and large, did not control for other influences, both institutional and macroeconomic, on a country's unemployment rate.

More recent work has advanced our understanding of international differences in unemployment. First, Nickell (1997, 1998) and Nickell and Layard (1999) have examined the determinants of differences across countries in average unemployment in the 1980s and 1990s. In an accounting sense, we found that their estimates for the United States imply that lower unemployment there is explained by lower labor taxes and less-generous UI systems, and, to a lesser extent, the net effect of the lower U.S. level of unionization and its decentralized union wage setting.

Second, Blanchard and Wolfers (2000) studied unemployment over the period 1960 to 1996 and found evidence consistent with the idea that macroeconomic shocks interact with labor-market institutions to affect unemployment. To account for the reversal in unemployment rates in the United States compared to the other OECD countries between 1970 to 1975 and 1995 to 1996, we used results from Bertola, Blau, and Kahn (2002), which builds on Blanchard and Wolfers (2000), taking into account demographic as well as macroeconomic shocks. As we noted in chapter 2, the United States had higher unemployment than did most other countries in the earlier period and considerably lower unemployment than most during the 1980s and 1990s. We found that macroeconomic and demographic shocks and institutional changes were more employment friendly in the United States and can, thus, explain a modest portion of the fall in the U.S. unemployment rate relative to that in other OECD countries. However, when we allowed for interactions between macroeconomic and demographic shocks and institutions, we found evidence that these shocks had a much larger effect in raising unemployment in the other countries than they did in the United States. This pattern appears largely due to the fact that the United States has more flexible labor-market institutions, allowing real wages rather than employment to bear the burden of adjustment. A framework that allows for interactions between macroeconomic shocks and labor-market institutions can account for most of the fall in the U.S. relative-unemployment rate.

A very similar pattern was found using an alternative approach suggested by Ball (1997): shocks are part of the picture, but most of the U.S.–other-country differences are tied to the interaction of shocks and institutions. An additional implication of Ball's (1997, 1999) work is that these effects can persist for a very long time.

While the findings reported in this chapter are remarkably consistent with the unified theory, introduced in chapter 1, we must be careful not to overinterpret them. In particular, many of the research-design concerns discussed in chapter 4 are applicable to the macroeconomic literature surveyed here. For example, many of the explanatory variables themselves can be affected by unemployment: higher unemployment may lead to changes in monetary policy and might even affect productivity growth. Moreover, the generosity of UI benefits or even individual workers' decisions to become union members may be affected by the extent of unemployment. These considerations suggest that the regressions discussed in this chapter may suffer from endogeneity biases and that, therefore, so may our estimates of the importance of shocks and institutions in explaining U.S. unemployment performance.

The macroeconomic research designs discussed in this chapter also do not directly test the mechanisms that are, in principle, behind the unified theory. First, the theory holds that some labor-market institutions affect absolute and relative wages and keep them rigid in the face of economic forces that would otherwise change absolute and relative pay levels. Second, the unified theory posits that these rigid wages lead to unemployment as firms move along their labor-demand curves. There is nothing in the macroeconomic evidence reviewed in this chapter that can speak to these mechanisms directly, even if the data do provide plausible evidence consistent with the theory. In the chapters to follow, we examine microeconomic evidence that sheds light on the specific mechanisms that macroeconomic observers believe to be an important part of the story.

APPENDIX 5A

TABLE 5A.1 **Selected Regression Results for the Determinants of Unemployment with Fixed Institutions: 1960 to 1995**

Explanatory Variables	Shocks Only		Shocks Interacted with Institutions	
	Coeff.	S.E.	Coeff.	Asymp. S.E.
Labor demand shift	.194	.085	.031	.037
Real interest rate	.294	.175	.234	.082
TFP growth	−.190	.178	.203	.131
Change in inflation	1.249	.594	1.061	.419
Birth/pop., fifteen to twenty-four years earlier	4.843	1.408	4.582	1.330
Interactions of shocks with				
UI replacement ratio	. . .	. . .	.050	.026
Maximum UI duration	. . .	. . .	.588	.213
Union coverage	. . .	. . .	−.065	.031
Employment protection	. . .	. . .	.248	.111
Active labor-market policies	. . .	. . .	.004	.027
Union density	. . .	. . .	.002	.023
Total labor-tax rate	. . .	. . .	.062	.035
Coordination index	. . .	. . .	.743	.375
Sample size	103		103	

Source: Bertola, Blau, and Kahn (2002).
Notes: Regressions also include country and period fixed effects. For variable definitions, see the notes to tables 5.1 and 5.2.

Following Blanchard and Wolfers (2000), all macroeconomic and demographic shock and institutions variables have been signed so that we expect a positive effect on unemployment. This means that the labor-demand-shift, TFP-growth, change-in-inflation, active-labor-market-policies, and coordination-index variables are all multiplied by −1. The "shocks-only" model is based on an OLS regression. The "shocks-interacted-with-institutions" model is estimated with nonlinear least squares. The model assumes that the form that the shocks-institution interactions take is a linear combination of the five shocks, which is then interacted with each institution separately. The weights in this linear combination are the shock-main-effect parameters.

Specifically, each institution is interacted with a linear combination of the four macroeconomic shocks:

$$a \times \text{labor-demand shift} + b \times \text{real interest rate} + c \times \text{TFP growth} + d \times \text{change in inflation} + e \times (\text{births/population}),$$

where the parameters a, b, c, d, and e are, respectively, the main effects for labor-demand shift, real interest rate, TFP growth, change in inflation, and births/population fifteen to twenty-four years prior to the current period.

TABLE 5A.2 **Selected Regression Results for the Determinants of Unemployment with Time-Varying Institutions: 1960 to 1995**

Explanatory Variables	Shocks and Institutions, Main Effects Only		Shocks Interacted with Institutions	
	Coeff.	S.E.	Coeff.	Asymp. S.E.
Main effects				
Labor-demand shift	.3093	.0978	.1763	.0612
Real interest rate	.4242	.1408	.3828	.1179
TFP growth	.1735	.2087	.0529	.1317
Change in inflation	1.9540	.6721	2.3455	.6871
Birth/Pop., fifteen to twenty-four years earlier	.8599	1.3967	1.9944	1.1261
UI replacement ratio	.0007	.0003	.0014	.0003
Union coverage	−.0007	.0007	−.0012	.0006
Employment protection	−.0067	.0079	−.0184	.0071
Union density	.0006	.0005	.0002	.0005
Coordination index	.0164	.0196	.0164	.0197
Interactions of shocks with				
UI replacement ratio	. . .	. . .	.0134	.0098
Maximum UI duration	. . .	. . .	.2108	.1893
Union coverage	. . .	. . .	.0333	.0196
Employment protection	. . .	. . .	−.0714	.2155
Active labor-market policies	. . .	. . .	−.0065	.0195
Union density	. . .	. . .	−.0319	.0155
Total labor-tax rate	. . .	. . .	−.0070	.0234
Coordination index	. . .	. . .	.8268	.5139
Sample size	103		103	

Source: Bertola, Blau, and Kahn (2002).
Note: Regressions also include country fixed effects.

Chapter 6

Labor-Market Institutions, Relative Wages, and Employment: Microeconomic Evidence

IN THIS CHAPTER and the next, we take a close look at a variety of research examining the effect of institutions on relative wages and relative employment. As we noted in chapter 4, the most-convincing evidence on the importance of institutions must take into account other possible causes of wage and employment outcomes. And, while the macroeconomic evidence discussed in the last chapter is consistent with the notion that institutions affect unemployment, it cannot easily account for alternative explanations. Evaluating the effect of other causes is crucial in reaching an accurate assessment of the effect of institutions. For example, given the results of the last chapter, we might be tempted to conclude that, if the high-unemployment countries of the OECD had adopted American-style, noninterventionist labor-market institutions, their unemployment rates would not have risen so high in the 1980s and 1990s. Or, considering the wage patterns shown in chapters 2 and 3, one might be tempted to argue that, if the United States encouraged more-extensive union coverage, perhaps through legislation, the American wage distribution would become less unequal.

While both these conclusions about European unemployment and American wage inequality may be true, it is also possible that characteristics of the population are an alternative explanation for the patterns that we have uncovered. For example, it is possible that Americans at the bottom of the skill distribution are less skilled relative to the middle than is the case in other countries. This difference could conceivably explain higher levels of wage inequality in the United States. Further, perhaps the skills of those at the bottom have deteriorated since the 1970s in the United States relative to the skills of those at the bottom in other countries, providing an alternative explanation for rising wage inequality in the United States relative to that in other countries since the 1970s. Alternatively, it is possible that the young in the United States, whose relative employment-to-population ratios have fallen much less than have those of the young in Europe, improved their relative labor-market qualifications compared to those of their counterparts in Europe. In this case, the composition of the labor force could explain rising youth unemployment in Europe relative to that in the United States during this period.

Such considerations motivate our examination of microeconomic evidence on the effect of labor-market institutions on relative pay and on employment among particular groups.[1] Micro data enable us to account for the types of alternative explanations discussed in the preceding paragraphs, through controls for individual-productivity characteristics. In this chapter, we consider relative wages and relative employment generally, while, in the next chapter, we examine the effect of institutions on the gender pay gap.

This chapter begins with an examination of the determinants of relative wages, focusing on the United States in comparison to other OECD countries. The unified theory suggests that real and relative wages are more flexible with respect to market forces in the United States than in other countries. We, therefore, investigate whether the rewards to human capital and the returns to being in favored sectors of the economy are, indeed, higher in the United States than elsewhere. We term these rewards *labor-market prices*. And we do, in fact, find that these rewards are substantially higher in the United States, even after accounting for the characteristics of the labor force.

Higher rewards in the United States are consistent with that country's more laissez-faire labor-market institutions in the face of widespread economic forces, such as technology or international trade, that would increase the rewards to skill in the absence of market intervention. However, it is also possible that differences in the supply and demand conditions for skilled labor between the United States and other OECD countries could cause the observed price differences. For example, perhaps the less skilled are more abundant in the United States, a factor that would raise the price of skill. If this is true, then it is possible that institutions do not have a major effect on relative wages, calling into question some of the logic of the unified theory. We, therefore, next examine direct evidence on the effect of labor-market institutions on wage inequality and on employment as well.

Evidence on the effect of institutions on employment is, of course, extremely important in and of itself. Further, a finding of employment effects of collective bargaining provides indirect evidence on institutions' wage effect as well: as we saw in chapter 4, under a monopoly-union model, we expect groups whose wages are raised the most by unions to have the most problems finding work. We examine results both from detailed comparisons of two or three countries and from several case studies of countries in which these institutions were radically and abruptly changed. These latter studies are particularly convincing because, by definition, such an approach enables one to control for national norms and culture. We find that, while institutions almost invariably affect the wage distribution, there is mixed evidence on their employment effects. In some cases, evidence of negative employment consequences of administered wages is obtained, while, in others, there is little evidence of such effects.

Taken together, these country studies and comparisons suggest strong evidence of an effect of collective-bargaining institutions on wage inequality and mixed evidence of an effect on relative employment of particular groups. This conclusion is bolstered by a review of results from statistical analyses of cross-sectional data from a large number of countries that examine the effects of institutions on wage inequality and relative employment among different skill groups while controlling for market forces (that is, supply and demand). We conclude that there is strong evidence that collective bargaining has an influence through its effect on labor-market prices and that, overall, collective bargaining is negatively associated with the relative employment of lower-skilled men (where skill embodies both experience and schooling), with weaker effects for women, other things equal. Further examination indicates that the negative employment effects of collective bargaining are concentrated among the young; in contrast, collective bargaining is not found to have a statistically significant effect on the relative employment of the less educated.

Finally, we also examine some microeconomic evidence on the effect of unemployment-insurance (UI) systems. Many believe that UI is an example of a labor-market institution that, when interacted with a recession, can lead to longer unemployment duration and, thus, hysteresis effects (Ball 1997, 1999). We find that UI-benefit levels and the potential duration of benefit receipt both have important effects in raising the duration of unemployment but that there are also some effective ways of reforming these systems in order to limit these effects.

DOES THE UNITED STATES HAVE HIGHER LABOR-MARKET PRICES THAN OTHER COUNTRIES?

In order to know whether wage setting and other labor-market institutions have affected the U.S. distribution of pay compared to that in other countries, we need to know how labor-market rewards stack up in the United States in contrast to those elsewhere. Even if it is true that rewards are higher in the United States, this outcome could have been caused by supply and demand or by institutional interventions, or some combination of both. A first step toward evaluating the importance of these factors is to determine whether the U.S. labor market does, indeed, yield higher returns to education or experience as well as to employment in favored sectors of the economy. We can then investigate the effect of institutions and market forces on these returns.

Evidence on Labor-Market Prices Controlling for Individual Characteristics

In assessing the role of labor-market prices in affecting wage inequality in different countries, we can decompose international differences in wage inequality into three components.[2] First, there is a portion due to differences in the distribution of productivity characteristics. A country might have a wider distribution of pay because the qualifications of its working population are more diverse. In one country, for example, the age of the workforce may be largely concentrated between thirty and fifty years, while, in another, workers' ages may range more widely. Because wages rise with experience in every country, this difference in the age distribution would produce a difference in wage inequality.

Second, wage inequality may be affected by measured labor-market prices. For example, in one country, the rate of return to an additional year of schooling may be 9 percent, while, in another, it may be only 4 percent. Or working in a high-paying industry like transportation may provide workers with a 15 percent pay premium in one country but only a 3 percent premium in another. Both these cases are examples of labor-market prices. And, depending on the distribution of workers by education level and industrial employment, these price differences will produce differing levels of wage inequality.

Labor-market prices are crucial to the workings of the economy because they provide workers with incentives to acquire skills and firms with incentives to hire various types of workers. For example, we might expect incentives to attend college to be low if there is a small wage return to attending college and jobs are plentiful for people without a college education. At the same time, if the relative price of highly skilled workers falls, then we would expect employers to demand relatively more of them. As we will show below, both these outcomes appeared to characterize Sweden in the 1970s and early 1980s (Edin and Holmlund 1995; Edin and Topel 1997).

Third, there may be unexplained differences in wage inequality across countries. For example, we may not be able to measure workers' ability and motivation adequately or to know the size of the firm at which a worker is employed. And we would expect abler workers and those working in large firms to earn more than others, all else equal (Neal and Johnson 1996; Brown and Medoff 1989). Differences in both the distribution of these unmeasured factors and the labor-market prices associated with them will contribute to international differences in wage inequality. One country may have a more concentrated distribution of firm sizes or individual-worker motivation than another. And one country may have especially large interfirm wage differentials or a high wage return to motivation. Thus, in some sense, this unexplained component combines the quantity and the price aspects of the first two for factors that are not explicitly measured.[3]

In measuring the contributions of these three factors to the higher U.S. levels of wage inequality, we make use of a statistical-decomposition technique devised by Juhn, Murphy, and Pierce (1993) in their study of rising American wage inequality from the 1960s through the 1980s. Table 6.1 shows the results of this decomposition from a study that we conducted (Blau and Kahn 1996a) that addressed the question of whether the United States had higher labor-market prices among men in the 1980s than was the case in a sample of nine other countries. The study is based on several nationally representative micro-data sources. Earnings, work hours, age, marital status, schooling, industry, occupation, and union membership are measured in comparable ways, and we can, thus, parcel out the effects of population heterogeneity and labor-market prices on wage inequality across countries.[4] We separately examined wage compression at the bottom (50–10) and at the top (90–50) of the distribution because of the importance of wage floors in highly unionized countries. Moreover, we measure labor-market prices on the basis of two specifications for wage determination. First, we estimated a "human-capital specification" (table 6.1, panel A), in which we controlled for education, potential experience, and marital status in our underlying wage regressions. Second, we estimated a "full specification" (table 6.1, panel B), in which we augmented these human-capital variables with industry, occupation, and union-status indicators. Comparison of the results across the two specifications can highlight the importance of industry, occupation, and union wage effects in explaining the higher American level of wage inequality.

Table 6.1, panel A, shows that, in the 1980s, the United States had a far larger men's 50–10 wage gap than did other countries. The average differential of 0.576 log points corresponds to a ratio of 1.8, meaning that the 50–10 ratio in the United States was 1.8 times the 50–10 ratio elsewhere. In contrast to the large difference in the 50–10 gap, the 90–50 gap was only slightly larger in the United States than elsewhere. OECD data for the 1980s also show

TABLE 6.1 **Decomposition of the U.S.–Other-Country Differences in the 50–10 and 90–50 Differentials in Men's Log Wages, 1980s**

	U.S. Differential–Other-Country Differential	Measured-Characteristics Effect	Wage-Coefficients Effect	Wage-Equation-Residual Effect
A. Human-capital specification				
50–10 log wage differential				
Germany 1985 to 1988	.584	.312	−.019	.291
Britain 1985 to 1989	.446	.083	.089	.274
Austria 1985 to 1987, 1989	.649	.299	−.005	.355
Switzerland 1987	.576	.254	.053	.269
Sweden 1980	.658	.385	.034	.239
Norway 1982	.668	.331	−.013	.350
Australia 1986	.285	.069	.068	.148
Hungary 1986 to 1988	.578	.158	.038	.382
Italy 1987	.562	.246	.041	.275
Norway 1989	.816	.338	−.037	.515
Sweden 1984	.518	.225	.018	.275
Non-U.S. average (unweighted)	.576	.245	.024	.307
90–50 log wage differential				
Germany 1985 to 1988	.013	−.183	.095	.101
Britain 1985 to 1989	−.131	−.134	−.043	.046

Austria 1985 to 1987, 1989	.044	−.199	.121	.122
Switzerland 1987	−.225	−.300	.046	.029
Sweden 1980	.100	−.075	.078	.097
Norway 1982	.170	−.132	.086	.216
Australia 1986	.113	−.067	.054	.126
Hungary 1986 to 1988	−.109	−.190	.208	−.127
Italy 1987	.066	−.151	.114	.103
Norway 1989	.027	−.104	.065	.066
Sweden 1984	.158	−.190	.152	.196
Non-U.S. average (unweighted)	.021	−.157	.089	.089

B. Full specification

50–10 log wage differential

Germany 1985 to 1988	.584	.301	.067	.216
Britain 1985 to 1989	.446	.010	.192	.244
Austria 1985 to 1987, 1989	.649	.208	.144	.297
Switzerland 1987	.576	.218	.170	.188
Sweden 1980	.658	.294	.205	.159
Norway 1982	.668	.370	.057	.241
Australia 1986	.285	.127	.046	.112
Hungary 1986–1988	.578	.145	.174	.259
Italy 1987	.562	.233	.092	.237
Norway 1989	.816	.212	.129	.475
Sweden 1984	.518	.164	.104	.250
Non-U.S. average (unweighted)	.576	.207	.125	.243

(Table continues on p. 176.)

TABLE 6.1 *Continued*

	U.S. Differential–Other-Country Differential	Measured-Characteristics Effect	Wage-Coefficients Effect	Wage-Equation-Residual Effect
90–50 log wage differential				
Germany 1985 to 1988	.013	−.177	.091	.099
Britain 1985 to 1989	−.131	−.149	−.056	.074
Austria 1985 to 1987, 1989	.044	−.151	.093	.102
Switzerland 1987	−.225	−.231	−.049	.055
Sweden 1980	.100	−.091	.080	.111
Norway 1982	.170	−.191	.166	.195
Australia 1986	.113	−.129	.098	.144
Hungary 1986 to 1988	−.109	−.206	.196	−.099
Italy 1987	.066	−.108	.048	.126
Norway 1989	.027	−.132	.056	.103
Sweden 1984	.158	−.140	.132	.166
Non-U.S. average (unweighted)	.021	−.155	.078	.098

Source: Based on table 3 from Blau & Kahn, "International Differences in Male Wage Inequality," *Journal of Political Economy* 104(1996): 812–13. © University of Chicago Press.

Note: The human-capital specification includes education, potential experience and its square, and marital status as explanatory variables. The full specification includes these variables and adds a vector of one-digit industry dummy variables, a vector of one-digit occupation dummy variables, and a union-status indicator where available (union-status information was not available for Australia, Italy, or Sweden). In all cases, a U.S. equation was estimated with the same explanatory variables as the indicated country so that the decomposition could be performed. U.S. data are for 1985 to 1989.

that U.S.–other-country differences in the men's 50–10 wage gap were larger than the 90–50 differences. However, since the mid-1980s, wage inequality in the United States has risen especially rapidly at the top of the distribution. Thus, the extent of the difference in the male wage distribution between the United States and the other countries has become more similar at both the top and the bottom of the distribution, although, as the OECD data presented in chapter 2 indicate, the U.S.–other country difference in the men's 50–10 wage gap remains larger than the 90–50 difference.

The importance of population heterogeneity in explaining the higher level of U.S. wage inequality is given in the column reporting the measured-characteristics effect. The entries there show the differences in wage differentials that would exist between the United States and the indicated other country if both countries had the same measured labor-market prices and distribution of residual wage inequality but their actual distribution of productivity-related characteristics. The wage-coefficients effect, shown in the next column, tells us how inequality would differ between the United States and the indicated other country if both had the same distribution of measured characteristics and wage residuals but had their own actual wage coefficients. Finally, the wage-equation residual effect indicates the differences in inequality that would exist between the United States and the indicated other country if both had the same distribution of characteristics and wage coefficients but their own actual distribution of wage residuals.[5]

Looking first at the measured-characteristics effects, the positive effects for the 50–10 differentials for both specifications indicate that the U.S. distribution of measured characteristics widens the 50–10 gap compared to that in each country. These effects— 0.245 log points for the human-capital specification and 0.207 log points for the full specification, on average—are large indeed. A comparison of the results for the two specifications indicates that it is the U.S. distribution of human-capital characteristics that is relevant in explaining the international differences, with the U.S. distribution of industry, occupation, and union status slightly lowering the 50–10 gap compared to that in other countries.[6] On average, measured characteristics are estimated to account for 35.9 to 43.4 percent of the higher U.S. 50–10 differential. In contrast, the distribution of measured characteristics lowers the 90–50 wage differential in the United States compared to that in other countries. The effect is negative, with an unweighted average effect of about −0.16 log points in both specifications.

The findings for the measured-characteristics effects imply that a considerable portion of the wider 50–10 gap relative to the 90–50 gap in the United States is accounted for by differences in the distribution of productive characteristics. With the same distribution of measured characteristics, the average difference between the U.S. 50–10 gap and that for the other countries would decline to 0.331 to 0.369 log points (from 0.576), while the figure for the 90–50 gap would increase to about 0.18 (from 0.021).

These results highlight the importance of controlling for personal characteristics. The inclusion of these controls reveals the widening effect of U.S. prices for the 90–50 gap, an effect that is not apparent if one merely compares the raw 90–50 differential in the United States with that in other countries. It also reduces the likelihood of our overstating the compression at the bottom in the other OECD countries compared to that in the United States (which would occur if we merely examined the raw 50–10 differentials).

However, the results also highlight the importance of wage structure or labor-market rewards in explaining the higher level of U.S. inequality. If we consider the part of the differential that is not accounted for by measured characteristics (that is, the sum of the wage-coefficients and wage-equation-residual effects) as being potentially due to wage structure, we find that, in every case, the U.S. wage structure widens both the top and the bottom of the wage distribution relative to that in other countries. And, even after taking the distribution of productivity-related characteristics into account, the U.S. wage structure continues to widen the wage distribution more at the bottom than at the top. This is true on average and in nine (full specification) or ten (human-capital specification) of eleven possible cases. Such an effect is consistent with government and trade-union wage policies in other countries having their biggest effect in bringing up the bottom of the wage distribution.

The last two columns of table 6.1 show the effects of wage coefficients and wage residuals separately. For the 50–10 gap, the

U.S. human-capital wage coefficients usually have a small widening effect compared to the other countries (accounting for 4.2 percent of the U.S.–other-country difference, on average), although the effect is negative in four cases. The wage-coefficients effect is notably increased when the full specification is employed (accounting for 21.7 percent of the difference, on average), suggesting that it is the prices associated with the industry, occupation, and unionism variables that are particularly high in the United States. One interpretation of the rise in the size of the wage-coefficients effect when we control for industry, occupation, and unionism is that, in other countries, centralized union contracts and contract extensions to nonunion workers reduce the extent of interindustry, interoccupation, and union-nonunion wage differentials relative to those in the United States. In both the human-capital and the full specifications, however, the wage-equation-residual effect accounts for a substantial share (42.2 to 53.3 percent) of the U.S.–other-country difference. In contrast, for the 90–50 gap, the wage-coefficients and wage-equation-residual effects are generally positive and do not differ very much between the two specifications, suggesting that the effect of measured prices at this end of the distribution primarily reflects higher prices of the human-capital variables in the United States. In this case, the wage-coefficients and wage-equation-residual effects are of roughly equal size, on average.

The results reported in table 6.1 suggest that, even after accounting for differences in the distribution of personal characteristics, there is substantially more wage inequality in the United States than elsewhere. Yet even these differences in qualifications—particularly schooling—may indirectly be influenced by labor-market institutions. Recall from chapter 3 that it has been argued that welfare-state benefits and programs are likely to be more extensive where wage setting is conducted on a very centralized basis (Summers, Gruber, and Vergara 1993). If this is the case, it is possible that school systems in corporatist societies are themselves more centralized and, therefore, turn out a more homogeneous group of graduates than do those in countries where wages are set in a less centralized way. Thus, at least for the 50–10 comparisons reported in table 6.1, where the United States was seen to have a more diverse workforce than other countries, some of the measured-characteristics effect may have reflected the ultimate effect of labor-market institutions. Further, while, for the 90–50 gap, the United States actually had a less-diverse workforce than did the other countries, labor-market institutions may have prevented an even larger difference in the measured-characteristics effect between the United States and the other countries from emerging.

Evidence of Industry Wage Effects

The decompositions reported in table 6.1 show that labor-market prices and the distribution of workers' characteristics both contribute to higher wage inequality in the United States. And there was some indication that prices associated with industry, occupation, and union membership were particularly important in explaining the higher degree of wage inequality at the bottom. Such outcomes would be expected in light of the presence of binding wage floors in many highly unionized countries. An additional dimension of these wage-setting institutions that we discussed in chapter 3 is the high degree of coordination of wage setting across sectors of the economy that characterizes the Scandinavian countries as well as others in continental Europe, such as Austria and Germany. To the extent that wages are coordinated across sectors, we expect smaller wage effects associated with working in a relatively high wage industry than we do where wage setting is decentralized, as in the United States. Britain may represent an intermediate case of coordination between the United States and the countries of continental Europe.

In the absence of some coordinating mechanism such as collective bargaining, firms in different industries may choose to pay similarly skilled workers different wages for several reasons. High wages allow firms to recruit higher-quality workers, reduce turnover, obtain more effort from workers, and improve employee morale. For these reasons, paying above-market wages may be profit enhancing for a firm, a practice that has been termed *paying efficiency wages* since high pay levels may improve the firm's efficiency (that is, profitability) (see, for example, Shapiro and Stiglitz 1984; and Krueger and Summers 1988). Firms in different industries may have different incentives to pay efficiency wages to the extent that the differing production technologies across industries imply different gains to reducing turnover, recruiting high-quality labor, and so on. For example, firms in some industries may require extensive firm-specific training for their workers and, thus, will especially benefit from pay policies that lower workers' propensity to quit. This discussion of possible reasons for paying efficiency wages suggests that there may be many possible reasons for interindustry wage differentials, and just what the ultimate reasons behind these wage differences are remains a source of controversy.[7] Nonetheless, an international comparison of interindustry wage differentials can shed light on the extent of coordination of wage setting across industries. The economywide importance of interindustry wage differentials may be estimated by asking how much variation there is in average industry wage levels for workers of the same level of skill.

Table 6.2 shows results from a variety of such studies. The entries are the standard deviations of industry wage effects from each study, where the industry wage effects are estimated controlling for other personal characteristics.[8] Looking first at studies in which men and women are pooled (panel A of table 6.2), we see that the standard deviation of industry wage effects is between 0.119 and 0.140 for the United States and between 0.013 and 0.077, with an average effect of 0.048, for the other countries, substantially smaller than the U.S. figures. These other countries include the Scandinavian countries and Austria, all of which traditionally have had high levels of union coverage and relatively centralized wage-setting institutions compared to those in the United States.

When we allow the wage-determination process to differ by gender (panel B of table 6.2, which summarizes Kahn's [1998b] results), we reach a similar conclusion. Namely, industry wage effects are much larger in the United States than elsewhere. Specifically, the average of the estimates for U.S. men is 0.122, while, for U.S. women, it is 0.137. For the other countries, the average effect for men is 0.057, and the average effect for women is even smaller, 0.038. To assess the magnitude of these U.S.–other-country differences, note that Blau and Kahn (1996a) found that, in the 1980s, the standard deviation of the log of men's wages was 0.311 log points higher (or, taking antilogs, about 36 percent higher) for

TABLE 6.2 Estimates of the Standard Deviation of Industry Wage Effects Based on Micro Data

A. Studies Pooling Men and Women				B. Estimates for Men and Women Separately			
Study	Country	Year	S.D. of Industry Log Wage Effects	Study	Country	Year	S.D. of Industry Log Wage Effects
Krueger and Summers (1988)	United States	1984	.140	Kahn (1998b)	United States, men	1985 to 1989	.119–.128
Edin and Zetterberg (1992)	Sweden	1984	.013		United States, women	1985 to 1989	.111–.159
Barth and Zweimüller (1992)	Austria	1983	.032		Norway, men	1987	.064
	Norway	1989	.053		Norway, women	1987	.026
	United States, union	1983	.141		Germany, men	1985 to 1988	.033
	United States, nonunion	1983	.119		Germany, women	1985 to 1988	.061
Albaek et al. (1996)	Denmark	1990	.057		Austria, men	1985 to 1987, 1989	.062
	Finland	1987	.072		Austria, women	1985 to 1987, 1989	.036
	Norway	1989	.077		Britain, men	1985 to 1989	.088
	Sweden	1981	.031		Britain, women	1985 to 1989	.062
					Sweden, men	1984	.040
					Sweden, women	1984	.003

Source: Authors' compilation.

American men than it was, on average, for Austrian, British, German, Norwegian, and Swedish men. Looking at the results reported in panel B for these countries, we see that the standard deviation of industry wage effects for men was about 0.065 log points higher in the United States than in these five other countries. By this rough comparison, industry wage effects account for about 21 percent (that is, 0.065/0.311) of the higher wage dispersion among American men, a substantial contribution.

A further interesting point to note about table 6.2 is that, apart from the United States, industry wage effects are largest for Britain. As the data presented in chapter 3 showed, compared to Austria, Germany, and the Scandinavian countries, Britain is much less unionized and has less-centralized wage setting, although not compared to the United States, which has the least and most-decentralized union coverage. The ranking of industry wage effects across countries is quite consistent with these rankings of the degree of coordination of wage setting. Finally, while the industry wage effects were, on average, slightly higher for men than for women in the other countries but slightly higher for women than for men in the United States, the effects move together across countries. For example, industry wage effects are higher for both men and women in the United States than in any other country, as they are in Britain compared to the other European countries. This consistency suggests that men's and women's wages within a country are affected by similar economic forces. This point is relevant to our examination of gender and wage determination in the next chapter.

Table 6.2 shows that industry wage differentials for similarly qualified workers are larger in the United States than in countries with more centralized wage-setting processes and more union coverage. To the extent that highly centralized wage setting results in binding wage floors, we would expect to see an especially large coordination effect in such economies for pay levels across industries at the bottom of the distribution of each industry's scale. For example, in an economy with a national wage bargain that calls for the same high wage floor for different industries, we should see a particularly small degree of dispersion of industry wage effects among the less skilled.

Kahn (1998b) analyzed these issues by using quantile regression analysis, a technique that allows one to estimate the effect of industry on wages at different points in the wage distribution, controlling for other personal characteristics. Looking at the same countries as are shown in panel B of table 6.2, he compared the standard deviation of industry wage effects at the 10th percentile of the distribution of wages, conditional on the other factors that affect pay. For U.S. men, the dispersion was 0.175 log points, while, for men in the other countries, it was only 0.073 log points, a larger gap than the overall U.S.–other-country gap in industry wage effects, which, as we have seen, averaged 0.065 log points. Thus, for men, the evidence is consistent with disproportionately more coordination of wages across industries among those at the bottom of the distribution in other countries than in the United States. However, for women, the results did not support this hypothesis. In the United States, industry wage dispersion at the 10th percentile was 0.149 log points, and it averaged 0.069 log points elsewhere, a smaller gap (0.080 log points) than that for the average industry wage differentials, 0.099 log points. Perhaps, given that the female wage distribution lies below the men's distribution in all countries, European women higher up in the wage distribution are also affected by industry wage floors.

The Role of Cognitive Ability in Explaining the High Level of U.S. Wage Inequality

The evidence presented in tables 6.1 and 6.2 strongly suggests that labor-market rewards serve to widen wage distribution in the United States compared to that in other countries. These patterns are consistent with the idea that collective bargaining or other labor-market institutions narrow the dispersion of pay in these other nations compared to that in the United States. However, attention has recently been focused on what could be a competing explanation for these patterns. Specifically, as we show below, data from the 1990s suggest that, at a given level of education, American workers have a lower level of cognitive skills than do workers in other countries and that this is particularly true at the bottom of the distribution of test performance. Furthermore, as pointed out by Nickell and Layard (1999), countries with greater wage returns to education, like the United States, also have larger cognitive-test-score differentials across education groups. This raises the possibility that evidence that appears to indicate higher labor-market prices in the United States may actually be due to greater variation in cognitive skills. Of course, more homogeneous distributions of cognitive skills in countries outside the United States may reflect the influence of union movements on government education policies. But the question of whether the distribution of cognitive skills explains higher U.S. wage inequality is still extremely important in evaluating the direct influence of institutions. For example, there may be institutional interventions that change the nature of wage setting in a country without changing the underlying education system, and we would like to know the effect of such a change on the wage structure.

Recently, micro data that allow us to examine the effect of cognitive skills on the wage structure in several countries have become available in the form of the International Adult Literacy Survey (IALS).[9] The IALS is the result of an international cooperative effort, conducted over the period 1994 to 1996, to devise an instrument to compare the cognitive skills of adults across a number of countries. The sampling frame was similar across countries, with the target population being those sixteen years and older who were not in institutions or in the military. Of unique interest in the IALS is its measurement of cognitive skills. This was accomplished through three tests that were administered to all respondents in their home-country languages. These tests were designed to measure the following:

a) Prose literacy—the knowledge and skills needed to understand and use information from texts including editorials, news stories, poems and fiction;

b) Document literacy—the knowledge and skills required to locate and use information contained in various formats, including job applications, payroll forms, transportation schedules, maps, tables, and graphics; and

c) Quantitative literacy—the knowledge and skills required to apply arithmetic operations, either alone or sequentially, to numbers embedded in printed materials, such as balancing a checkbook, calculating a tip, completing an order form, or determining the amount of interest on a loan from an advertisement. (Statistics Canada 1998)

Proficiency in each of the three test areas was scored on a scale of 0 to 500, after the tests were read by several graders from the respondent's own country. The IALS provides five alternative estimates of proficiency for each test, which were computed from raw test-performance information using a multiple-imputation procedure developed by Rubin (1987). These alternative estimates are, in fact, highly correlated. We found that, within each of the three types of test, the five estimates of the score were correlated at 0.90.[10] Further, to ensure comparability of grading across countries, an average of 9.4 percent of the tests for each country were regraded by personnel from another country; interrater agreement with respect to this regrading was 94 to 99 percent.

Although, in principle, interpreting prose or documents and using mathematics may each require different skills, we found that, as measured by the IALS, these skills are, in fact, highly correlated. Forming a score for each of the three tests (that is, quantitative, prose, and document literacy) based on the average of the five available estimates, we found that these scores were correlated at between 0.91 and 0.94. Owing to this high correlation, we focused on a measure of cognitive skill that is an average of the three average test scores for each individual. However, we also estimated models with the three average test scores entered separately, with very similar results.

Table 6.3 provides evidence on the distribution of cognitive test scores for men and women in the population across the full set of nine countries with test-score data (panel A) and for the wage sample in the five countries for which this information is available (panel B).[11] The wage sample is composed of full-time workers who worked at least twenty-six weeks during the year. Looking first at the full population (panel A), a striking pattern is the higher level of test-score inequality for both men and women in the United States than elsewhere, particularly at the bottom of the distribution. Americans do substantially worse than the non-U.S. average at the bottom, about the same at the median, and somewhat better at the top. The U.S. shortfall at the 10th percentile of the test-score distribution is 15.5 points for women and 23.7 points for men, while the U.S. advantage at the 90th percentile is 7.3 points for women and 8.3 for men. However, the men's 50–10 test-score gaps in Britain, Canada, and Ireland are more comparable to those in the United States than are those in the other countries. Among women, the 50–10 gap is higher in the United States than in every other country, with Belgium, Canada, and New Zealand having the gaps closest to that in the United States.

TABLE 6.3 **Distribution of Individual Average Literacy Test Scores by Country and Gender**

Country	Mean	S.D.	Percentile			Differential	
			10	50	90	50–10	90–50
A. Population							
Men							
Belgium	284.63	51.43	221.67	292.13	341.79	70.46	49.67
Britain	273.59	63.55	192.67	283.89	344.79	91.22	60.90
Canada	277.66	67.06	186.76	289.28	346.95	102.52	57.67
Ireland	264.47	59.47	185.76	273.26	329.88	87.50	56.62
Netherlands	289.13	43.97	231.60	295.47	338.00	63.87	42.53
New Zealand	273.12	57.00	200.09	279.71	340.49	79.61	60.78
Sweden	308.47	48.26	249.08	312.38	364.67	63.30	52.29
Switzerland	281.67	51.80	227.26	288.75	334.03	61.50	45.28
United States	275.60	65.54	188.13	287.05	350.89	98.92	63.85
Non-U.S. average	281.59	55.32	211.86	289.36	342.58	77.50	53.22
Women							
Belgium	270.46	57.02	194.14	282.25	334.63	88.11	52.38
Britain	261.81	58.33	187.80	267.18	329.75	79.38	62.58
Canada	281.88	60.16	204.25	288.78	349.56	84.53	60.77
Ireland	261.69	54.37	190.39	266.50	326.03	76.11	59.53
Netherlands	282.24	43.93	224.90	288.92	333.50	64.02	44.57
New Zealand	271.04	56.11	194.45	278.89	335.14	84.43	56.25
Sweden	300.17	48.70	238.98	304.97	356.93	66.00	51.95
Switzerland	271.12	50.81	212.72	278.34	324.78	65.63	46.44
United States	274.80	62.87	190.45	283.96	343.57	93.51	59.61
Non-U.S. average	275.05	53.68	205.95	281.98	336.29	76.03	54.31
B. Wage sample							
Men							
Canada	295.96	52.40	233.95	296.76	362.29	62.81	65.53
Netherlands	294.07	40.43	241.92	297.80	338.92	55.88	41.12
Sweden	311.60	46.37	256.31	313.94	365.97	57.63	52.03
Switzerland	283.79	51.32	227.65	291.01	334.86	63.36	43.85
United States	288.97	61.43	216.49	297.16	357.13	80.67	59.98
Non-U.S. average	296.35	47.63	239.96	299.88	350.51	59.92	50.63
Women							
Canada	299.11	56.19	225.92	307.46	365.08	81.53	57.62
Netherlands	300.53	34.17	251.05	303.85	340.39	52.80	36.54
Sweden	308.54	43.08	259.48	310.49	361.42	51.02	50.93
Switzerland	278.74	47.51	230.62	284.72	326.95	54.10	42.23
United States	289.56	58.79	221.53	294.54	352.88	73.01	58.34
Non-U.S. average	296.73	45.24	241.77	301.63	348.46	59.86	46.83

Source: International Adult Literacy Survey (IALS) data analyzed in Blau and Kahn (2000a).
Note: Individual scores are the average of quantitative, document, and prose test scores. Non-U.S. average is the unweighted average of the figures in the table. Wage sample includes full-time workers who worked at least twenty-six weeks.

When test-score differentials are computed for the subset of workers in the wage sample, roughly similar patterns are obtained (panel B). However, it is notable that, for the five countries for which we have wage data, wage-sample inclusion tends to be selective of individuals with higher test scores. The mean is higher and the standard deviation generally lower for the wage sample than for the full population, although the extent of these differences varies considerably across countries. We address the issue of sample selection later in this chapter.

These test-score patterns roughly mirror the differences between the United States and the other countries in wage distributions shown in chapter 2, at least in leading us to expect larger wage differentials between the middle and the bottom and between the middle and the top in the United States. However, test scores are likely to provide a better explanation for the greater U.S. gap at the bottom than for that at the top since the difference in dispersion of test scores between the United States and the other countries in the upper ranges is relatively small.

In Blau and Kahn (2000a), we undertook to shed light on the effect of the distribution of cognitive skills on wage inequality in the United States compared to that in other countries, using the IALS data. We focused on a comparison of the United States to Canada, the Netherlands, Sweden, and Switzerland—the countries for which wage data were available. We found that the measured return to education remains considerably higher in the United States than elsewhere, even after controlling for test score: a one-standard-deviation increase in schooling is estimated to raise the wages of U.S. men by 16.6 percent and U.S. women by 26.4 percent, compared to a non-U.S. average of 6.4 percent for men and 10.3 percent for women.[12] With the inclusion of test scores, the ratio of the average return to education among the other countries to the U.S. return increases only slightly, from 36.9 to 38.6 percent, among men and actually falls slightly, from 41.9 to 38.9 percent, among women. Thus, the greater dispersion of test scores in the United States does little to account for the higher return to education there. Among both men and women, education is considerably more highly rewarded in United States than in other countries, even controlling for test scores. In addition, in regression specifications that include education, the estimated U.S. returns to cognitive test scores are higher than is the non-U.S. average, considerably so for men. This is in line with higher rewards to skills in the United States than elsewhere.

While the dispersion in test scores and the regression results suggest that cognitive skills play a role in explaining the higher level of U.S. wage inequality, how quantitatively important are they? We addressed this question using the same decomposition technique employed in table 6.1 to explain U.S.–other-country differences in the distribution of wages. Again, we assessed the relative importance of differences in the distribution of characteristics (in this case, including test scores), as well as labor-market prices and residual inequality, in explaining higher U.S. wage inequality.

We found that, while the greater dispersion of cognitive test scores in the United States plays a part in explaining higher U.S. wage inequality, higher labor-market prices (that is, higher returns to measured human capital and cognitive skills) and greater residual inequality still play important roles for both men and women. Moreover, we found that, on average, prices are quantitatively considerably more important than differences in the distribution of test scores in explaining the relatively high level of U.S. wage inequality.[13]

It is possible that a given test score may not mean the same thing for an immigrant as it does for a native, given differences in language ability and other factors. If this is the case, our results may in part reflect the native-immigrant composition of each country's wage samples. For this reason, we examined international differences in the sources of wage inequality for a sample that was restricted to natives in each country. Our results regarding the importance of higher labor-market prices in the United States in explaining higher U.S. wage inequality remained the same for these natives-only samples.

While it might be tempting to conclude that poor-quality education is responsible for low U.S. test scores at the bottom of the test-score distribution, consideration of the native sample suggests that this argument applies only partially to men and perhaps not at all to women. Native U.S. men at the 10th percentile of the test-score distribution scored only 7.9 points below those in other countries, in contrast to the overall population difference at the 10th percentile of 23.7 points. And native U.S. women at the 10th percentile actually outscored their counterparts in other countries by 4.5 points.[14]

As can be seen in table 6.3, test scores are higher and less dispersed for our wage sample (this is, workers employed full-time) than for the population in general. This pattern raises the possibility that wage inequality is higher in the United States, not because of higher labor-market prices, as we have claimed, but rather because a larger share of those at the bottom of the skill distribution are not employed in the other countries than in the United States. This means that we do not observe wages for them.

To examine this possibility, we corrected our samples for selectivity. To illustrate the adjustment, consider the comparison of U.S. and Canadian men. Among the population of Canadian men, 63.9 percent were employed full-time and worked at least twenty-six weeks in the past year, while the figure was 71.1 percent in the United States, or 10.1 percent higher—that is, $(71.1 - 63.9)/71.1 = 0.101$. To correct for selection, we first compute a predicted probability of being in the wage sample for each U.S. male in the population on the basis of a probit model for U.S. men in which the probability of being in the wage sample is a function of age, education, and test score. Since Canadian men are 10.1 percent less likely than are American men to be in the wage sample, we then exclude from the original U.S. men's wage sample the 10.1 percent with the lowest predicted probabilities of inclusion. We then reestimated the U.S. wage equations on this reduced sample and performed the Juhn, Murphy, and Pierce (1993) decomposition for the selectivity-adjusted U.S. sample and the original Canadian sample. This procedure provides some adjustment for selectivity bias both in our estimation of overall wage inequality and in our estimation of the wage equation itself.[15] A similar adjustment was made for each pairwise (that is, U.S.–other-country) comparison for men and for women. After correcting our samples for selectivity in this way, we obtained results that were very similar to those reported earlier. We conclude that the United States has higher labor-market prices than other countries do even accounting for labor-force selectivity.

Higher U.S. Wage Inequality:
Transitory or Permanent?

We have presented a considerable body of evidence suggesting that, at a point in time, U.S. wages are much more unequal than are those in other countries and that higher U.S. rewards to skills and employment in favored sectors are an important reason for these differences. It is possible, however, that individual wage mobility over time is greater in the United States than elsewhere and, thus, that lifetime earnings in the United States may be no more unequally distributed than are lifetime earnings elsewhere. If this were true, then we would need to reevaluate our conclusions about the degree to which the U.S. labor market delivers more unfavorable wage outcomes for those at the bottom. One recent study concerned with this question compared individual earnings mobility in the United States and West Germany in the 1980s (Burkhauser, Holtz-Eakin, and Rhody 1997). Workers were followed over a period of years, and the degree to which they moved up the wage distribution was assessed. A similar degree of mobility was found in both countries, as was a high level of persistence in individuals' relative earnings outcomes over time. While this study compared only the United States and West Germany, it does suggest that our focus on annual earnings inequality gives results that are similar to those that would be obtained by a focus on long-term earnings inequality.

CAUSES AND CONSEQUENCES OF INTERNATIONAL DIFFERENCES IN LABOR-MARKET PRICES: INSTITUTIONS, MARKET FORCES, WAGE INEQUALITY, AND RELATIVE EMPLOYMENT

High labor-market prices in the United States could be the result of the more laissez-faire labor markets there or of market forces, or a combination of both. We have already discussed in detail the ways in which centralized wage-setting institutions in many other countries could lead to wage compression and, therefore, to lower levels of wage inequality than we find in the United States. However, it is also possible that a relatively high supply of less-skilled workers in the United States, as suggested by the relatively low test scores at the 10th percentile of the test distribution shown in table 6.3, could depress the relative pay of those at the bottom (Leuven, Oosterbeek, and van Ophem 1998). In this section, we provide more-direct evidence on institutions and market forces as factors influencing wage inequality and on the employment consequences of these wage outcomes.

We begin with an examination of the role of collective bargaining in wage inequality and then turn to an assessment of the relative strength of institutions and market forces. An important conceptual consideration in gauging these two types of explanation is to note that, if wages are compressed as a result of institutional interventions such as collective bargaining or minimum-wage laws, and if employment is demand determined, then we expect to observe employment problems among those whose wages are raised the most. Of course, according to the theories of efficient bargaining and monopsony discussed in chapter 4, wage-setting institutions can affect relative pay without affecting relative employment. But a finding that collective bargaining or minimum wages are associated with employment problems among the less skilled, as well as with wage compression, would be strong evidence that these interventions actually do affect labor-market prices. On the other hand, if the market forces of supply and demand are the main factors affecting wage inequality, then groups whose wages are raised the most, for example, by high relative demand, will also have abundant employment opportunities. Therefore, an examination of employment across different groups in the labor force can, in addition to being of major policy interest in itself, also shed considerable light on the question of whether institutions have an important effect on the wage structure.

Accounting for the Effect of Unionization on Wage Inequality

There are several routes through which the industrial-relations system can affect overall wage inequality. First, unions may increase the difference between their members' average wages and those of nonunion workers. All else equal, the larger the union-nonunion wage gap, the larger the country's overall wage variance will be. And, as we show later in this chapter, this gap is much higher for the United States than for other countries.[16]

Second, unions typically negotiate contracts that allow for less variation in pay than occurs in the nonunion sector (Freeman

1982; Blanchflower and Freeman 1992). Unions are much less prevalent in the United States than elsewhere; thus, the lower union variance in pay would receive a smaller weight in the United States. Hence, we would expect a higher overall variance in wages in the United States even if the variance of wages within the union and nonunion sectors were identical across countries. However, there are strong reasons for expecting both these within-sector variances to be higher in the United States than elsewhere. These higher within-sector variances constitute a third route by which the U.S. industrial-relations system raises wage inequality relative to that in other countries.

With respect to the union sector, as we have noted, collective bargaining in the United States is relatively decentralized, with an emphasis on single-firm agreements that, in most cases, are not firmwide (Hendricks and Kahn 1982). In contrast, in many other countries, bargaining is conducted on an industrywide or even an economywide level. Thus, there appears to be more scope for interfirm and interindustry wage differentials in the United States than elsewhere, and a substantial portion of the wage inequality that we observe in the United States is associated with such firm or industry wage effects (Blau 1977; Groshen 1991; Davis and Haltiwanger 1991; Krueger and Summers 1988).

While a lower variance in the union sector of other countries could be achieved either by raising the bottom or by restraining the top, or by doing both, centralized bargains often emphasize the setting of wage minima across diverse units. For example, in Austria, Germany, Italy, Sweden, and Switzerland (as well as in several other European countries), collective-bargaining agreements, generally at the industry level, set minimum rates for the lowest pay group in a collective agreement ("Minimum Pay in 18 Countries" 1992). To the extent that such minima are binding, they will tend to bring up the floor among workers covered by the contract. In the limiting case, a contract that covered all workers in the economy might be expected to compress the bottom of the distribution, just as would a high national minimum wage. Thus, we expect to find greater narrowing at the bottom than at the top in the union sector in most countries compared to the United States, but we regard this as, to some extent, an empirical question.

Several factors also lead us to expect more dispersion of non-union wages in the United States than elsewhere. These include the practice in many other countries of extending the terms of collective-bargaining agreements to nonunion workers. Such contract extensions blur the distinction between union and nonunion wage setting. To the extent that unions in all countries tend to compress wages at the bottom in the union sector, contract extension will not only reduce wage variation in the nonunion sector, but compress wages at the bottom as well. In addition, the higher degree of union organization outside the United States should produce more "voluntary" imitation of union pay structures by nonunion firms than is found in the United States.[17] Finally, the effect of these factors has been further strengthened by explicit union and government policies in some countries to bring up the bottom of the wage distribution. This appears to have happened, for example, in Italy, Norway, and Sweden as well as in Germany (Hibbs 1990; Edin and Topel 1997; Edin and Holmlund 1995; Kahn 1998a; Erickson and Ichino 1995; Blau and Kahn 1996a).

Table 6.4 presents some descriptive information on union density (membership) and wage inequality. It is based on micro data for twelve OECD countries over the period 1990 to 1994 from the International Social Survey Programme (ISSP), although, as the notes to the table indicate, the country coverage is not complete in each year (for a description of these data, see Blau and Kahn forthcoming). Several interesting patterns emerge. First, for both men and women, the variance of log wages is much greater in the United States than elsewhere. Among men, the variance is 0.603 log points in the United States but, on average, only 0.250 elsewhere. For women, the comparisons are similar, with the United States having a far higher level of wage variance, 0.652 log points, than other countries, where this measure of inequality averaged 0.274 log points.

Second, in every country for both men and women, union wages show less dispersion than do nonunion wages. This pattern supports the idea that unions tend to narrow pay differentials within their jurisdictions. Although table 6.4 does not control for other causes of wage compression, Blau and Kahn (1996a) and Kahn (1998b) have found that, controlling for individual-productivity characteristics, union members generally experience less

TABLE 6.4 **Unions and Wage Dispersion, Descriptive Statistics: 1990 to 1994**

	Variance of Log Wages	Variance of Log Nonunion Wages	Variance of Log Union Wages	Union-Nonunion Log Wage Differential	Union Density
Men					
Australia	.351	.495	.199	.032	.486
West Germany	.217	.244	.172	.062	.388
Britain	.268	.331	.178	.092	.423
Austria	.237	.308	.156	.109	.485
Italy	.143	.183	.090	.121	.461
Norway	.175	.263	.113	.091	.596
New Zealand	.272	.313	.183	.033	.319
Canada	.261	.297	.173	.066	.296
Japan	.316	.381	.205	.027	.365
Ireland	.341	.387	.227	.254	.378
Sweden	.170	.365	.109	.117	.766
Non-U.S. average	.250	.324	.164	.091	.451
United States	.603	.650	.329	.224	.168
Women					
Australia	.404	.425	.369	.065	.383
West Germany	.204	.225	.124	.057	.217
Britain	.296	.313	.249	.212	.428
Austria	.230	.255	.154	.237	.374
Italy	.217	.242	.128	.230	.321
Norway	.215	.324	.144	.197	.653
New Zealand	.298	.352	.210	.119	.401
Canada	.267	.283	.211	.192	.338
Japan	.423	.409	.292	.486	.248
Ireland	.337	.384	.215	.315	.417
Sweden	.127	.315	.104	−.002	.886
Non-U.S. average	.274	.321	.200	.192	.424
United States	.652	.683	.386	.284	.133

Source: Authors' computations using International Social Survey Programme (ISSP) micro data.
Note: The following years are used: Australia (1990, 1991 and 1994); West Germany (1990 to 1993); Britain (1990 to 1994); USA (1990 to 1994); Austria (1991 to 1992, 1994); Italy (1990, 1992 to 1994); Norway (1990 to 1994); New Zealand (1991 to 1994); Canada (1992 to 1994); Japan (1993 to 1994); Ireland (1990, 1993 to 1994); Sweden (1994).

wage inequality than do nonunion workers across several OECD countries, including Austria, Britain, Norway, the United States, and West Germany. (We will present results corroborating this later in this chapter.) A further important union-nonunion pattern revealed in table 6.4 is that the variance of wages is much higher in the United States than elsewhere among both union and nonunion workers. Moreover, the gap between the United States and other countries is larger for nonunion workers than for union workers. For example, the variance was 0.326 log points higher in the United States than in other countries, on average, among male nonunion workers, compared to 0.165 log points higher in the United States among male union workers. The corresponding comparisons for women were a 0.362 log points higher variance in the United States among nonunion workers and a 0.186 log points higher variance among union workers. These patterns are consistent with the effect of contract extension in many non-U.S. countries as well as the possibility that, in these more highly unionized countries, nonunion firms voluntarily imitate union pay scales to a greater extent than they do in the United States.

A third important pattern to be found in table 6.4 is that the union-nonunion wage differential is much higher in the United States than elsewhere, a finding that also suggests greater spillovers to nonunion workers in many countries outside the United States. Finally, as we have already seen using OECD data in chapter 3, union density is far lower in the United States than elsewhere.

All these patterns—higher variances of wages within the union and nonunion sectors, a higher union-nonunion wage differential, and a lower union density—could potentially contribute to a higher wage variance in the United States than in other countries. Table 6.5 tells us how important each of these factors was for the period 1990 to 1994. In performing this decomposition, we make use of the following statistical relation:

$$v_i = \alpha_{ai} v_{ai} + (1 - \alpha_{ai}) v_{ni} + \alpha_{ai}(w_{ai} - w_i^*)^2 \\ + (1 - \alpha_{ai})(w_{ni} - w_i^*)^2, \tag{6.1}$$

where, for country i, v is the overall variance of log wages, α_a is the fraction of workers unionized, v_a and v_n are the variance of

TABLE 6.5 **Decomposition of the U.S.–Other-Country Differences in Log Wage Variances by Union Status, 1990 to 1994**

	U.S. Variance– Other- Country Variance	Within- Sector- Variance Effect	Within- Sector- Composition Effect	Between- Sector- Wage- Differential Effect	Between- Sector- Composition Effect
Men					
Australia	.2522	.1513	.0941	.0079	.0000
West Germany	.3860	.3641	.0158	.0074	−.0002
Britain	.3347	.2905	.0391	.0064	−.0003
Austria	.3661	.3135	.0483	.0053	−.0001
Italy	.4595	.4287	.0273	.0049	−.0003
Norway	.4275	.3584	.0641	.0055	.0007
New Zealand	.3311	.3046	.0196	.0080	−.0001
Canada	.3417	.3197	.0158	.0075	−.0002
Japan	.2868	.2451	.0346	.0080	.0000
Ireland	.2618	.2358	.0336	−.0036	−.0033
Sweden	.4327	.2743	.1530	.0014	.0043
Non-U.S. average	.3527	.2987	.0496	.0053	.0000
Percentage due to	100.00	84.69	14.06	1.51	.01
Women					
Australia	.2477	.2259	.0140	.0085	−.0003
West Germany	.4482	.4316	.0085	.0089	−.0002
Britain	.3556	.3390	.0189	.0002	−.0019
Austria	.4218	.4019	.0242	−.0005	−.0034
Italy	.4354	.4167	.0214	.0014	−.0035
Norway	.4367	.3436	.0933	−.0057	.0062
New Zealand	.3540	.3105	.0381	.0067	−.0007
Canada	.3855	.3702	.0148	.0035	−.0025
Japan	.2289	.2503	.0135	−.0210	−.0137
Ireland	.3150	.2817	.0479	−.0101	−.0047
Sweden	.5245	.3562	.1590	.0093	.0000
Non-U.S. average	.3776	.3389	.0412	.0001	−.0022
Percentage due to	100.00	89.74	10.92	.03	−.59

Source: Authors' computations using ISSP microdata.
Note: For specific years of data availability, see the note to table 6.4.

log union and nonunion wages, w_a and w_n are average log union and nonunion wages, and w^* is the country's average log wage level.[18]

Table 6.5 indicates that the overwhelming portion of the gap between the United States and other countries in the variance of wages—about 85 percent for men and 90 percent for women, on average—is due to higher U.S. variances within the union and nonunion sectors (that is, the within-sector-variance effect). Another substantial proportion, about 14 percent, on average, for men and 11 percent for women, comes from the within-sector-composition effect. That is, a higher proportion of U.S. workers are nonunion, and this sector has a larger wage variance in all countries. The higher union-nonunion wage differential in the United States causes a small widening of the U.S. variance relative to that in other countries, with the between-sector-wage-differential effect (that is, the portion explained by the United States' larger union-nonunion wage differential) accounting for, on average, about 1.5 percent of the average U.S.–other-country variance gap for men and less than this for women. Finally, the between-sector-composition effect, which measures the contribution to the U.S.–other-country difference in the variance of wages of a higher representation of employment in the sector with wages relatively far from the average, is found to be negligible.[19]

Table 6.5 implies that the key to understanding U.S.–other-country differences in wage inequality is to explain higher U.S. inequality within the union and nonunion sectors. Table 6.6 provides some suggestive evidence here by comparing union and nonunion wage inequality at the bottom (50–10 gap) and the top (90–50 gap) of the wage distribution. In light of our earlier discussion of the importance of wage floors in many OECD countries, we focus particularly on the 50–10 gap. Mirroring the results for wage-variance patterns, the 50–10 gap is much larger in both the union and the nonunion sectors in the United States than in the other countries, on average. For example, among union members, the 50–10 gap is 0.109 (men) to 0.279 (women) log points higher in the United States than in other countries, while, among non-union workers, the United States has a higher 50–10 gap by 0.387 (men) to 0.406 (women) log points. The 90–50 gaps are also larger in the United States than elsewhere, but the contrasts are less dramatic than they are for the 50–10 gap. Specifically, for union members, the 90–50 gap is 0.051 (men) to 0.137 (women) log points higher in the United States than elsewhere, while, for nonunion workers, the 90–50 gap is 0.150 (women) to 0.171 (men) log points higher. This comparison of middle-bottom and top-middle wage differentials implies relatively more compression among both union and nonunion workers at the bottom of the distribution in other countries. Moreover, these contrasts show much larger U.S.–other-country differences in the 50–10 gap for the nonunion sector than for the union sector.

Table 6.6 provides evidence consistent with the idea that wage compression at the bottom of the distribution among nonunion workers in other countries is a particularly salient difference between wage setting in the United States and that elsewhere. While it suggests the importance of contract extensions and voluntary imitation of union-contract provisions in these countries, table 6.6 does not control for individual-productivity characteristics, which could also conceivably explain the wage patterns.

Table 6.7, from a study by Lawrence M. Kahn (1998b), provides sharper evidence on the connection between unionization and wage compression by reporting the effect of union membership on log wages, controlling for individual characteristics (education, experience and its square, marital status, occupation, and industry). It shows that the union wage effect overall ("all workers") is much higher in the United States than it is in other countries, a result similar to those obtained in previous research (Blanchflower and Freeman 1992; Blanchflower 1996). More important, the table shows the effect of union membership on wages at different portions of the conditional distribution of wages. The method of quantile regression, which we discussed earlier in this chapter, was used to estimate these effects. The most dramatic contrasts between the United States and other countries in the union wage effect come at the 10th percentile of the wage distribution. At this location near the bottom of the wage distribution, the average effect of unions is 0.224 to 0.260 log points higher in the United States than elsewhere; in contrast, at the median (the 50th percentile), the U.S. union wage effects are 0.134 to 0.183 log points larger, and, at the top (90th percentile), they are only 0.108 to 0.138 log points larger. This pattern of especially large differences between the United States and other countries at the bottom of the wage distribution suggests the importance of wage floors for low-skilled nonunion workers in other countries.

The union-nonunion comparisons offered in this section provide strong evidence that, among workers in the industrialized countries, low-skilled nonunion workers in the United States are the least protected by wage floors. This conclusion was suggested

TABLE 6.6 Union and Nonunion Log Wage Inequality at the Bottom and the Top of the Wage Distribution, 1990 to 1994

	Men				Women			
	50–10		90–50		50–10		90–50	
Country	Nonunion	Union	Nonunion	Union	Nonunion	Union	Nonunion	Union
Australia	.833	.447	.696	.419	.861	.592	.649	.526
West Germany	.530	.405	.532	.410	.539	.381	.587	.353
Britain	.688	.471	.707	.553	.593	.656	.786	.601
Austria	.579	.414	.651	.469	.560	.379	.585	.516
Italy	.438	.264	.446	.407	.651	.347	.557	.402
Norway	.609	.321	.449	.379	.857	.420	.491	.333
New Zealand	.711	.529	.721	.495	.765	.628	.601	.452
Canada	.745	.618	.589	.423	.620	.520	.631	.541
Japan	.615	.643	.882	.569	.839	.637	.833	.678
Ireland	.560	.648	.944	.594	.734	.418	.728	.669
Sweden	.831	.374	.762	.564	.723	.434	.610	.288
Non-U.S. average	.649	.467	.671	.480	.704	.492	.642	.487
United States	1.036	.576	.842	.531	1.110	.771	.792	.624

Source: Authors' computations using ISSP micro data. For specific years of data availability, see notes to table 6.4.

TABLE 6.7 **Union-Membership Regression Coefficients, 1980s (Standard or Asymptotic Standard Errors in Parentheses)**

Country and Sample	All Workers	Union Effect at Various Levels in the Conditional Wage Distribution		
		10th Percentile	50th Percentile	90th Percentile
United States				
ISSP, men	.230	.377	.180	.108
	(.043)	(.077)	(.030)	(.032)
ISSP, women	.201	.437	.169	.165
	(.062)	(.151)	(.055)	(.055)
PSID, men	.263	.342	.263	.179
	(.027)	(.054)	(.029)	(.030)
PSID, women	.278	.335	.241	.234
	(.034)	(.071)	(.037)	(.046)
CPS, men	.186	.276	.185	.120
	(.004)	(.007)	(.004)	(.007)
CPS, women	.181	.243	.179	.112
	(.005)	(.007)	(.005)	(.009)
Average U.S. effect: men	.226	.332	.209	.136
	(.025)	(.046)	(.021)	(.023)
Average U.S. effect: women	.220	.338	.196	.170
	(.034)	(.076)	(.032)	(.037)
Norway, men	.007	.026	.017	.023
	(.019)	(.031)	(.016)	(.035)
Norway, women	.019	.050	.017	−.0001
	(.018)	(.032)	(.016)	(.025)
Germany, men	.030	.044	−.002	.017
	(.020)	(.039)	(.021)	(.025)
Germany, women	.125	.184	.058	.091
	(.041)	(.083)	(.042)	(.054)
Austria, men	.061	.133	.043	−.001
	(.025)	(.028)	(.026)	(.041)
Austria, women	.103	.090	.096	−.002
	(.032)	(.044)	(.032)	(.028)
Britain, men	.065	.085	.047	.072
	(.021)	(.030)	(.023)	(.031)
Britain, women	.076	.133	.075	.040
	(.026)	(.041)	(.018)	(.054)
Average non-U.S. effect: men	.041	.072	.026	.028
	(.021)	(.032)	(.021)	(.033)

TABLE 6.7 *Continued*

		Union Effect at Various Levels in the Conditional Wage Distribution		
Country and Sample	All Workers	10th Percentile	50th Percentile	90th Percentile
Average non-U.S. effect:	.081	.114	.062	.032
women	(.029)	(.050)	(.027)	(.040)

Source: Kahn (1998b).

Note: United States data sources are the following: ISSP (1985 to 1989); PSID = Michigan Panel Study of Income Dynamics (1988); and CPS = Current Population Survey (May 1989). Norwegian data come from the 1987 Level of Living Survey. Austrian (1985 to 1987, 1989), British (1985 to 1989), and West German (1985 to 1988) data come from the ISSP. The entries are based on regressions of log wages on education, potential experience and its square, marital status, and vectors of industry and occupation dummy variables in addition to union membership. The entries for "all workers" refer to OLS regression coefficients, while the entries for the 10th, 50th, and 90th percentiles come from quantile regressions.

in the descriptive data reported in tables 6.4 to 6.6 and also by the regression results presented in table 6.7, which control for worker characteristics.

Evidence on the Effect of Collective Bargaining

The previous section built a strong "circumstantial" case for the claim that union wage floors are an important source of greater wage compression in other countries than in the United States. In this section, we first review evidence from studies of the effect of episodic change in wage-setting institutions within particular countries or within regions within a country. As discussed earlier in this chapter, the research designs utilized in these studies are especially attractive since, within a country, many factors are, in effect, held constant when one particular aspect of the wage-setting environment is changed. A focus on changes over time allows any unmeasured characteristics of a given country that would otherwise affect its wage distribution to be "differenced out," enabling us to concentrate more precisely on the effect of the institutional change in question. Next, we examine detailed comparisons of two or three countries. Overall, these studies show strong evidence that collective bargaining affects the wage distribution but mixed evidence that it affects relative employment.

Evidence from Changes in Collective-Bargaining Institutions
Sweden has experienced episodes in which institutional changes
occurred that would be expected to decrease wage inequality as
well as episodes in which institutional changes occurred that
would be expected to increase it, making this country particularly
interesting to study. While Sweden has had relatively centralized
wage setting since at least the 1950s, during the period 1964 to
1983, its major blue-collar union, the LO, embarked on a "solidarity-wage" policy promoting the radical equalization of pay by
giving especially large increases to the lowest-paid workers. This
new wage policy involved equal krona per hour wage increases
instead of percentage increases and special funds to raise the
wages of low-paid workers (Edin and Topel 1997). Hibbs (1990)
shows that the coefficient of variation of blue-collar union wages
took an abrupt and large downturn precisely in the mid-1960s,
following an eight-year period of gradually rising dispersion. Further, Edin and Topel (1997) and Edin and Holmlund (1995) document the sharp decline in the returns to education in Sweden following the 1960s, while Edin and Topel (1997) and Steven Davis
and Magnus Henrekson (2000) present evidence that interindustry
wage differentials contracted sharply between 1960 and 1970. The
abrupt nature of the changes in bargaining practices and the correspondingly sudden decrease in wage inequality following these
changes constitute fairly strong evidence that institutional change
did, indeed, cause changes in wage inequality.

These studies also found important employment effects of these
changes. Edin and Topel (1997) and Davis and Henrekson (1997,
2000) found strong allocative effects of Sweden's solidarity-wage
policy of the late 1960s and early 1970s. Specifically, relative wages
in low-paying industries were sharply raised during this time, and
increases in out-migration from areas where these industries were
located as well as decreases in relative employment in these industries were observed. Further, this relation was strongest during the
period of most-intense wage compression as compared to later
periods, providing some further evidence that there were negative
relative-employment effects of this wage policy. An additional response to Swedish wage compression was low enrollment in higher
education. This occurred as the wage returns to education were
sharply reduced and jobs were plentiful (Edin and Holmlund 1995).

As noted in chapter 4, the reduction in interindustry wage differentials in Sweden was positively associated with labor-productivity gains. An interpretation of this finding that is consistent with the employment responses to wage compression in Sweden is that the reduction in interindustry wage differentials caused the low-productivity sectors to shrink, raising the average overall level of labor productivity (Hibbs and Locking 2000). It is also possible that, by reducing the differences in the marginal productivity of labor across sectors, the economy's overall efficiency was raised. However, Hibbs and Locking (2000) found that reducing wage differentials within industries, for example, by reducing occupational or educational differentials, was negatively associated with labor productivity. An interpretation of this finding is that, by compressing market-based occupational or educational wage differentials, the solidarity-wage policy hindered the allocative function of relative wages.

Perhaps in response to the strains caused by wage leveling, the Swedes abandoned the country's economywide wage-setting practices in 1983 and moved toward a system of industrywide wage bargains (Freeman and Gibbons 1995). In principle, this structure can allow more interindustry wage variation than the more-centralized system did. And the Swedish wage distribution did abruptly become more dispersed following 1983 (Hibbs 1990; Edin and Holmlund 1995). Although this pattern is consistent with a real effect of changes in bargaining institutions on the wage distribution, Edin and Holmlund (1995) suggest that, in the 1980s, supply and demand were changing, to the detriment of low-skilled workers, and that this could be a competing explanation for rising wage inequality in Sweden during this period. However, Davis and Henrekson's (2000) findings that, after 1983, Swedish relative employment grew in the industries whose relative pay was allowed to fall (compared to similar industries in the United States) implies that institutions were an important part of the story. This pattern is the mirror image of what happened during the solidarity-bargaining period of 1968 to 1983, in which, as noted earlier, the industries whose relative pay was raised the most experienced relative-employment declines. If employment is demand determined, we would expect institutional wage interventions to cause relative employment to move in the opposite direction from relative pay. These findings for employment during the periods 1968 to 1983 and 1983 and after in Sweden provide some strong evidence that interventions in wage-setting institutions have important effects on wage structure and relative employment.

The Swedish experience of the 1980s illustrates a difficulty involved in estimating the effect of changes in wage-setting institutions when supply and demand forces go in the same direction as the institutional changes and may, in fact, have contributed to the institutional changes themselves. Indeed, in the Swedish case, Edin and Topel (1997) note that excess demand for skilled workers in the early 1980s, an excess demand due partly to wage leveling in encompassing labor agreements, contributed to the end of economywide bargaining in 1983.

In contrast, the case of Norway in the period 1987 to 1991 provides an interesting instance in which institutions changed in the direction opposite to supply and demand forces and opposite to the direction of institutional change in virtually all other advanced countries (Kahn 1998a). Until 1982, Norway's collective-bargaining system was quite similar to Sweden's in that there were economywide centralized negotiations between national union and employer federations. And, as in Sweden, as well as in several other countries,[20] collective bargaining became less centralized in Norway during the 1980s. Decentralization took the same form as it did in Sweden—industrywide bargains replaced the economywide agreement. However, spurred by the recession brought on by reduced oil prices after 1986, in 1988 the national government in Norway took steps to recentralize the country's bargaining system. The government's goal was wage restraint, and recentralizing negotiations with special wage increases for the low paid was deemed necessary in order to obtain union cooperation in the effort (Kahn 1998a). In 1988 and 1990, negotiations returned to the nationwide level, and low-paid workers received higher absolute (and, therefore, higher percentage) wage increases than others did.

Supply and demand for low-skilled labor in Norway changed during the late 1980s and early 1990s in ways similar to the change in supply and demand in other countries, notably Sweden (Kahn 1998a). And, at a time when bargaining structures were breaking apart in several other countries, Norway's was becoming more monolithic. Consistent with this change, Norway was the only OECD country with a sharply narrowing gap between the middle and the bottom of the wage distribution during the period 1987 to 1991. And Kahn (1998a) finds that a fall in the price of skills contributed importantly to this reduction in inequality, as would be expected given the wage policies adopted by the union federation in this period. Moreover, while the supply of and demand for skills in Norway changed similarly in both the period 1980 to 1983 and the period 1987 to 1991, in the earlier period, when bargaining was being decentralized, the return to skills rose. These comparisons of Norway with Sweden and of Norway during a period of recentralization with Norway during a period of decentralization provide evidence that the change in Norway's bargaining structure did narrow wage differentials.

As was the case in Sweden, this intervention in wage-setting procedures in Norway during the period 1987 to 1991 also appears to have had relative-employment effects. Specifically, less-educated workers, whose relative wages were sharply raised, suffered relative-employment declines during these years. It is possible that these relative-employment changes were due to the recession that occurred at that time rather than to the wage policy. However, during an earlier recessionary period (1980 to 1983), when bargaining had become less centralized, the relative wages of less-educated workers declined, and relative-employment levels actually increased among less-educated men while remaining constant among less-educated women. Again, the differences-in-differences framework provides some support for the notion that there are negative employment effects of union wage policies.[21]

Two cases in which the government passed laws that were apparently designed to reduce union power—the United Kingdom in the 1980s and New Zealand in 1991—enable us to examine the effect on employment of reductions in the extent of collective bargaining. While the U.K. intervention appears to have affected the wage structure, it is less obvious that New Zealand's reforms did. Further, the effects of these reforms on employment are also mixed.

In the United Kingdom, the Thatcher reforms constituted a

multifaceted program designed to move the economy toward a laissez-faire ideal (Blanchflower and Freeman 1994), including such policy interventions as abolishing closed shops, limiting union picketing, reducing the generosity of the welfare state by lowering the UI replacement ratio (that is, after-tax UI benefits as a fraction of after-tax wages), and eliminating wages councils. The fact of many reforms along a variety of dimensions makes it difficult to single out the effect of any one reform. Nonetheless, the Thatcher programs together appear to have had a strong negative effect on union coverage in the United Kingdom (Freeman and Pelletier 1990).

For example, data presented in chapter 3 show declines in union density in the United Kingdom from 50 percent in 1980 to 39 percent in 1990, with an even-larger absolute and relative fall in collective-bargaining coverage during this time from 70 to 47 percent. And there is evidence of an effect on wages of these changes. Blanchflower and Freeman (1994) find that the responsiveness of wages and employment at the micro level to demand changes increased. Moreover, the wage-inequality data presented in chapter 2 indicate a sharp increase in inequality in the United Kingdom during this period. Using micro data that allow him to control for worker heterogeneity, John Schmitt (1995) attributes a moderate portion (13 to 21 percent) of the increase in British wage inequality in the 1980s to declining unionization.

In contrast to the evidence that the reduction in unionization in the United Kingdom raised wage inequality, there is mixed evidence on the employment effects of the Thatcher program. On the one hand, a study from the early 1990s found that this program was not successful in lowering unemployment generally or in raising transitions out of unemployment (Blanchflower and Freeman 1994). Moreover, in the early 1990s, union relative-wage effects remained at about 10 percent, a relatively high level by international standards (see the relevant discussion earlier in this chapter), implying that the power of union members was still a force with which to contend (Blanchflower 1996).

On the other hand, a more recent study (Nickell and van Ours 2000) notes that, in the United Kingdom, the OECD-standardized unemployment rate fell from 10.9 percent in 1983 to 1988 to 8.9 percent in 1989 to 1994 and was further reduced by early 1999 to

6.2 percent. This is one of the largest cumulative reductions in unemployment in the OECD. The authors attribute important portions of this unemployment decline to reductions in union density and union coverage, with smaller contributions from reductions in taxes and in UI-benefit replacement ratios. It is possible that the Thatcher reforms had delayed effects in lowering unemployment. For example, with such a comprehensive reform program, it may have taken several years for workers' and firms' norms of wage setting to shift to the new freer-market environment. Thus, developments in the United Kingdom in the late 1990s may be an example of social norms changing in response to changing economic incentives, as discussed by Assar Lindbeck, Sten Nyberg, and Jorgen Weibull (1999).

Like the Thatcher reforms, the New Zealand Employment Contracts Act (ECA) of 1991 appears to have substantially reduced union power. However, while it is not clear whether the ECA has caused a widening of the wage distribution, there is some evidence suggesting that, unlike the Thatcher reforms, it did have some immediate positive employment effects. The ECA legislation outlawed compulsory unionism and abolished national wage awards (Maloney 1994). Union density declined precipitously after 1991, presumably in response to the legislation. For example, prior to the ECA, union density had risen slightly, from 43.5 percent in December 1985 to 44.7 percent in September 1989, before falling modestly, to 41.5 percent, in May 1991, the month during which the ECA took effect (Crawford, Harbridge, and Walsh 1999). However, after the passage of the ECA, union density plummeted, reaching 28.8 percent by December 1992 and 17.7 percent, only slightly above the U.S. level, in December 1998. Collective-bargaining coverage also plunged, going from 67 percent in 1990 to 31 percent in 1994 (table 3.1).

One would, of course, expect this legislation to have also increased wage inequality. And there is, indeed, some evidence that the returns to human capital and residual inequality both increased in New Zealand over the period 1984 to 1997 (Dixon 1998). But wage inequality overall and the returns to human capital rose substantially faster during the pre-ECA years of 1984 to 1990 than over the period 1990 to 1997, a comparison that does not suggest a major effect of the ECA on the wage distribution

(Dixon 1998).[22] It is still possible that the ECA had some effect on wage inequality since, during the period 1984 to 1990, New Zealand instituted many market-oriented reforms that would themselves have been expected to raise wage inequality. For example, industrial subsidies were reduced, exchange controls were eliminated, import protection was decreased, capital markets were deregulated, and many government enterprises were privatized (Evans et al. 1996; Cowen 1993; Lang 1998). It is, therefore, possible that both the 1984 to 1990 reforms and the ECA raised wage inequality, with the earlier legislation having a larger effect. But the direct evidence in favor of an effect of the ECA on wage inequality is not overwhelming.

In contrast to this mixed picture, there does appear to be some evidence that the ECA generated employment. Since, because of different contract-expiration dates, the ECA was implemented starting in May 1991 at different rates across different industries, one can estimate its effect by using the industries that had not yet implemented the changes as a control group. Employing this research design, Maloney (1994) found that the law sharply reduced union coverage and raised employment. However, relative wages were unaffected, implying that fringe benefits or changes in work rules were the mechanism for increasing employment.

Finally, there are two additional interesting case studies examining the effect of wage-setting interventions through the collective-bargaining system. First, Stephen Nickell and Jan van Ours (2000) studied the steady, remarkable fall in Dutch unemployment from 10.5 percent in 1983 to 1988 to 3.4 percent in early 1999. Nickell and van Ours attributed the largest portion of this decline to the agreement by Dutch unions in the early 1980s to practice wage restraint, an agreement whose implementation was facilitated by the centralized wage-setting institutions in the Netherlands. A smaller role in explaining the falling unemployment rate there was played by a combination of an expansion of active labor-market policies, a reduction in UI-benefit replacement ratios, and a reduction in labor-tax rates. Second, Steven Allen, Adriana Cassoni, and Gaston Labadie (1996) studied wages and employment in Uruguay from 1983 to 1991, a period before and after the 1985 relegalization of collective bargaining, which had been outlawed after the establishment of a military regime in 1973. Allen, Cassoni, and Labadie found that wages grew more and employment grew less in more-unionized industries, a result consistent with a negative union employment effect.

Evidence from Specific Country Comparisons   Several studies of the effect of institutions have made detailed comparisons using micro data for two or three countries that have different institutions or different types of changes in their wage-setting institutions. This research uses one country as a control for another that has more-interventionist institutions or a larger increase in the degree of intervention in the labor market. One of the best examples of such an analysis is work that compares Canada and United States, two countries that have similar economic and labor-force structures and are major trading partners but have very different degrees of unionization. For example, as may be seen in table 3.1, not only are union density and collective-bargaining coverage substantially higher in Canada than in the United States, but these indicators have also remained stable since 1980 in Canada while both have decreased substantially in the United States. Specifically, over the period 1980 to 1994, both union density and collective-bargaining coverage remained relatively constant in Canada at between 36 and 38 percent, but both fell in the United States, union density from 22 to 16 percent and collective-bargaining coverage from 26 to 18 percent.

Thomas Lemieux (1993) studied the effect of unionization on the differences between Canadian and American wage inequality in the 1980s and on the change in inequality in the two countries over the 1980s. He found that, among men, U.S.-Canadian differences in union coverage accounted for 40 percent of the difference in wage dispersion between the two countries in the 1980s.[23] Over the 1980s, wage inequality increased by considerably more in the United States than in Canada. For example, between 1979 and 1987, the variance of the log of men's full-time, full-year earnings rose by 0.034 in the United States but by only 0.018 in Canada (Blackburn and Bloom 1993, 254). And, as we have seen, union density fell in the United States relative to that in Canada over the 1980s. Using an accounting framework similar to the one underlying table 6.5, Lemieux finds that this decrease was responsible for 40 to 45 percent of the growth in wage inequality in the United States relative to that in Canada. This closely matches the magnitude of his estimate of the effect of union density in explaining the difference in wage dispersion between the United States and Canada at a point in time.[24]

While Lemieux's results suggest that unionization is an important factor explaining differences in wage inequality between the United States and Canada, it is possible that the differences in the degree of unionization between the two countries represent, at least in part, the effect of different market forces. If this is true, it is, thus, possible that Lemieux's results are upper bounds for the true effect of unionization. In this regard, some recent results for the U.S.-Canadian comparison provide some reassurance. Craig Riddell (1993) finds that the higher degree of unionism in Canada than in the United States is primarily due to the more favorable legal environment there rather than to differences in the structure of the economy. For this case at least, we have some confidence that there really is an independent effect of unionization.

Four comparisons of wage and employment changes across labor-force groups in Germany and the United States or Canada, France, and the United States reach conflicting conclusions about whether the decentralized wage-setting environment in the United States has contributed to better relative-employment outcomes for the less skilled in the United States over the 1980s and 1990s. However, they all agree that the U.S. wage-setting system contributed to faster growth in wage inequality in the United States than elsewhere. First, Freeman and Schettkat (2000) found that, in the 1990s, low-skilled male workers in Germany had high wages but low employment relative to men with middle levels of skills in comparison to the analogous contrasts in the United States. They also found that, from the 1970s to the 1990s, the relative wages of low-skilled men fell in the United States compared to those in Germany while their relative employment fell in Germany compared to that in the United States. These findings were interpreted as reflecting the effects of German unions in pushing up the wages of the less skilled but causing employment problems for them. While unions evidently had an effect on relative employment in Germany, Freeman and Schettkat found that this effect could account for only a relatively small portion of the higher overall German unemployment rate relative to that in the United States in the 1990s.

In contrast to Freeman and Schettkat's (2000) findings, studies by David Card, Francis Kramarz, and Thomas Lemieux (1999) for Canada, France, and the United States and Alan Krueger and Jörn-Steffen Pischke (1997) for Germany and the United States produced results that do not suggest negative union employment effects. These authors compared the change in relative employment and wages by skill level in the 1980s in heavily unionized and less-unionized countries under the premise that the decline in the demand for low-skilled workers was common to all these nations but that wage-setting institutions would moderate the effects of this decline. It was found that relative wages were, indeed, more rigid in the more-unionized countries (France relative to Canada and the United States, Canada relative to the United States, and Germany relative to the United States); however, the relative employment of low-skilled workers compared to that of high-skilled workers in Canada and France did not fall in comparison to that in United States. In fact, relative employment among the low skilled generally fell in the United States compared to that in the other two countries. And low-skilled workers' relative employment actually rose in Germany, in contrast to its fall in the United States. The authors conclude that, while unions can reduce or even eliminate the effect of adverse demand shifts on low-skilled workers' relative wages, the point estimates generated by their studies offered no evidence of adverse relative-employment effects that could be attributed to such union policies.

Finally, Blau and Kahn (2000b) also found that, among young Germans and young Americans over the period 1984 to 1991, the less skilled did better with respect to both relative wages and employment in Germany than in the United States. We speculated that differences in public-sector employment could be partly responsible for this difference (we elaborate on this point later in this chapter).

It is possible that the contradictory findings of the various U.S.-German studies could be due in part to differences in the definition of skill or in the samples studied. However, overall, these intercountry comparisons provide mixed evidence on the employment effects of centralized wage-setting systems over the 1980s and 1990s.

UI Systems and Unemployment Duration

A large body of research using microeconomic data on individual workers has examined the effect of UI-benefit levels or the duration of benefit eligibility on the duration of unemployment. Theory predicts that more-generous benefit levels or longer durations of entitlement to benefits will make unemployed workers choosier about accepting new job offers and, thus, increase the duration of unemployment. Much of the research conducted on this question is surveyed by Anthony Atkinson and John Micklewright (1991), who report that, for the United Kingdom and the United States, a higher UI replacement ratio (that is, UI benefits as a percentage of wages, after taxes) has a modest positive effect on the duration of unemployment. However, evidence from other OECD countries such as Australia, Canada, the Netherlands, and West Germany found either very small or imprecisely estimated effects of replacement ratios on unemployment duration. Atkinson and Micklewright also surveyed a more limited set of studies on benefit-duration eligibility for Canada and the United States. These studies uniformly find that a longer potential duration of benefit collection raises the actual duration of unemployment.

Some more-recent microeconomic evidence than that included in the Atkinson and Micklewright survey also finds that, within countries, a longer potential duration of UI-benefit collection raises unemployment duration. First, Hunt (1995) studied the effect of Germany's 1985 to 1988 enactment of expansions in the potential duration of benefits for older workers. She found that this legislation did, indeed, cause rising unemployment duration among the targeted group. Second, George Sheldon (1997) studied the effect of Switzerland's increase in benefit duration during the period 1990 to 1995 and also found a positive effect on actual unemployment duration. As noted previously, this legislation was likely passed in response to that country's relatively high unemployment rates (by historical standards) and illustrates the idea that the parameters of social programs are endogenous.

While much of this research indicates that more-generous UI systems raise the duration of unemployment, this outcome could be helpful for an economy if longer search duration leads to better post-unemployment job matches. However, as pointed out by Ronald Ehrenberg (1994), most studies find that more-generous UI systems do not ultimately lead workers to find better-paying jobs, suggesting a more-negative evaluation of the longer unemployment duration that more-generous systems encourage. Of course, UI systems may also have insurance value. Owing to the standard insurance problems of moral hazard, adverse selection, and correlated risks discussed in chapter 4, UI might not exist or might not be provided in sufficient quantity in the absence of government intervention. Thus, it is possible that, even if UI programs raise the duration of unemployment, they may still, on net, produce economic benefits because of their insurance value (Gruber 1997a).

Nonetheless, perhaps in light of findings like those cited in Ehrenberg (1994), several countries have experimented with a variety of policies designed to lower unemployment duration without changing the basic structure of benefit levels and duration eligibility. In the United States, research analyzing experiments in which UI recipients are given a bonus if they find work early has found that these interventions lower the duration of unemployment (Meyer 1995). In addition, experimental data from the United Kingdom and the United States indicate that counseling UI recipients about effective job-search methods also leads to reduced durations of unemployment (Meyer 1995; Dolton and O'Neill 1996). Finally, imposing sanctions (that is, temporary reductions in benefit levels) in the event that a UI recipient does not comply with job-search requirements has been found to reduce unemployment duration in the Netherlands (Nickell and van Ours 2000). These modifications in the delivery of UI-system benefits show that it is possible to reduce some of the adverse effects on unemployment duration of these systems without changing the underlying benefit structure. Whether these reductions are worth the administrative costs (for example, counseling) is an open question.

The Effect of Government Intervention in Wage Setting: Wage Indexation and Minimum Wages

While collective-bargaining institutions have received the most attention in research on wage inequality and employment, two other institutions have also apparently exerted an important effect on the wage structure. First, Italy's system of wage indexation, the scala mobile, which was in place from 1975 to 1992, evidently led to considerable wage compression. This was a nationally mandated cost-of-living adjustment that explicitly gave low-paid workers larger relative increases than it did others (Erickson and Ichino 1995). Evidence of the effect of this policy is provided by comparing Italy to other countries. There was rapid inflation from 1975 to 1983 in Italy, averaging 10 to 20 percent per year, yet wage inequality fell sharply during this time, in contrast to virtually all other OECD countries (OECD 1993). Moreover, through 1987, the wage distribution in Italy did not widen, in contrast to that in the United States and many other countries, even though the supply of and demand for skills changed in qualitatively similar ways in Italy and the United States (Erickson and Ichino 1995, 296). And wage inequality in Italy sharply increased after 1992, when the scala mobile expired (OECD 1996), again suggesting an effect of this institution on the wage structure. A study of the employment effects of Italy's indexation system would be very interesting and informative; unfortunately, one has not yet been undertaken.

Second, minimum-wage legislation clearly affects the bottom of the wage distribution and, therefore, is expected to have a disproportionate effect on low-wage workers, including youths and women. Much research on the effect of minimum wages looks for spikes in the wage distribution around the legal required minimum. For example, Card and Krueger (1995) find that, for U.S. teenagers, there was a spike at $3.35 in 1989, when the federal minimum wage was $3.35 per hour, that was the largest mass point in the teenage wage histogram; by 1991, when the minimum wage had risen to $4.25 per hour, there was again a spike in the teenage wage distribution at the new minimum wage that was higher than any other spike in the histogram. This evidence provides a prima facie case for an effect of minimum wages on the teenage wage distribution. Further, using a full-distributional simulation technique, DiNardo, Fortin, and Lemieux (1996) attributed 30 to 70 percent of the 1979 to 1988 widening in the 50–10 log wage gap in the United States to falling real minimum wages. And Blau and Kahn (1997) concluded that falling real minimum wages over this period retarded the progress of low-skilled women's wages relative to low-skilled men's.

Similar findings are obtained in studies analyzing the effect of minimum wages in other countries. A study by Stephen Machin and Alan Manning (1994) of the effect of wages councils in the United Kingdom for the period 1979 to 1990 found that, when minimum wages were raised, the distribution of pay among affected workers became more compressed. Similarly, Lawrence Katz, Gary Loveman, and David Blanchflower (1995) concluded that rising minimum wages in the 1980s were an important reason why France's wage distribution was stable in the face of demand shifts that were similar to those in other countries where wage inequality widened.

Other evidence that minimum wages have had an effect on the wage distribution in several OECD countries is presented in Juan Dolado et al. (1996). For example, these authors show that, in France, regional wage dispersion fell dramatically when the national minimum wage was raised sharply in the 1980s. Or, as another example, in the Netherlands, between 1981 and 1983, official youth subminimum wages were substantially lowered: for example, the minimum for twenty-year-olds fell from 77.5 percent of the adult minimum to 61.5 percent, and that for sixteen-year-olds fell from 47.5 to 34.5 percent. As a consequence, while average nominal wages rose 9 percent from 1980 to 1984 for those aged twenty-three and older who were not affected by these changes, they fell for those under twenty-three (Dolado et al. 1996, 345).

In general, the effect of minimum-wage mandates on wage distributions has not been the subject of much controversy. Most economists believe that a minimum wage that is binding will bring up the bottom of the wage distribution. Considerably more controversy has surrounded the issue of the employment effects of increases in the minimum wage. Generally, the minimum wage is too low to affect major portions of the labor market, although specific subgroups such as teenagers may be more directly affected by legislated minimum-wage increases than are workers in general. Most of the research on the effect of minimum wages finds little evidence of negative employment effects, and, when these have been found, they are generally too small to have an important effect on the labor market.[25]

Early research in a time-series framework for the United States, based on minimum-wage changes in the 1960s and 1970s, found that, for teenagers, a 10 percent increase in the minimum wage led to a 1 to 3 percent fall in teenage employment. However, this research has been criticized on the grounds that the measure of minimum-wage changes was itself negatively confounded with overall demand changes since it included average wages in the denominator. This could have induced a negative estimated employment effect even if, in fact, minimum wages had no effect on employment (Card, Katz, and Krueger 1994; Card and Krueger 1995).

More recent research looks for appropriate control groups against which to compare the employment changes of teenagers or other low-wage workers who are most likely to be affected by minimum-wage increases. Much of this work finds either no effect[26] or, in some cases, a positive effect on employment of increasing the minimum wage (Card and Krueger 1995, 2000). Some recent research on minimum wages in the United States continues to find negative effects, including David Neumark and William Wascher (1992, 2000), Donald Deere, Kevin M. Murphy, and Finis Welch (1995), and Richard Burkhauser, Kenneth Couch, and David Wittenburg (2000), although only the Deere, Murphy, and Welch (1995) study reports large disemployment effects. Specifically, Deere, Murphy, and Welch find that, after the 1990 and 1991 minimum-wage increases in the United States, youth employment fell sharply relative to adult unemployment. However, such an outcome could also have been explained by the recession of the early 1990s having a disproportionate negative effect on youths. When a positive effect on employment of increasing the minimum wage has been found, this has been interpreted as possible evidence of employer monopsony, as have similar findings by Manning (1996) on the employment effect of policies designed to combat sex discrimination in the United Kingdom (we discuss these findings in the next chapter). Of course, a zero effect on employment is also consistent with employer monopsony but not with the conventional competitive-demand model.

Minimum-wage research for other countries has also produced mixed results, finding evidence of negative effects in some cases and little reported effect in others. For example, John Abowd et al. (2000) report that minimum-wage increases in France in the 1980s lowered the employment of workers at the minimum relative to a control group just above the minimum. The effects on workers at the minimum were large, but, since these workers constituted only a small portion of the labor force, the effect on total employment was small. However, an alternative analysis of France during the period 1967 to 1985, when minimum wages were substantially raised, found that employment growth was actually higher in regions most affected by minimum-wage increases (Dolado et al. 1996). While such a finding could have been caused by the relocation of businesses to low-wage regions (a long-run adjustment that could occur even if minimum-wage increases affected these regions disproportionately), it does not suggest a negative employment effect of raising the minimum wage.

Some evidence compatible with negative employment effects of the minimum wage comes from the Netherlands, where, from 1981 to 1983, youth subminimum wages were sharply lowered. Dolado et al. (1996) do find that, relative to youth-employment changes in the economy overall, youth relative employment generally rose in low-paying occupations, the ones most likely to be affected by minimum-wage changes. However, as the authors note, given the aggregate level of the data used, it is not clear whether such differences were statistically significant. In addition, if changes in the minimum wage in the Netherlands had an effect on youth employment, it must be the case that employers were taking advantage of the youth subminimum. Yet previous work on the United Kingdom and the United States finds that employers do not appear to use the subminima in those countries (Machin and Manning 1994; Katz and Krueger 1992). If employers in the Netherlands also do not in general utilize the youth subminimum, the findings reported in Dolado et al. (1996) must have been caused by some factor(s) other than the change in the minimum-wage law.

Evidence consistent with a negative effect of the minimum wage was also found for Spain, which sharply raised the minimum wage for those sixteen years of age and younger in 1990. Dolado et al. (1996) find that this policy led to a substitution of adults for youths but that, paradoxically, it also led to increased total employment. Mixed evidence is also obtained for Canada using the traditional time-series approach. Summarizing Canadian research, Card and Krueger (1995) report that, while negative effects on teenage employment were estimated for the period 1956 to 1975, the effects were not statistically significant for 1976 to 1988, with a negative point estimate for men and a positive one for women. A more recent study of Canadian minimum-wage effects over the period 1975 to 1993 (Baker, Benjamin, and Stanger 1999) finds a significant, modest negative minimum-wage-employment elasticity for teenagers. Finally, Machin and Manning's (1994) findings on the effect of wages councils on employment in the United Kingdom are consistent with the recent U.S. findings of no or even positive employment effects of minimum-wage increases.

Institutions and Market Forces: Toward Some Generalizations

The research on wage and employment effects of institutions reviewed and summarized thus far has consisted, by and large, of country studies or comparisons across a small number of countries and has not infrequently obtained conflicting results, particularly with respect to employment effects. In this subsection, we discuss results from three recent studies that attempt to make some generalizations about the effects of institutions and market forces on wage inequality (Brunello, Comi, and Lucifora 2000), wage and employment inequality (Kahn 2000), or youth employment (Neumark and Wascher 1999), drawing on comparisons across a large set of countries.

First, Giorgio Brunello, Simona Comi, and Claudio Lucifora (2000) used micro data from ten European countries to attempt to explain changes in the wage return to a college degree among men between the 1980s and the 1990s.[27] Pooling the changes in these returns for different cohorts and countries, the authors regressed these changes on: union density, a cohort dummy, the change in the relative supply of the education group, the growth of labor productivity, the change in a demand index for the group, and indicators for whether employment protection became more strict and whether bargaining became more centralized.[28] Although the regression had only twenty observations, the findings with these seven variables proved remarkably strong. Falling supply, rising demand, rising labor productivity, less-strict employment protection, less-centralized bargaining, and falling union density each had a positive effect on the college wage premium, and these effects were usually statistically significant. Brunello, Comi, and Lucifora, thus, found evidence that both institutions and market forces influenced relative wages in the expected direction.

Second, using ISSP data for fifteen countries from the period 1985 to 1994, Kahn (2000) formed skill groups—separately by gender for each country and year[29]—that were based on such measured human-capital characteristics as education, age, and marital status. He then analyzed the determinants of wage inequality and differences in the log of the employment-to-population ratio across these skill groups. For each year, skill groups were formed using the distribution of predicted wages from wage regressions estimated on a sample of workers pooled across countries (each country received the same weight). The low-skilled group consisted of the bottom third, the middle-skilled group consisted of the middle third, and the high-skilled group consisted of the top third of the predicted wage distribution. These fractions were computed with respect to the entire multicountry sample of men and women for that year, with each country receiving the same weight. Thus, for example, one country might have had more or less than a third of its men or women in the low-skilled group.

Given the evidence linking union pay setting to wage floors that have their largest effects on the bottom of the pay distribution, Kahn concentrated on comparing the middle to the bottom third of the predicted wage distribution (that is, the middle-skilled to the low-skilled groups).

In order to determine whether there was a general relationship between collective-bargaining institutions and wages and employment, Kahn estimated a variety of regression models separately by gender. The dependent variable was either the middle-low log wage differential or the middle-low log employment-to-population ratio differential for a given country in a given year. The major explanatory variables of interest were measures of unionization such as collective-bargaining coverage, union density, and indicators of the degree of coordination of wage setting. Kahn also included a variety of control variables that allow one to place a sharper interpretation on the unionization indicators, including the overall unemployment rate, year dummy variables, characteristics of the UI system, the degree of mandated job protection, and characteristics of the retirement system as well as indicators of the supply of and demand for workers in the two skill groups.[30]

The results of these regressions provide considerable evidence for the importance of wage-setting institutions in influencing relative wages among both men and women and relative employment, particularly among men. First, for both men and women, moving from U.S. to other-country averages for union coverage, union density, and coordination caused a statistically significant reduction in middle-low wage differentials in every case. Second, in most cases, changing from U.S. values of the unionization variables to the other-country averages widened the employment differential between middle- and low-skilled men, all else equal. Third, there was mixed evidence of a similar employment effect among women, with four of six effects positive but only two statistically significant.

The stronger effects obtained for men than for women in this study may reflect stronger collective-bargaining institutions in sectors of the economy such as manufacturing and construction that are traditionally dominated by men. In addition, while we would like to interpret the relative-employment effects as indicating employer demand, it is also possible that they are influenced by movements along labor-supply schedules: higher relative wages may bring people into the labor force. This effect is likely to be stronger among women, whose labor supply is known to be more elastic than men's (Killingsworth 1983). It is, thus, possible that higher relative wages could actually raise women's employment-to-population ratio.

In evaluating these findings, we note that it is possible that interventionist collective-bargaining institutions are negatively correlated with unmeasured heterogeneity of skills of the population. If so, this could help explain Kahn's finding of a negative effect of these institutions on wage differentials. However, such reasoning cannot explain the positive effect of collective bargaining, coordination, and so on on employment differentials by skill group.

Finally, Kahn found that, while the wage-compression effects were very strong for both younger and less-educated workers, the employment problems identified in the results described above were concentrated among the young for both men and women. Collective-bargaining institutions did not, in fact, lead to relative-employment problems for the less educated. These differential effects by age and education will be relevant later on when we consider alternative public-policy and market responses to employment loss.

The United States has a relatively high employment-to-population ratio for less-skilled men—0.79, according to Kahn (2000), compared to a non-U.S. average of 0.68. However, it is well-known that a larger fraction of the male population is incarcerated in the United States than elsewhere, and this difference is likely to be particularly large among those with low labor-market skills (Freeman 1996; Western and Beckett 1999). Specifically, Bruce Western and Katherine Beckett (1999) estimate that, during the period 1992 to 1993, 519 adults per 100,000 were incarcerated in the United States, compared to an average of only 78 across a sample of thirteen other OECD countries. Further, over 90 percent of these individuals were men. It is, therefore, possible that the relatively high employment-to-population ratio for less-skilled U.S. men reflects the U.S.–other-country difference in prison populations rather than labor-demand effects.

To see whether this factor could explain his results, Kahn performed some calculations making the extreme assumptions that all inmates are low skilled and that, if they had been released from prison, none of them would have found jobs. He further assumed that all inmates were men. Under these assumptions, the U.S. employment-to-population ratio for the less skilled fell from 0.79 to 0.77, or about 18 percent of the difference in employment-to-population ratios between the United States and the other countries. Thus, even making the most extreme assumptions about the employability of the prison population, the high incarceration rates in the United States can account for at most a small fraction of that country's higher employment-to-population ratio. Of course, the currently incarcerated probably would have had lower wage offers as well as lower employment levels than those not in prison. So were the currently incarcerated included in the estimates, wage differentials between the middle and the low skilled in the United States would likely be raised even further.

Finally, David Neumark and William Wascher (1999) use aggregate data to study the impact of minimum wages across sixteen OECD countries over the 1975 to 1997 period. They find that higher minimum wages reduce youth employment, particularly when these wages are set in collective bargaining agreements.

Policy and Behavioral Responses to Employment Problems

As previously outlined, there is mixed evidence on the effect of wage-setting institutions on the relative employment of the less skilled. As we noted in chapter 3, countries differ greatly in the degree to which they use government as a tool to bolster the employment of workers who are having trouble finding work. These active labor-market policies include a variety of measures meant to improve the chances that these workers will find employment, such as training and relocation subsidies for workers, hiring subsidies for firms, and direct job creation in the public sector.

Several country studies indicate that government employment may camouflage some of the negative effects on employment of wage-setting institutions that we would otherwise observe. Moreover, an additional response to employment problems is to share the work, and it appears that a greater emphasis is placed on work sharing in European countries than in the United States. Also, as noted in chapter 2, temporary-employment contracts, which may provide another way in which to bolster employment among particular groups in the face of rigid wages, appear to be more prevalent in Europe than in the United States. Finally, in some countries, particularly Italy and Spain, there is a very large unregulated sector that can serve as an outlet for workers and firms shut out of the regulated sector by the high cost of doing business by the rules. This unregulated sector includes both those employed in the underground economy, where employment regulations are flouted, and the self-employed, who are, by and large, exempt from these regulations. European labor markets may, thus, be more flexible in practice than they would appear at first blush. And actual employment-to-population ratios may be higher in such countries than official statistics and survey data indicate.

One mark of flexibility is the degree to which labor inputs are allowed to vary in response to changes in demand. And job creation and job destruction are both much less rapid in Europe than in the United States, implying less-flexible labor allocation in Europe. However, Katharine Abraham and Susan Houseman (1994) and Marc Van Audenrode (1994) note that, in several European countries, workers can collect short-time compensation from the government much more easily than they can in the United States. An implication of this difference is that hours per worker adjustments are, in fact, more cyclically sensitive in Europe than in the United States, in contrast to the greater sensitivity of employment to demand in the United States. The result of these offsetting patterns is that, in the 1980s, the adjustment of total production-worker hours in Belgium, France, and West Germany was similar to that in the United States (Abraham and Houseman 1994).

The European practice of hours flexibility may actually provide more income insurance than does the U.S. practice of employment adjustment since, under the former, a 10 percent cut in total labor input, for example, gets shared among all workers while, under the latter, it is more likely to be concentrated among those who are laid off.[31] And, of course, as discussed previously, UI benefits are more generous in Europe than in the United States. Further, the greater incidence of national health insurance in Europe implies that finding work is less important there—at least in terms of obtaining health care.[32] Therefore, while unemployment is much more prevalent in Europe than in the United States, it appears to have less-severe consequences for poverty.

While Europe appears better able to tolerate high unemployment, it is also true that European governments intervene to a greater extent in order to shore up employment than does the U.S. government. Chapters 2 and 3 showed that the public sector is larger in several European countries than in the United States, and many of these countries spend considerably larger amounts per unemployed worker (in relation to output per worker) on training and relocation programs than does the United States.[33] And, although the size of the public sector undoubtedly reflects the demand of the electorate for publicly produced services, the government has also been explicitly used in some countries to provide employment for those out of work.

For example, in Sweden and Norway, government employment of unskilled workers has been found to increase during periods of wage compression, in which the wages of workers at the bottom of the distribution have been raised the most. Such government hiring may serve to limit the disemployment effects of union wage bargaining (Edin and Topel 1997; Björklund and Freeman 1997; Kahn 1998a). Similarly, in the late 1980s, government employment has been found to be more prevalent, both absolutely and relative to other groups, among less-skilled youths in Germany than among such young people in the United States (Blau and Kahn 2000b). Again, the group most likely to be shut out by high union wages for the low end of the wage distribution was more likely to find government employment. We will return to the issue of these responses to employment problems shortly. Here we note that the prevalence of these responses may partly explain why there is mixed evidence on the effect of wage-setting institutions on employment.

Can we generalize about the use of public employment for the less skilled as a way in which to alleviate potential employment problems where there are high wage floors? Kahn (2000) investigated this issue by estimating the effect of a country's level of unionization on the relative propensity of the young or the less educated to be employed by the government. He found only limited evidence that such behavior characterized countries with high levels of collective-bargaining coverage or union density in general. Most of the time, the effects were insignificant, but there were some positive effects in some models for young men, less-educated women, and less-educated men. While the latter two findings are not robust, they may help explain why Kahn did not find that unionization negatively affected the relative employment of the less educated even though it raised their relative wages. The government may be picking up the slack. Nonetheless, overall, the evidence that public employment is disproportionately an outlet for the young or the less educated in highly unionized countries is fragile. This response to employment problems, then, appears to be concentrated in the Scandinavian countries and, perhaps, Germany.

In addition to public-sector employment, another possible response to problems in the job market, at least for younger individuals, is to stay in school longer. Kahn (2000) investigated this by estimating the determinants of a country's average incidence of school enrollment among men and women aged eighteen to thirty as a function of the same kinds of explanatory variables used to study wages and employment among these groups. Collective-bargaining coverage had a large, positive effect on school enrollment that was usually statistically significant.

These results for enrollment indicate that, in more heavily unionized economies, school attendance is more prevalent among younger individuals, other things equal. This is a striking finding given that Kahn found strong evidence that unions raise the relative pay of young men and some evidence that they increase the pay of young women and the less educated as well. If there were no constraints on finding a job, we would expect these wage results to lead to *less* school enrollment. As noted above, this appears to have happened in Sweden in the solidarity-wage period (1968 to 1983), when relatively high-paying jobs for the less skilled were abundant (Edin and Holmlund 1995).

The difference between Kahn's findings and those of Edin and Holmlund is likely due to the fact that, in contrast to the experience in Sweden during the solidarity-wage period, young people, especially young men, in highly unionized economies in the OECD countries faced severe employment problems over the 1980s and 1990s. Not only is the opportunity cost of attending school lower when few jobs are available, but obtaining higher levels of education may be the only way for many to eventually get a job at all. Such reasoning holds strongly among younger men but less strongly among younger women, for whom Kahn found the negative relative-employment effects of unionization to be less often statistically significant.

The basic finding that union wage setting is positively associated with school attendance is consistent with Agell and Lommerud's (1997) theoretical model of human-capital investment in an economy with high minimum (that is, administered) wages. In particular, Agell and Lommerud argue that schooling can raise one's employability when jobs are rationed as a result of wage floors.[34]

CONCLUSIONS

In this chapter, we have examined microeconomic evidence on the effect of institutions on the wage structure and on the relative employment of different skill groups. We have found abundant evidence that collective bargaining and minimum-wage laws lead to wage compression and help explain the higher level of wage inequality in the United States than in other countries. Collective bargaining appears to have stronger effects on the overall labor market than minimum wages do. We have also found that the distribution of labor-market skills is more diverse in the United States than elsewhere and that, in relation to the demand for their services, workers with low skill levels are more abundant in the United States than elsewhere. While these market-oriented factors are important, there is also strong evidence of an effect of wage-setting institutions on the wage structure that remains after these factors are taken into account.

Our examination of the effect of institutions on employment yielded less clear-cut results than did our examination of the effect of institutions on the wage structure. In many cases, union- or minimum-wage-induced wage compression was seen to lower the relative employment of the less skilled. In other cases, such effects were not evident. What negative employment effects unions have appear to be concentrated among the young. And, as we saw in chapter 2, the young had lower relative employment in 1998 and more adverse changes in their relative employment over the period 1979 to 1998 in the European Union than in the United States. Increasingly in the high-unemployment European economy of the 1980s and 1990s, the young were outside the protected labor markets that provide high wages and benefit levels. Integrating the young into work will be a major challenge for these countries in the coming years (Blanchflower and Freeman 2000). Conversely, in the United States, wage inequality has increased both absolutely and relatively over the 1980s and the 1990s and is currently the highest in the industrialized world. Raising the living standards of the less skilled in the United States, without causing major damage to the job-generation process, is, thus, a major challenge facing the United States.

——— Chapter 7 ———

Labor-Market Institutions and the Gender Pay Gap

V IRTUALLY EVERY INDUSTRIALIZED country has passed laws mandating equal treatment of women in the labor market. Yet, despite this universal concern on the part of policy makers and, implicitly, the citizenry whom they represent, while the gender wage gap is on the decline in many countries, it is a persistent feature of the labor market in virtually every nation. Moreover, the extent to which men outearn women varies substantially across countries as well.

For example, the data reported in chapter 2 indicate that, in the 1990s, the gender pay ratio was relatively high in countries such as Australia, Belgium, France, Italy, New Zealand, and Sweden, with female-male pay ratios among full-time workers of more than 80 percent, while it was relatively low in nations such as Austria, Canada, and Japan, with ratios of under 70 percent. Moreover, the United States lagged well behind most other countries in 1980 with a gender pay ratio of only 62.5 percent, compared to an average of 71.2 percent in the other OECD countries. By the 1990s, the United States had virtually caught up and had a gender pay ratio of 76.3 percent, which was only slightly below the average for the other countries of 77.4 percent. Nonetheless, the gender earnings ratio was higher in eight of sixteen other countries than it was in the United States, often considerably so. How do we explain why U.S. women do not rank higher relative to their counterparts in other advanced countries? And what accounts for the faster narrowing of the gender pay gap in the United States?

In addressing these questions, we will pay particular attention to the effect of labor-market institutions on the gender pay gap. As was the case in chapter 6 when we evaluated the effect of institutions on wage inequality, we must account for differences in labor-force composition in attempting to explain international differences in the gender pay gap. The female-male pay ratio may be higher in some countries simply because women there have better labor-market skills, although institutions can affect the development of these skills. Alternatively, even at similar levels of skills, there may be large differences across countries or over time in the gender pay gap.

Economists have traditionally looked to "gender-specific" factors such as women's shortfalls in human capital or employer discrimination against women to explain the size of the gender pay gap and its evolution over time. However, beginning with the work of Juhn, Murphy, and Pierce (1991), it has been recognized that the overall wage structure, or the prices that the labor market attaches to skills and the pay premiums accruing to those in favored sectors, can have a major effect on the relative wages of different subgroups in the labor market. The logic behind this insight is straightforward. Considering changes over time in the gender wage differential, for example, since women have, on average, less labor-market experience than do men and tend to work in different occupations and industries, an increase in the return to experience or in sectoral differentials will raise the gender pay gap, all else equal.

As we have pointed out in our earlier work (Blau and Kahn 1992, 1995, 1996b, forthcoming), the same reasoning applies across countries: nations with relatively high rewards to skill and relatively large sectoral differentials will tend to have larger gender pay gaps, all else equal. International comparisons provide a particularly fertile field in which to study the effects of wage structure on pay differentials between men and women because, owing in part to substantial international differences in wage-setting institutions (see chapter 3), they provide greater variation in wage dispersion and labor-market rewards than may generally be obtained by changes over time within a country. An important implication of this approach is that the factors that influence overall wage structure, such as the supply of and demand for skills and wage-setting institutions, may well be extremely important determinants of international differences in the gender pay gap and, by implication, of trends in the gender pay gap within countries as well.

In this chapter, we find that, influenced importantly by the kinds of wage-setting institutions analyzed in earlier chapters, overall wage compression has a powerful effect in lowering the gender pay gap. This can be seen in analyzing why the U.S. gender pay gap has, until very recently, been larger than that in most other Western countries and, even now, falls roughly at the average for advanced countries. As shall be seen, there seems to be little reason to believe that U.S. women either are less well qualified compared to men than are women in other countries where the gender pay gap is considerably smaller, nor do they appear to encounter more discrimination than do women elsewhere. And the American commitment to equal employment opportunity (EEO) for women predates that in most other countries as well. Thus, gender-specific factors appear unlikely to account for the mediocre ranking of the U.S. gender earnings ratio.

The data presented in this chapter suggest that this puzzle may be resolved by taking into account the effect of wage structure: overall wage compression appears to be the major reason why the gender pay gap has traditionally been lower in other countries than in the United States and has only recently attained the average level. We also find that market forces, particularly women's relative levels of skills and the relative supply of women, have important effects on the gender pay gap. Finally, as was the case when we examined the effects of wage compression on the employment of the low skilled, we find some mixed evidence on the question of whether such interventions in wage setting adversely affect job opportunities for women.

THE INSTITUTIONAL SETTING

In this section, we briefly summarize international differences in gender-specific policies and basic wage-setting institutions and their expected effects on the gender pay gap. Human capital is also a major determinant of gender pay gaps, and, later in this chapter, we discuss the effect of differences between men and women in human capital. However, international differences in policies and institutions appear to be more dramatic than are those in women's relative-human-capital levels. Further, human capital can be affected by the policies and institutions to be discussed. Differences across countries in institutions that affect the gender pay gap may be classified into those that are gender specific and those that affect the wage structure in general.

Gender-specific policies include EEO and antidiscrimination laws as well as laws and policies governing maternity and family leave. The expected positive effect of the former on the female-male earnings ratio is reasonably straightforward, although that effect will most likely depend on the effectiveness of the legislation's enforcement as well as its provisions. In general, it is expected that, given considerable segregation of women by occupation, industry, and firm, equal-pay laws mandating equal pay for equal work within the same occupation and firm will have a relatively small effect. Laws requiring equal opportunity, hiring preferences, and/or "comparable worth" (that is, equal pay for work of equal value to the firm, regardless of specific occupational category) have potentially larger effects. In addition, since EEO laws involve occupation shifts, they may require considerable time to have an effect on pay. Thus, the comparable-worth approach, which provides for immediate increases in relative pay in occupations dominated by women, may be expected to have the largest initial wage effect, possibly accompanied by a negative effect on women's employment.[1]

Virtually all OECD countries had passed equal-pay and equal-opportunity laws by the mid-1980s, although the United States implemented its antidiscrimination legislation before most other countries did (OECD 1988, 167–68; Simona 1985). One country with perhaps the strongest intervention against gender discrimination is Australia, the only one to have implemented a national policy of comparable worth through its labor courts (Gregory and Daly 1991; Killingsworth 1990).[2] Comparable-worth pay policies remain rare in the U.S. private sector, although they have been adopted by a number of state governments (Blau, Ferber, and Winkler 1998).

The expected effect of family leave (disproportionately taken by women even when it is available to men) is unclear a priori.

Jane Waldfogel (1998b) details the prevalence of a "family penalty" in many advanced countries, that is, lower earnings among
women with children, other things equal. This likely reflects the
loss of their attachment to the firm and associated firm-specific
skills when they withdraw from the labor force on the birth of a
child.[3] On the one hand, it is possible that the availability of family
leave would raise the relative earnings of women by encouraging
the preservation of their ties to particular firms and, hence, increasing the incentives of employers and women workers to invest in firm-specific training. On the other hand, the existence of
such policies could increase the incidence and/or duration of temporary labor-force withdrawals among women, raising the gender
pay gap for the affected group. Further, the incremental costs associated with mandated leave policies may increase employers'
incentives to discriminate against women. In Germany, for example, where mandated parental leave is of long duration, Nora
Demleitner (1992) reports that it was legal for employers to discriminate against pregnant women.

Some evidence suggests that family leave could reduce the
size of the family penalty. For example, Waldfogel (1998b) reports
evidence from analyses of micro data for Britain, Japan, and the
United States indicating that women who were covered by maternity leave were considerably more likely to return to their prior
employer after childbirth. And women who return to their employer after a birth have higher subsequent wages. Consistent
with these results, Christopher Ruhm (1998) finds, using aggregate
data on nine countries during the period 1969 to 1988, a positive,
but not significant, effect of 1 percent on women's wages relative
to men's of short leave entitlements (one to thirteen weeks), although longer leave entitlements (over twenty-six weeks) had a
significantly negative effect of 3 percent. The negative effect of
longer leaves could indicate that such leaves encourage women to
extend their time away from the firm. It is also possible that the
higher costs of long mandated leaves provide employers with
greater incentives to discriminate against women in terms of
wages or job assignments.

The data presented in chapter 3 showed that, at only twelve
weeks, America's family-leave entitlement was lower than that in
each of the other nineteen OECD countries under consideration,
often substantially so. For example, the non-U.S. average entitle-

ment was about sixty-five weeks, or over one year longer than that in the United States. However, in light of the mixed findings in the research on the effect of family leave on women's relative wages, we cannot be certain whether the relatively short leave entitlement in the United States raises or lowers women's relative pay.

Child care is another important area of public policy that particularly affects women, but it is one that is more difficult to summarize across a large set of countries. Some available evidence suggests that, as of the mid-1980s, the United States had a smaller share of young children in publicly funded child care than did many other OECD countries but provided relatively generous tax relief for child-care expenses (Gornick, Meyers, and Ross 1997).

With respect to wage structure, in chapter 6 we surveyed a considerable body of evidence showing that wage-setting institutions affect a country's level of wage inequality. These institutions take the form of collective-bargaining conventions, minimum-wage laws, and government-mandated extensions of the terms of collective-bargaining agreements to nonunion workers (Blau and Kahn 1999). We showed that, in general, more heavily unionized economies in which collective bargaining takes place at highly centralized levels have been found to have the lowest overall wage dispersion.

It seems likely that systems of centrally determined pay also entail smaller gender wage differentials for a number of reasons. First, in the United States, a significant portion of the male-female pay gap is associated with interindustry or interfirm wage differentials that result from relatively decentralized pay-setting institutions (Blau 1977; Johnson and Solon 1986; Sorensen 1990; Groshen 1991; Carrington and Troske 1995; Bayard et al. 1999). Thus, centralized systems that reduce the extent of wage variation across industries and firms are likely to lower the gender differential, all else equal. Second, since in all countries the female wage distribution lies below the male distribution, centralized systems that consciously raise minimum pay levels, regardless of gender, will also tend to lower male-female wage differentials. Finally, the effect of gender-specific policies meant to raise women's wages may be greater under centralized systems, where such policies can be more speedily and effectively implemented.[4]

As discussed in chapters 3 and 6, there is considerable variation across countries, both in collective-bargaining coverage and in the degree of centralization of wage setting in both the union and the nonunion sectors. We showed, for example, that the Scandinavian countries and Austria stand at one extreme, with their high degree of collective-bargaining coverage and union-negotiated wage agreements at the economywide or industrywide level, while the United States stands at the other, with an especially low rate of collective-bargaining coverage and pay setting that is often determined at the firm or plant level even within the union sector. Moreover, in many of the OECD countries, but not in the United States, formal or informal mechanisms exist to extend union-negotiated pay rates to nonunion workers.

Systems of pay compression may influence workers' incentives to invest in skill acquisition, although the direction of these effects is theoretically ambiguous. On the one hand, if the return to experience is reduced by wage compression, women will have less incentive to remain employed during periods of childbearing and childrearing than they would if there was a larger penalty for time out of the paid labor force. On the other hand, high wage floors may disproportionately encourage women's labor-force participation, raising their relative experience levels. Of course, these wage floors could still reduce women's employment if labor-demand effects are important. In any case, wage-induced changes in women's qualifications could provide a further avenue along which wage-setting institutions can affect the gender pay gap.

Another institution that directly affects the wage distribution is mandated minimum-wage coverage. As we discussed in chapter 6, studies of the effect of minimum wages on the wage distribution in various countries invariably find that such regulation compresses the bottom of the distribution. International differences in minimum wage levels, which we surveyed in chapter 3, can, therefore, lead to international differences in the gender pay gap. In particular, we saw that, in 1997, the national minimum wage in the United States was only 38 percent of the full-time median wage while it averaged 48 percent in the other countries. Thus, minimum-wage laws, like collective-bargaining coverage and the centralization of wage setting, are another factor tending to raise the gender pay gap in the United States compared to that in other countries.

GENDER DIFFERENCES IN
WORKER CHARACTERISTICS

While the U.S. gender pay gap is currently about average among other Western countries, women appear to be better qualified relative to men in the United States than in most other countries. In most Western countries, men and women have roughly comparable levels of education, although men tend to have a slight advantage, one that, in some, including Australia, Austria, Germany, the Netherlands, and Switzerland, exceeds half a year.[5] The United States has among the smallest disparities in educational attainment between men and women, and, in recent years, women in the United States have actually become more likely than men to attend college.

In addition to being well qualified in terms of their educational attainment, American women appear to have a higher level of labor-force commitment than do women in most other countries. For example, data presented in chapter 2 indicate that, while both men and women in the United States have higher labor-force-participation (LFP) rates than do their counterparts in the European Union, the participation-rate advantage of American women exceeds that of American men considerably. For example, in 1998, U.S. women had an LFP rate of 70.7 percent, in comparison to an EU average of 58 percent; the corresponding figures for men were 84.2 percent in the United States and 77.8 percent in the European Union. Moreover, U.S. women were more likely to work full-time when they were employed: in 1998, 8.2 percent of male and 19.1 percent of female workers were employed part-time in the United States; the corresponding EU figures were 5.9 percent for men and 28.1 percent for women.

While U.S. women's LFP rates are higher than those of women in most of the other countries, this does not necessarily imply that the average employed American woman has more labor-market experience. It is possible that, in a country with a high women's LFP rate, recent entrants constitute a larger proportion of the labor force and, thus, that women workers have less experience, on average, than do women in a country with a low women's LFP rate. On the other hand, it may be that a country's high women's

LFP rate is due to more-continuous labor-force attachment among women (Blau and Ferber 1992; O'Neill and Polachek 1993).

Lacking complete international data on actual experience, we tentatively conclude that U.S. women are at least as oriented toward market work as women in most other countries are. This conclusion is supported by data on actual experience, which is available to us for Sweden, the United States, and West Germany for 1984. These data indicate that the male-female gap in actual experience in 1984 was about six years in the United States and five years in Germany and Sweden (Blau and Kahn 1996b; Blau and Kahn 2000b). Thus, in terms of actual experience among the employed, women in Sweden, the United States, and West Germany faced fairly comparable shortfalls relative to men in 1984. And the male-female experience gap in the United States declined steadily over the 1980s (Blau and Kahn 1997).

Continuing our assessment of American women's relative qualifications and treatment in the labor market, table 7.1 presents data from Richard Anker (1998) on occupational segregation, where the index of segregation has been defined on the basis of seventy-five nonagricultural occupations.[6] The index can range from 0 to 100, and it indicates the percentage of women (or men) who would have to change jobs for the occupational distribution of men and women to be the same. As may be seen in the table, only one of the seventeen countries for which data are available has a lower level of segregation than does the United States. The average of segregation indexes among the other countries, 56.5 percent, is fully 10 percentage points higher than the U.S. level, 46.3 percent. Notably, several countries with substantially lower gender pay gaps than that in the United States, such as Finland, France, New Zealand, and Sweden, have higher levels of occupational segregation. A country's level of occupational segregation is likely to reflect both women's relative training levels and labor-force commitment, as well as the effect of employer, government, and union policies (Reskin and Hartmann 1986; Blau and Ferber 1992). To the extent that it reflects training and commitment, we may again conclude that the workforce credentials of U.S. women relative to those of U.S. men equal or exceed those of women in other countries.

TABLE 7.1 Occupational Segregation Index by Gender, 1990

Country	Index	Country	Index
Australia	58.1	New Zealand	58.2
Austria	60.7	Norway	57.3
Canada	54.1	Spain	56.9
Finland	61.6	Sweden	58.1
France	55.6	Switzerland	63.0
West Germany	52.3	United Kingdom	56.7
Italy	44.9		
Japan	50.2	Non-U.S. average	56.5
Luxembourg	58.9	United States	46.3
Netherlands	56.7		

Source: Anker (1998). © International Labor Organization; for full citation see references.
Note: As indicated, data are for 1990, with the following exceptions: West Germany (1989); Italy (1981); New Zealand (1986); Sweden (1991); Switzerland (1980); and the United States (1991).

ASSESSING THE RELATIVE EFFECTS OF WAGE STRUCTURE AND GENDER-SPECIFIC CAUSES OF INTERNATIONAL DIFFERENCES IN THE GENDER PAY GAP

In order to understand differences across countries in the gender pay gap, we need to account for the gender-specific and overall wage-structure effects discussed earlier. In much of our research on this topic (Blau and Kahn 1992, 1995, 1996b), we have been guided by a framework developed by Juhn, Murphy, and Pierce (1991) to analyze changes in racial pay differentials in the United States. Across countries, we view gender-specific factors, including differences in qualifications and the effect of labor-market discrimination, as determining the percentile ranking of women in the male wage distribution and the overall wage structure as determining the wage penalty or reward associated with this position in the wage distribution. The basic premise is that men at the same percentile ranking as women may be viewed as comparable in the eyes of employers. Thus, the same set of factors will determine the relative rewards of women and of these comparable men. In each country, for example, women are disproportionately employed in relatively low-paying occupations. In labor markets

TABLE 7.2 **Female Wages Relative to the Male Distribution, Actual and Wage-Distribution-Corrected Gender Wage Ratios, 1985 to 1986 and 1993 to 1994**

	Average Female Percentile in Male Wage Distribution	Actual Female-Male Wage Ratio	Female-Male Wage Ratio at U.S. Male Wage Distribution
1985 to 1986			
Australia	33.4	.716	.555
West Germany	28.4	.702	.536
Britain	25.8	.660	.471
Austria	31.0	.718	.515
Italy	40.5	.808	.672
Non-U.S. average	31.8	.721	.550
United States	31.9	.637	.637
1993 to 1994			
Australia	34.7	.773	.667
West Germany	21.5	.693	.368
Britain	35.1	.782	.689
Austria	33.3	.797	.605
Italy	35.2	.795	.622
Non-U.S. average	32.0	.768	.590
United States	36.9	.729	.729

Source: Blau and Kahn (2000c, 94).
Note: The years covered for each country are as follows: Australia (1986, 1994); West Germany (1985 to 1986, 1993); Britain (1985 to 1986; 1993 to 1994); United States (1985 to 1986; 1993 to 1994); Austria (1985 to 1986, 1994); Italy (1986, 1993 to 1994). Earnings are corrected for weekly hours differences. For details, see Blau and Kahn (forthcoming).

where there is a large penalty to working in a low-paying sector, we would expect to see a larger gender pay gap, other things equal.

Table 7.2 presents some descriptive information that allows us to make an initial determination of the relative strength of gender-specific factors and overall wage structure in explaining international differences in the gender pay gap. It is based on calculations made using International Social Survey Programme (ISSP) micro data and presents information on the United States and five major Western countries for the periods 1985 to 1986 and 1993 to 1994. These five countries are a subset of those included in the

ISSP for which data are available in both the 1980s and the 1990s. Our findings were similar, however, when we considered the full set of countries. These two periods allow us to observe how the changing economic environment of the 1980s and 1990s affected women in the United States compared to those elsewhere. Earnings are corrected for differences in weekly hours worked.[7]

Our results for the ranking of the U.S. gender wage ratio compared to the non-U.S. average are qualitatively similar to those presented in chapter 2, which were based on OECD data on the weekly earnings of full-time workers. We again find that, in the mid-1980s, the U.S. ratio lagged behind that of the other countries substantially (top panel, middle column). By 1993 to 1994, however, the United States had closed much of this gap (bottom panel, middle column). The average female percentiles[8] presented in the first column of the table are of interest as an indicator of gender-specific factors. In 1985 to 1986, the wages of U.S. women ranked at the 31.9th percentile of the male wage distribution, virtually the same ranking as the average for the other countries. By 1993 to 1994, the percentile ranking of the wages of U.S. women, 36.9, was considerably higher than the non-U.S. average ranking of 32.0. The percentile rankings suggest that the relative qualifications and treatment of U.S. women were similar to those of women in the other countries in the mid-1980s and actually more favorable by the mid-1990s.

Although the percentile rankings are suggestive, in order to determine the relative strength of gender-specific factors and wage structure, we need to ascertain the wage consequences of women's placement in the male wage distribution. The hypothetical gender pay ratios shown in the last column of table 7.2 enable us to do just that. They show what the gender pay ratio would be if men and women in each country had their own relative position in the wage distribution *but if overall wage inequality was at U.S. levels.* So, for example, a man or woman at the 25th percentile of the male wage distribution in Australia would receive a wage equal to that of a man at the 25th percentile of the U.S. male wage distribution in the same year. For these hypothetical wage ratios, we find that the U.S. gender ratio is higher than the non-U.S. average of the distribution-corrected ratios in both periods: 8.7 percentage points higher in 1985 to 1986 and 13.9 percentage points higher in 1993 to 1994.

This simulation implies that gender-specific factors in general explain none of the higher U.S. overall actual pay gap. On average, the gender-specific factors go the wrong way, as implied by our earlier discussion of full-time work, labor-force commitment, occupational segregation, and EEO legislation. We conclude that, compared to women in the other countries, U.S. women are better qualified relative to men and/or encounter less discrimination. The mediocre ranking of the U.S. gender ratio in the face of these favorable gender-specific factors is a consequence of the higher level of wage inequality in the United States, which places a much higher penalty on being below average in the wage distribution.

The effect of the more-compressed wage structures in the other countries can also be seen by comparing the hypothetical gender pay gap for each country shown in the third column of table 7.2—where workers are evaluated at their actual percentile in the wage distribution of their own country but the distribution itself is shifted to reflect the U.S. level of wage inequality—to its actual gender pay gap as shown in the middle column of the table. In every case, the gender pay ratio would be higher using own-country wage distributions, usually substantially so. On average, the more-compressed wage distributions in these countries increased the gender wage ratio from 55 to 72.1 percent in the 1980s (top panel, sixth row) and from 59 to 76.8 percent in the 1990s (bottom panel, penultimate row).

The results reported in table 7.2 also suggest in several ways that the relative qualifications or treatment of U.S. women compared to women in other countries improved between the 1980s and the 1990s. First, the average female percentile in the male wage distribution rose from 31.9 to 36.9 in the United States, but the average for the other countries was relatively stable (as shown in column 1). Second, the gender pay ratio evaluated at the U.S. male wage distribution rose by 9.2 percentage points in the United States, in comparison to a smaller average rise of 4 percentage points in the other countries (as shown in column 3). While women in Australia, Austria, Britain, Italy, and West Germany were, on average, improving their qualifications and/or treatment relative to that of men between the 1980s and the 1990s, American women were improving theirs faster.

A final indication that the narrowing difference in the gender pay gap between the United States and the other countries was due to gender-specific factors rather than changing wage structure is that the effect of the higher level of wage inequality in the United States was fairly stable over the period: if the other countries had the U.S. men's wage structure, the non-U.S. average gender ratio would have decreased by 17.1 percentage points in 1985 to 1986 and 17.8 percentage points in 1993 to 1994 (comparing columns 2 and 3). The similar effects of the U.S. wage structure in 1985 to 1986 and 1993 to 1994 make sense in the light of Lawrence Katz and David Autor's (1999) observation that much of the increase in U.S. wage inequality over the 1980s and 1990s occurred between 1979 and 1983.

Unfortunately, this analysis cannot tell us exactly which factors improved more rapidly for American women than for women in the other countries over this period. However, a recent study that we performed of trends over time in the U.S. gender gap does suggest some possible candidates (Blau and Kahn 1997). We analyzed women's wage gains over the 1980s and found that, although rising wage inequality retarded wage convergence during this period, this effect was more than offset by improvements in gender-specific factors, especially a decline in the gender gap in full-time experience (see also O'Neill and Polachek 1993) and an upgrading of women's occupations as their relative employment as professionals and managers rose and their relative employment in clerical and service jobs fell.

Also working to reduce the gender pay gap was a decrease in the size of the unexplained gap that could reflect either an upgrading of women's unmeasured labor-market skills or a decline in labor-market discrimination against women, or a combination of the two. Both interpretations are credible during this period. Since women improved their relative level of measured skills, it is plausible that they also enhanced their relative level of unmeasured skills. And, as women increased their commitment to the labor force, the rationale for statistical discrimination against them carried less weight; thus, it is plausible that this type of discrimination declined. The decrease in the size of the unexplained gender pay gap may also reflect favorable shifts in the demand for female versus male workers as the demand for blue-collar workers in manufacturing shrank.

While similar changes may have occurred in other countries during this time period, the faster narrowing of the gender pay gap in the United States suggests that they occurred at a faster pace in the United States than elsewhere. In particular, it may well be that the relative qualifications and experience of American women improved faster than did those of women in other countries. And, if women's labor-force attachment increased more in the United States than elsewhere, the associated reductions in statistical discrimination against women could well also have been larger.

The simulations in table 7.2 suggest a determining role for wage structure in raising the U.S. gender pay gap relative to that in other countries at each point in time. We should point out, however, that these simulations assume that the entire difference in men's wage inequality across countries is due to labor-market prices and rents rather than population heterogeneity. However, as we discussed at length in chapter 6, higher U.S. prices are, in fact, an important reason for higher men's wage inequality in the United States, although population heterogeneity also plays a role. Moreover, in earlier research on the 1980s (Blau and Kahn 1992, 1995, 1996b), we controlled for the distribution of personal characteristics and obtained results very similar to those reported in table 7.2 in explaining why the United States had a higher gender pay gap than did most other countries in the 1980s. Results for one of our comparisons, namely, that between Sweden and the United States, illustrate the effect of labor-force characteristics very pointedly.

This comparison is of particular interest because, in the 1980s, Sweden and the United States represent cases at the extremes of an international ranking of both wage centralization and the female-male wage ratio, the United States having highly decentralized wage setting and a high gender pay gap, the opposite holding for Sweden. Moreover, our analysis was based on data sets for each country that allow for more-accurate measures of wage rates and qualifications than do most other sources. In particular, we were able to measure hourly earnings and actual labor-market experience as well as schooling, industry, and occupation. The earnings variable represents an advance over the ISSP data in table 7.2, where data on annual earnings were corrected for time input

TABLE 7.3 **Gender Wage Ratios and Female Percentiles in the United States and Sweden, 1984**

	United States	Sweden
Female-male log wage ratio		
Unadjusted	66.9	82.7
Adjusted[a]	82.2	90.9
Mean female percentile in		
Male log wage distribution	29.6	29.9
Male residual distribution[a]	36.6	37.4

Source: Blau and Kahn (1996b). Data sources are Michigan Panel Study of Income Dynamics for the United States and the Swedish HUS (Household Market and Nonmarket Activities Survey).
[a]Based on hourly earnings adjusted for education, actual experience and its square, major industry, and occupation.

using a regression approach.[9] And the control for labor-market experience (which is not available in the ISSP data) is extremely important since experience differences have been found to be a major cause of gender pay gaps (Mincer and Polachek 1974; O'Neill and Polachek 1993; Blau and Kahn 1997).

Table 7.3 shows some summary results from our U.S.-Swedish comparison of the gender pay gap in 1984. The table indicates that the gender ratio was 16 percentage points higher in Sweden than in the United States and that it remained 9 percentage points higher after adjusting for gender differences in measured characteristics.[10] Insight into the role that wage-setting institutions play in producing these large differences in the gender pay gap may be gained by looking at the percentile rankings of women in each country's male wage distribution. Recall that gender-specific factors—that is, gender differences in qualifications and the extent of labor-market discrimination—will influence the placement of women in the male wage distribution and that wage structure will determine the size of the wage penalty associated with this placement.

Surprisingly, given the large differences in gender wage ratios shown in table 7.3, the mean percentile of women in the overall male wage distribution and in the male distribution of wage residuals from a male wage regression[11] was virtually identical in the two countries. These two measures correspond, respectively, to

FIGURE 7.1 **Cumulative-Distribution Function, Women's Wages Relative to the Men's Wage Distribution: Sweden and the United States, 1984**

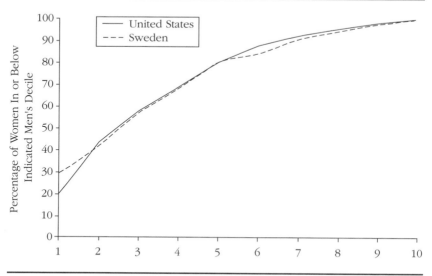

Source: Blau and Kahn (1996b).

the unadjusted and adjusted wage ratios, where the latter controls for gender differences in measured characteristics. These findings suggest that the large difference in the gender pay gaps between the two countries is entirely due to the larger wage penalty placed on women's lower position in the male wage distribution in the United States than in Sweden.

Figure 7.1 further illuminates the effect of wage compression at the bottom of the distribution in producing this outcome. It presents the female cumulative-distribution functions that result from placing women in male wage deciles on the basis of men's log wage cutoffs. While the U.S. women's cumulative-distribution function is quite similar to that of Swedish women, a larger proportion of women are in the lowest male wage decile in Sweden (29 percent) than in the United States (20 percent). This suggests that the wage floors in Sweden raise women's relative pay to a greater extent than equivalent floors raise women's relative pay in the United States. Our detailed decomposition results confirmed that more than the entire U.S.-Swedish difference in the gender pay gap was accounted for by Sweden's more-compressed men's wage structure. Our estimates indicated that, with the same wage structure, the gender pay gap in Sweden would actually have been slightly higher than that in the United States.

Other analyses of women's relative wages come to largely the same qualitative conclusion regarding the importance of wage-setting institutions. First, in a comparison of Australia and Canada using data for 1989 to 1990, Michael Kidd and Michael Shannon (1996) found that the Australian gender pay gap was considerably smaller than that in Canada (by about 0.14 log points). Australia's more-compressed wage structure explained 37 to 66 percent of this difference. Australia's institution of nationally binding wage awards issued by government tribunals as well as its higher level of unionization likely help cause its lower wage dispersion. Second, Per-Anders Edin and Katerina Richardson (forthcoming) studied the effect of Sweden's solidarity bargaining on the gender pay gap. During the key period 1968 to 1974, when collective-bargaining agreements were compressing the wage distribution at the bottom, the gender pay gap in Sweden fell by 0.062 log points. Of this decline, 82 percent was due to the compression of the wage structure, which raised the pay of low-wage workers in general, including women. Finally, Hunt (forthcoming) finds that the extension of western Germany's relatively high union wages to eastern Germany with monetary union reduced the gender pay gap by roughly 10 percentage points.

As discussed above, the basic framework of several of these studies assumes that gender-specific factors such as male-female differences in qualifications or discrimination are indicated by women's placement in the distribution of male wages and that a country's degree of wage compression determines the wage penalty that women pay for their specific placement in the male wage distribution. A possible objection to this kind of analysis is that the presence of discrimination and the particular form that the discrimination takes can complicate the interpretation of the simulation.[12] Specifically, Wing Suen (1997) suggests a model in which discrimination takes the form of a fixed deduction from every woman's pay, say, 20 percent. This may produce a mechanical positive relation between male wage inequality and the average female percentile: under these assumptions, anything that increases male wage inequality will have no effect on the gender pay gap but will push more men's pay below that of the average woman. On the other hand, suppose that discrimination primarily takes the form of women being confined to lower-paying firms, industries, and occupations but then being treated the same as similarly situated men. This is similar to our assumption, based on Juhn, Murphy, and Pierce's (1991) framework (noted earlier) that women are treated the same as men who are "comparable" in the employer's eyes— that is, men at the same percentile in the male wage distribution. In these latter cases, higher labor-market prices will raise the gender pay gap by increasing the penalty associated with being in low-paying sectors, as our framework in this chapter has assumed.

This discussion of discrimination implies that the degree to which we can rely on the female percentile as an indicator of gender-specific factors and the degree to which we can speak of wage structure having an effect on the gender pay gap are empirical questions. We note in this regard that a number of empirical findings give credence to the framework that we have posed for understanding the gender pay gap.

First, a number of studies have found that the segregation of women in low-paying occupations is an important factor in producing the male-female pay differential, while other research indicates that, when men and women do work within the same detailed occupation, most of the gender pay gap is associated with women's location in low-paying firms rather than with unequal pay within firms.[13] This implies that the model in which the female percentile reflects women's gender-specific treatment or qualifications has some validity.

Second, in our work on trends over time in the U.S. gender gap (Blau and Kahn 1997), we found that the gender pay ratio increased as the mean female percentile rose. This suggests that the increase in the female percentile is not simply an artifact of widening male inequality, but rather that it contains information about women's relative qualifications and treatment.

Third, the international data presented in chapter 2 show that male and female wage inequality in a country are highly correlated, suggesting that overall labor-market prices are similar for men and women in a country.

Finally, across the sample of countries included in the ISSP, we found little statistical relationship between the average female percentile in the male distribution and the standard deviation of the log of male wages (an indicator of male wage inequality), providing further evidence against the idea of the mechanical relation posited in Suen's model.[14] This again suggests that the female percentile is not merely an inverse indicator of male wage inequality, but that it likely conveys important information about women's relative qualifications and treatment.

While the results presented in tables 7.2 and 7.3 suggest an important role for wage structure in raising the U.S. gender pay gap relative to that in other countries, it is possible to test this relation more directly. And we have done so in a recent paper (Blau and Kahn forthcoming). Using micro data for each country and year from the 1985 to 1994 ISSP data files mentioned earlier (one hundred country-year observations in all),[15] we found strong evidence that higher inequality of male wages (controlling for the distribution of men's productivity characteristics) and higher women's labor supply had large, statistically significant, positive effects on the gender pay gap. The differences in inequality of male wages were quantitatively more important than was women's labor supply in explaining differences across countries in the size of the gap.

The contribution of higher wage inequality and higher women's labor supply in the United States to the larger U.S. gender pay gap can, on the basis of these regression estimates, be estimated. We found that both helped explain the higher U.S. gap, with wage inequality being considerably more important. Interestingly, these variables were more than sufficient to account for the higher U.S. gender pay gap, suggesting that unmeasured factors—perhaps higher women's qualifications or less discrimination—favored U.S. women. However, most important, this analysis provided strong, direct evidence that wage structure was overwhelmingly the most important factor causing a higher gender pay gap in the United States than in other countries during this period. In addition, the strong results that we found for the effect of wage inequality on the gender pay gap indirectly provide support for the Juhn, Murphy, and Pierce (1991) decomposition technique that we and others employed in the earlier work previously summarized, work that yielded very similar results.

In evaluating these findings, it could, of course, be argued that there may be problems of reverse causation; that is, the gender pay gap could affect both male wage inequality and women's net supply. On the former effect, see Fortin and Lemieux (1998), which presents a model in which a lower gender pay gap causes higher male wage inequality as women take jobs that men would otherwise have held. And general economic reasoning suggests that men and women's labor-supply decisions could be affected by the wages that they are offered.

However, if a reduction in the gender pay gap does raise male inequality to some extent, this implies that our estimated effect of male wage inequality on the gender pay gap is biased downward and that the true effect of wage compression is even larger than the substantial estimates that we found. And, although women's labor supply may to some extent be endogenous, controlling for it is especially helpful in that it standardizes for the relative selectivity of the female labor force in each country and, thus, sharpens our interpretation of the male wage-inequality variables.

However, recognizing that the explanatory variables may be endogenous, we estimated reduced-form models in which male wage inequality and women's labor supply were replaced by institutional variables such as collective-bargaining coverage. We found that more highly unionized countries had much smaller gender pay gaps, all else equal, an effect that is quite consistent with the positive effect of wage inequality on the gender gap that we estimated.

Finally, our basic results were robust to the inclusion of a variety of controls, including statutory minimum-wage laws, mandated parental-leave length, an occupational segregation measure, controls for unemployment-benefit-system characteristics, indicators of job-protection regulations for both regular and temporary employment, and the incidence of employment in very small firms.

WAGE AND EMPLOYMENT EFFECTS OF SPECIFIC LABOR-MARKET INTERVENTIONS DESIGNED TO LOWER THE GENDER PAY GAP

While changes or differences in union wage-setting arrangements appear to have an important effect on the gender pay gap, in several instances governments have explicitly intervened on behalf of women through antidiscrimination policy. It is likely that the nature of wage-setting institutions can have an important influence on the effect of antidiscrimination policies. If there are mechanisms through which wages can be centrally altered, then a policy designed to reduce gender wage differentials can have a more immediate effect than it can when wage setting is decentralized. Evidence suggests that this interaction between the gender-specific policy of antidiscrimination laws and general wage-setting mechanisms may help explain the relative effectiveness of government attempts to reduce the gender pay gap in Australia, the United Kingdom, and the United States.

In the United States, the Equal Pay Act of 1963 and the Civil Rights Act of 1964 broadly outlawed discrimination in pay, employment, layoffs, and promotion on the basis of race, gender, or national origin. Significantly, these laws predate those in other advanced countries. Enforcement was to be accomplished through individual or group lawsuits, some of which would proceed under the aegis of a government agency, the Equal Employment Opportunity Commission (EEOC). An additional measure was an executive order implemented on behalf of women in the early 1970s that added the threat that firms that discriminated would lose government contracts. There is some econometric evidence that, all else equal, government policy in the 1970s raised the female-male pay ratio (Beller 1979), and discrimination as conventionally measured declined in the 1970s and 1980s as well (Blau and Beller 1988; Blau and Kahn 1997). Moreover, in some local- or state-government jurisdictions, authorities have mandated comparable worth—equal pay for work of equal value—for government workers, with some positive earnings effects on disproportionately female public-sector jobs (Killingsworth 1990).

Nevertheless, it was not until the 1980s that the overall gender pay gap in the United States fell. It is, of course, possible that the removal of discriminatory barriers in higher education in the 1970s, as well as antidiscrimination legislation generally, indirectly encouraged women to accumulate higher levels of training and other human capital and, ultimately, contributed to the falling gender gap in the 1980s (Blau and Kahn 1997; O'Neill and Polachek 1993). Moreover, there is some evidence that the anticipated positive effects on women's relative pay of reductions in discrimination and women's rising labor-force attachment were delayed by a small decrease in women's *average* levels of labor-market experience in the 1970s. This decrease was due to a large increase in labor-force participation among younger women as women began to participate in the labor force more consistently over the life cycle (Goldin 1990). While this was a development that would raise women's average experience levels in the long run, it initially lowered them as the average age of employed women fell. Yet it is also possible that the immediate wage effects of the antidiscrimination legislation were small in part due to the individualistic nature of the enforcement of the law (that is, lawsuits were the basis of its enforcement), and in part because of the decentralized nature of U.S. wage setting itself. The implementation of antidiscrimination policies in the United States contrasts, therefore, with that in Australia and the United Kingdom, where more highly centralized wage-setting institutions appear to have resulted in much-larger immediate effects.

Australian government tribunal decisions mandating equal pay for equal work and equal pay for work of equal value were implemented during the period 1969 to 1975. The latter essentially involved implementing a policy of comparable worth on a nationwide basis. The enforcement mechanism was Australia's system of government tribunal awards, which set occupation pay rates and was estimated to cover about 90 percent of workers (Gregory and Daly 1991). And the female-male pay ratio rose from 65 percent in 1969 to 85 percent in 1975, an extremely rapid and large increase, likely caused by the implementation of these policies through tribunals (Blau and Kahn 1995; Gregory and Daly 1991). In the United Kingdom, equal-pay legislation was implemented during the period 1970 to 1975. It was initially enforced through collective-bargaining agreements, which removed differentiated male and female rates and, significantly, required that, in workplaces with collective bargaining, women could not be paid less than the lowest male wage rate (OECD 1988; Zabalza and Tzannatos 1985). The interaction between collective bargaining and the equal-pay law helped raise the female-male pay ratio sharply during the period of 1969 to 1977 by about 0.11 log points (Dolton, O'Neill, and Sweetman 1996).

These examples suggest that government intervention can affect the gender pay gap. However, such policies can also have unintended consequences for women's relative employment. Of particular concern is comparable worth, that is, government mandates that employers compensate workers equally for work of equal value to the enterprise, regardless of occupation. This policy is currently in effect nationwide in Australia as well as in one Canadian province (Ontario) for virtually all employers and in about twenty states in the United States for certain public-sector employees. It recognizes that men and women are, to a considerable degree, segregated in different jobs and that a simple policy of equal pay for equal work will leave a substantial portion of the gender gap in pay untouched, at least initially.[16] As we have seen, this policy appears to have been quite successful in Australia, raising the relative pay of women in a fairly short period of time through a realignment of pay in jobs traditionally segregated by gender. However, by increasing wages in occupations in which women predominate, this policy runs the risk of lowering women's relative-employment levels, at least assuming downward-sloping labor-demand curves.[17]

Economists have studied the employment effects of such comparable-worth interventions in the Australian case and in those of government employees in San Jose, California, Minnesota, and Washington State. In each case, comparable worth had a noticeably positive effect on women's relative wages, particularly in Australia (Gregory and Duncan 1981; Killingsworth 1990; O'Neill, Brien, and Cunningham 1989). And, in several cases, the implementation of comparable worth came at a time of rising relative employment among women, a rise that continued even after women's relative wages were increased. However, when each of these analyses controlled for the overall growth of women's employment, it was found that women's relative employment grew more slowly than it otherwise would have, although the effects were not large. One interpretation of these results is that any negative employment effects of comparable worth were not sizable enough to outweigh women's growing labor-market attachment or, in the case of public employees in the United States, to cause layoffs of female government workers.

In contrast to the research on comparable worth, which finds some evidence, albeit modest, of employment losses in response to administered wages, Manning's (1996) study of the effect of the U.K. Equal Pay Act of 1970 and Sex Discrimination Act of 1975 shows no employment losses for women despite the large gains in their relative wages that occurred. Manning finds that, after this legislation was passed, wage changes and employment levels by industry were strongly positively related for women but less so for men, a pattern that he interprets as being consistent with the notion that women face more monopsony power than men do. And the positive relationship became slightly less so after 1971, implying that monopsony power fell after the passage of the Equal Pay Act of 1970. Manning's (1996) results provide an explanation for why women's relative employment did not decline in the face of large exogenous increases in their relative pay. As we saw in chapter 6, some results for the effect of minimum-wage laws in the United States follow a similar pattern, again suggesting monopsony elements in the labor market.

Differential monopsony power facing men and women could help to explain the existence of gender discrimination (Madden 1973) as well as Manning's (1996) results of different wage-employment relationships for men and women. Although women's labor supply is, in general, more elastic to the economy than is men's (implying that men might face more monopsonistic exploitation), Manning (1996) argues that women's supply of labor to individual employers may be less elastic because, for family-related reasons, women are likely to be less mobile. While this appears plausible, this factor may or may not outweigh women's greater overall wage elasticity of labor supply.

Findings from studies of quitting in the United States do not support the idea that men's labor supply at the firm level is more sensitive to wages than is women's. For example, calculations based on results presented in Kip Viscusi (1980) and Blau and Kahn (1981) on the quit behavior of men and women in the 1970s indicate that the elasticity of quitting with respect to the wage was similar for men and women, which is, of course, counter to the monopsony story. And, for a later period, Audrey Light and Manuelita Ureta (1992) found that women's quit behavior was actually more responsive to wages than men's.[18] On the other hand, Erling Barth and Harald Dale-Olsen (1999) found that men's turnover is more wage elastic than is women's in Norway. On the assumption that turnover is primarily quitting, this result implies that, in Norway, men's labor supply is more wage elastic at the firm level than is women's. These findings suggest that Norwegian employers could potentially exercise differential monopsony power over women. Of course, the degree to which Norway's centralized wage-setting system would allow this to take place is an empirical question. These conflicting findings for the wage elasticity of labor supply at the firm level for the United States and Norway do not challenge Manning's (1996) basic finding for the United Kingdom that women's employment did not suffer despite the massive increase in their relative wages occasioned by the Sex Discrimination Act. They do, however, raise some question about the underlying mechanism that produced this result.

CONCLUSIONS

In this chapter, we have presented a variety of evidence indicating that the major factor raising the gender pay gap in the United States relative to that in other countries is the far lower degree of wage compression in the United States. In many other countries, women's wages are swept up by centrally negotiated wage floors. Thus, somewhat paradoxically, even though the labor-market qualifications of American women appear to be higher relative to those of men than do those of women in most other countries, the gender pay gap has, until recently, been higher in the United States than elsewhere. Of course, if wage-setting institutions become less centralized, as appears to be happening in several countries (for a discussion of this, see chapter 3), then women in many of these countries may suffer large declines in their relative wages.

The surest way in which to lower the gender pay gap is to reduce the gender-specific components of this gap: male-female differences in qualifications, experience, and discrimination. This appears to be the way in which American women have advanced from a place near the bottom of the OECD pack in 1980 to one roughly in the middle today. Moreover, while intervention in the form of wage-setting institutions can also lower the gender pay gap, there may be negative employment consequences of such intervention. Further, when there is little wage penalty for occupational segregation, women have less incentive to press to enter fields dominated by men. In the limit, with equal wages across sectors and skill levels, we may have a "separate but equal" labor market for women. But one may question whether such a separate arrangement can confer truly equal status on women.

—— Chapter 8 ——

Policy Implications and Future Research Directions

I N THE PRECEDING chapters, we have examined the effect of labor-market institutions on labor-market performance. The context has been the contrast between the excellent record of the United States on employment, especially in the 1990s, on the one hand, and the stagnating real wages and sharply rising wage inequality there in comparison to the situation in other Western nations, on the other. We have posed as a possible explanation of these trends the interaction between America's noninterventionist labor-market institutions and the macroeconomic shocks relating to productivity trends, globalization, technological change, and monetary policy that all Western nations have experienced since the 1970s.

We hypothesized that the flexible U.S. labor market was able to accommodate these strains by letting absolute and relative real-wage levels adjust, thus permitting the unemployment rate to stay low. In contrast, according to this framework, in most other OECD countries, collective bargaining and other labor-market institutions and government regulations kept overall real wages rising and prevented the relative wages of unskilled workers from falling as fast as they did in the less-interventionist U.S. labor market or, in some cases, preventing any decrease at all in the relative pay of low-skilled workers. The theory of labor demand predicts that such wage trends would help produce the sharp increases in unemployment that these nations experienced (Blanchard and Wolfers 2000; Freeman 1994).

255

This view has been termed the *unified theory* (Blank 1997), in the sense that the U.S. experience of declining unemployment, falling to steady real wages, and rapidly rising wage inequality and the EU experience of rising unemployment, rising real wages, and comparatively stable relative-wage levels are two sides of the same coin. The United States permitted real and relative wages to adjust, while many countries in Europe (and other countries such as Australia) chose to let employment take the brunt of the shocks.

We spent much of the book attempting to accumulate evidence testing the unified theory. We examined both macroeconomic- and microeconomic-level analyses of the role that institutions have played in explaining the differences between the United States and the rest of the OECD. At the macroeconomic level, we reviewed the findings of Nickell and Layard (1999), who examined the cross-national evidence on the determinants of average unemployment in the 1980s and 1990s. They found a strong association between labor-market institutions, such as collective bargaining, decentralized wage-setting institutions, generous unemployment-insurance (UI) systems, high labor taxes, and the like, and high unemployment. Our calculations based on their results indicate that, in an accounting sense, lower unemployment in the United States is explained by its lower labor taxes, less-generous UI systems, and low level of unionization, although decentralized union wage setting has a somewhat offsetting effect.

While these findings provide some suggestive evidence about the United States in the 1980s and 1990s, it is important to remember that, in the 1960s and 1970s, the United States had relatively high unemployment compared to that in these other countries. This state of affairs prevailed despite the fact that then, as is the case today, the United States had much less interventionist labor-market institutions. A convincing explanation of how the United States has fared since the 1960s must account for both periods. How was it that much of Europe had low unemployment in the 1960s and 1970s but persistently high unemployment ever since? Considerable insight on this question is provided by Blanchard and Wolfers (2000), who studied unemployment over the period 1960 to 1996. They found evidence consistent with the idea that macroeconomic shocks interact with labor-market institutions to affect unemployment, that is, evidence consistent with the unified theory.

We used parameter estimates from Bertola, Blau, and Kahn (2002), which built on Blanchard and Wolfers's work, to account for the reversal of unemployment fortunes of the United States compared to those of the other OECD countries between the early 1970s and the mid-1990s. In addition to macroeconomic shocks and labor-market institutions, Bertola, Blau, and Kahn considered the role of demographic shifts in accounting for unemployment changes, focusing particularly on the youth share of the population. We found that macroeconomic shocks and demographics, as well as institutional changes, were, on net, more employment friendly in the United States—and, thus, help explain a portion of the fall in the U.S. unemployment rate—than they were in other OECD countries. But we estimated that macroeconomic, demographic, and institutional changes by themselves could account for only about 30 percent of this decrease. However, when we allowed for interactions between shocks and institutions, we found evidence that these shocks had a much larger effect in raising unemployment outside than inside the United States. This pattern suggests that the United States has more-flexible labor-market institutions than other countries do, theoretically allowing real wages rather than employment to bear the burden of adjustment. A framework that allows for interactions between macroeconomic and demographic shocks and labor-market institutions can account for fully 63 percent of the decrease in the relative-unemployment rate of the United States.

While Bertola, Blau, and Kahn's results are remarkably consistent with the unified theory, macroeconomic evidence on the role of institutions is, in many ways, circumstantial. For example, many of the explanatory variables used in these analyses may themselves be affected by unemployment: higher unemployment may lead to changes in monetary policy and might even affect productivity growth through incentives to innovate. Moreover, the generosity of UI benefits or even individual workers' decisions to become union members could also be influenced by the extent of unemployment. These considerations suggest that, while the macroeconomic evidence is consistent with a strong interaction effect between institutions and economic forces, there are other plausible explanations for the empirical relations that we observe.

In addition to these potential problems of interpretation, the macroeconomic research designs do not directly test the mechanisms that are in principle behind the unified theory. First, the theory holds that some labor-market institutions affect absolute and relative wages and keep them rigid in the face of economic forces that would otherwise have resulted in changes in absolute and relative pay levels. Second, the unified theory posits that these rigid wages lead to unemployment as firms move along their labor-demand curves. Because of the concerns about the macroeconomic evidence, and because we are interested in disaggregated outcomes in their own right, we turned to a consideration of microeconomic evidence to shed light on the specific mechanisms that macroeconomic observers believe are an important part of the story.

We found very strong evidence that institutions such as collective bargaining do affect relative wages, particularly in reducing wage inequality. This narrowing of the wage structure occurs both across the wage distribution as a whole and between men and women in particular. This component of the unified theory seems to be valid: labor-market institutions exert a powerful influence on the wage structure and reduce the effect of market forces on relative wages, although we also found evidence that market influences are important as well.

Our examination of the effect of institutions on employment yielded less clear-cut results. In many cases, union- or minimum-wage-induced wage compression was found to lower the relative employment of the less skilled, as the unified theory would predict. The negative relative-employment effects of unions appear to be especially concentrated among the young. We also found some instances in which specific interventions designed to raise women's wages had negative employment effects for women. However, in other cases, such effects were not evident. One possible reason for ostensibly weak employment effects of wage-setting interventions is that, in several countries, government employment takes up the slack and prevents a loss of employment among the low skilled that would have otherwise resulted from very compressed wage structures. It is also possible that employers have market power and that, under such conditions, externally imposed wage floors may not cause employment to fall at all.

POLICY IMPLICATIONS

While interventions in wage setting or in insuring workers against income loss can improve the living standards of some participants in the economy, a major worry from a policy perspective is that some of these interventions may lead to a loss of jobs. Although the evidence on employment effects from microeconomic-level studies is somewhat mixed, there is enough evidence of adverse effects to suggest caution in this regard. In addition, even if the loss of jobs can be avoided, it is possible that such interventions can reduce economic efficiency, although, in chapter 4, we outlined some circumstances in which institutions that promote wage compression can enhance economic efficiency. Moreover, it is possible that, owing to failures in insurance markets, social-insurance programs deliver services whose benefits to society more than outweigh the costs that can be attributed to adverse incentive effects.

However, we should not underestimate the costs to society of high unemployment levels. In addition to the lost output and income associated with unemployment, joblessness is likely to have adverse psychological effects on the unemployed and adverse effects on the rest of society as well. Amaryta Sen (1997) and Arthur Goldsmith, Jonathan Veum, and William Darity (1996) survey a variety of evidence on many of these consequences of unemployment and find them to include social exclusion, loss of morale and motivation, deteriorating physical health (partly caused by the loss of income and partly caused by the mental-health problems associated with joblessness), and the deterioration of family relations. Freeman (1999) surveys evidence for the United States showing that joblessness contributes to crime.

This evidence on the effect of unemployment implies that many of these psychological problems would remain even if we provided more complete insurance for the incomes of the unemployed. If we could lower unemployment, society would gain by more than the increased production and reduced taxes necessary to support the unemployed. On the other hand, there is also evidence that low wages have adverse effects besides the obvious ones relating to lower living standards. For example, a variety of studies of the United States have found that a reduction in young men's real-wage opportunities will have a positive effect on their likelihood of committing crimes (Freeman 1999). Again, society gains by creating better wage opportunities.

Our evidence on wage inequality suggests that large-scale interventions in the form of high levels of collective-bargaining coverage can, indeed, raise the pay of the low skilled who still have jobs. However, we also found some evidence of negative effects of these interventions on the relative employment of the less skilled, particularly youths. Minimum wages at the current relatively low levels that prevail in the United States have not been found to have large disemployment effects on the young; however, our review of international evidence on collective bargaining suggests that raising these wages to European levels could well have some negative employment effects on young people.

A policy that would increase the living standards of the low skilled and not have negative employment consequences is an expansion of the earned-income tax credit (EITC). This is an American program that provides people with a refundable tax credit that increases with labor income over low ranges of earnings. As of 1999, for a qualifying family with two children, the EITC provided a tax credit on the first $9,500 of earnings of roughly 40 percent, yielding a maximum tax credit in this range of $3,816. The credit remained at $3,816 until earnings reached $12,500 and then declined at a rate of about 21 percent per additional dollar earned. The credit, thus, disappeared at an earnings level of $30,580.[1]

For example, suppose that a worker with two children earned the minimum wage of $5.15 per hour and worked 1,845 hours in a year, or roughly a thirty-five-hour workweek. Then the individual's pay would be roughly $9,500. If, however, he or she was the sole earner in the family and qualified for the EITC, the family's total income would be about $13,300. Moreover, at earnings levels up to $9,500, the credit augments the reward to working. In this example, a $5.15 per hour job becomes roughly a $7.21 per hour job from the worker's point of view. Put differently, the EITC in effect raises the minimum wage to a level that was higher in purchasing power than the actual minimum wage in all countries except for Australia, which had a minimum wage of $7.30 in 1998 U.S. dollars.

Thus, the EITC has the potential to raise the after-tax wages of low-wage workers substantially, but, unlike the minimum wage, it does not directly change the cost of labor to the employer. It is, thus, not expected to have an adverse effect on employer demand for the low skilled. Of course, it is possible that the added labor supply caused by the EITC could reduce wages and, hence, employer labor costs for the affected group, but it is, nonetheless, very likely to lead to higher net incomes for the target population.[2]

It should also be noted that anyone in a family with earned income greater than $9,500 would unambiguously have work disincentives due to income effects and to the benefit-reduction rate of 21 percent that starts at an income of $12,500. Moreover, expanding the EITC would be expensive, and the additional taxes necessary to pay for such expansion might cause some deterioration in economic performance. A matter of additional concern is that, as currently formulated, the EITC imposes a potentially large "marriage penalty" on low-income workers (Blau, Ferber, and Winkler 1998). This is the case because the maximum income level in the program is not adjusted for the number of adults in the family. Addressing this issue could impose further cost increases.

Nonetheless, considering the fact that the EITC increases the gain to working for those out of the labor market, it deserves serious consideration in the United States as a policy tool with which to raise the incomes of low-wage workers.

An additional, perhaps complementary, policy is the long-term strategy of upgrading the skills and training of the labor force. Such an investment would benefit the trained workers themselves, as suggested by the high returns that economists estimate for individuals' investment in formal education, at least in the United States (Card 1999). Moreover, there is evidence from a variety of sources that raising the share of the labor force consisting of skilled workers lowers wage differentials.

For example, Freeman (1976) attributes the falling return to education in the 1970s to the rapidly growing supply of highly educated labor. And Katz and Murphy (1992) suggest that decelerating growth in this supply helped cause the rising wage inequality of the 1980s. Moreover, in the 1980s, economists have attributed some of the more rapidly growing wage inequality in the United States than in Canada or Germany to the more-rapid increase in the supply of skilled workers in the latter two countries (Abraham and Houseman 1995; Murphy, Riddell, and Romer 1998). And a cross-country study discussed in chapter 6 (Brunello, Comi, and Lucifora 2000) provided some evidence that a higher relative supply of more-skilled labor lowered wage differentials across skill groups.

While the evidence on the effect of training programs is weaker than is that for the effect of formal schooling (for example, Heckman 1999), it is reasonable to pursue various routes to raising the supply of skilled workers—not only training programs for adults, but also early-intervention programs for children from disadvantaged families.[3] Not only can a policy of raising the supply of skilled workers contribute to the reduction of wage inequality, but, unlike the possible employment effects of high wage floors, it would also likely increase the employment opportunities of the less skilled rather than reduce them. Again, this policy may be expensive from a budgetary point of view. And the effects on the wage distribution of changes in supply and demand may take several years to be observed. But the high current rates of return to schooling that we observe in the United States suggest that this investment may be economically efficient as well as equitable.

Similar considerations apply to the gender pay gap as to the problem of low wages for the less skilled in general. The surest way to a low gender pay gap is to reduce the gender-specific components of this gap: male-female differences in qualifications and experience and labor-market discrimination. This appears to be the way in which American women have advanced from a gender pay ratio at the bottom of OECD pack in 1980 to one at the middle today. Moreover, while intervention in the form of wage-setting institutions can provide an alternative route to lowering the gender pay gap, we have seen that there may be negative employment consequences of such an approach. Further, when there is no wage penalty for occupational segregation, women have less incentive than they would otherwise to press to enter fields dominated by men.

Our analysis of the gender pay gap also indicates the importance of focusing on the gender-specific component of male-female pay differentials, in addition to the overall gender pay gap, in evaluating the effect of antidiscrimination policies. In particular, as we have shown, the overall wage structure can have a major influence on male-female pay differentials. Suppose, for example, that an antidiscrimination policy is implemented during a time of wage compression in which we would have expected the gender pay gap to fall even with no specific policy intervention on women's behalf. Then, if we concentrate only on the gender pay gap as an indicator of the effectiveness of policy, we may overestimate its effect. Conversely, if an antidiscrimination policy is implemented during a period of rising inequality, the raw gender pay gap will give an unrealistically pessimistic picture of its effect.

Finally, on the basis of recent experimental interventions in the design of social-insurance programs, the possibility of building in better incentive structures and support services for these initiatives also deserves consideration. Requiring UI recipients to receive job-search training, for example, appears to have reduced unemployment durations (Meyer 1995; Dolton and O'Neill 1996) and may be a good way in which to reduce the adverse incentive effects of UI without undermining its insurance value.

FUTURE RESEARCH DIRECTIONS

Our review of evidence on the effect of labor-market institutions has suggested several important areas in which our knowledge is insufficient. First, we need a better understanding of the determinants of institutional change. For example, as discussed in chapter 3, wage setting has become less centralized in several countries in the 1980s and 1990s, while, in other countries, these structures have been stable or become even more centralized. A better understanding of the fundamental causes of these changes would be useful for a number of reasons. It would enable us to obtain a more-accurate estimate of the true effect of institutions on labor-market outcomes. For example, if changes in institutions are themselves caused by economic factors such as technological change or globalization, then, by simply relating changes in institutions to changes in outcomes such as wage inequality, we may overestimate the effect of institutions. A better understanding of when institutions will change would also be useful in helping us form more-accurate predictions about future labor-market developments.

Second, in chapter 4, it was suggested that, in some circumstances, institutions such as wage compression, employment protection, or mandated family leave may enhance economic efficiency and that, in others, they may cause worse overall economic performance. We need additional serious empirical evaluations of these arguments for the obvious reason that tampering with such institutions may have unintended consequences if they do, in fact, contribute to economic efficiency.

Gruber (1997a), for example, provides estimates of the insurance value of UI by examining how the spending patterns of unemployed individuals are affected when they have better UI-benefit coverage. This value can be compared with the loss of output due to the additional weeks of unemployment caused by the benefits of the program. If the program's insurance value outweighs its costs, the UI program may be a desirable intervention, even if it does prolong unemployment. Or, as another example, mandated protections may, in some cases, be the political price that a country must pay to open itself up to international trade. In such instances, allowing imports in and compensating workers for the adverse consequences associated with more-open economies may be a package that, in its entirety, enhances economic efficiency (Krueger 2000).

While we have concentrated on wage and employment effects of institutional interventions, these economic-efficiency considerations imply a larger range of possible outcomes to study. These include labor-supply incentives, job creation and destruction, and the ability of the labor market to adjust to changing technology.

Third, European integration is an emerging phenomenon, and monetary union essentially removes one adjustment mechanism that individual countries could use in response to their own unemployment problems. As pointed out by Ronald Ehrenberg (1994) several years before monetary union, it was possible for countries with very different levels of mandated benefits and other regulations to coexist in the same world economy. Ehrenberg believed that this was the case because there were several escape mechanisms by which the costs entailed by these benefits and regulations could be prevented from detracting from an economy's competitiveness. For example, the costs of many mandated benefits can be passed back to workers in the form of lower wages, in effect allowing the workers themselves to pay for them. Overall labor costs need not be affected. Moreover, even in a case in which such benefits affect labor costs, when each country controls its own currency, it can devalue and remain competitive. Now, with monetary union, this second escape valve is no longer available for a single country in the European Union, although it is still available for the members of the monetary union in the aggregate.

Whether the new monetary environment in Europe will worsen the employment effects of labor-market interventions or cause a reduction in the intrusiveness of institutions is one of the most important research topics on the agenda. But the fact that countries with very different types of labor-market institutions have been able to coexist in the same world economy for so long is itself evidence supporting Ehrenberg's (1994) analysis. As Ehrenberg points out, there may be much to be learned from studying the effect of the social-insurance and -regulation systems of the individual states in the United States. In this country, each state has its own system for UI as well as for workers' compensation and welfare. In addition, employees in different states have different rights regarding unjust dismissals. The effect of these different laws under a common currency and a very mobile population may provide valuable insights for Europe under monetary union, and there is a large volume of this type of research to draw upon.

Fourth, as we saw in chapter 6, international differences in the distribution of cognitive skills have a noticeable effect on differences in wage inequality across countries. It would be very helpful to know what produces high levels of cognitive skills. Does having a more ethnically homogeneous population, as is the case in Sweden, facilitate the production of high measured cognitive-skill levels? Does spending more money on schools have this effect? If so, what types of spending are the most effective? For example, how should we trade off teachers' salaries and lower class size?

Precisely because there are such dramatic differences in the institutional makeup of otherwise culturally similar societies, there is much to be learned from international comparisons. At the level of basic research, this means that we have considerably greater variation in some key explanatory variables than we could obtain within any given country; this is extremely useful in ascertaining their effects. Moreover, from a policy perspective, examining the full range of international comparisons provides individual countries like the United States with a fresh perspective and gives us the opportunity to think outside the box in the best sense of this sometimes overused expression. We can learn from the experience of other nations, and, in the process, new options may be suggested to us for addressing shared problems. At the same time, we can avoid approaches that have been tried elsewhere and, while perhaps promising, produced serious adverse effects.

───── Notes ─────

Chapter 1

1. These figures are taken from OECD (1983).
2. According to the U.S. Bureau of Labor Statistics website (accessed October 15, 2001 on the World Wide Web at: *www.bls.gov*).
3. Earnings data are taken from unpublished OECD data; we are grateful to Jonas Pontusson for his help in obtaining this information. All figures are given in terms of 1998 U.S. dollars; foreign earnings figures are purchasing-power corrected using OECD (1998d).
4. These statements about real-wage levels depend, of course, on the way in which we correct for inflation. As discussed in more detail in chap. 2, we use the personal-consumption-expenditures deflator, which may or may not give an accurate picture of changes in living costs. However, as long as we use the same deflator to adjust each country's wage levels for inflation, relative comparisons are unaffected by the particular deflator used.

Chapter 2

1. An exception to the relative-employment story is the similarity of the relative-employment experience of less-educated workers in the United States and elsewhere. We will discuss this group extensively in later chapters.
2. According to the U.S. Bureau of Labor Statistics website (accessed October 15, 2001 on the World Wide Web at: *www.bls.gov*).
3. This evidence implies that, during a recession, the number of discouraged workers outweighs the number of so-called added workers who enter the labor force to make up for the income lost when other family members have been laid off. Note that the labor force

is defined as the sum of those with jobs (the "employed") and those who are actively seeking work (the "unemployed").

4. As we discuss later in this and subsequent chapters, there may be countervailing factors preventing a rise in the relative pay of the low skilled from causing a reduction in their relative employment.

5. Richard Freeman and Ronald Schettkat (2000) also make the case that what matters for measuring substitution on the demand side is relative-employment-to-population ratios (E/P) across groups rather than ratios of relative-unemployment rates (UR). Further, they show that absolute differences in unemployment rates are a better approximation of relative-demand effects than are ratios of unemployment rates. To see this, note that

$$E/P = (LF/P)(1 - UR),$$

where LF is the labor force, and UR is the fraction of the labor force that is unemployed. Then, if the labor-force-participation rate is fixed, and if UR is relatively small,

$$\ln(E/P) = k + \ln(1 - UR) \approx k - UR,$$

where $k = \ln(LF/P)$. Therefore, changes or differences in $\ln(E/P)$ are approximately the same magnitude as and opposite in sign to changes or differences in the unemployment rate (Freeman and Schettkat 2000, 15).

6. Our findings for the employment-to-population ratios were presented earlier in this chapter. For the share of the labor force that is employed (that is, 100 − unemployment rate), we find a youth–prime age ratio of 0.90 and 0.92 among men and 0.90 and 0.94 among women for the European Union and the United States, respectively.

7. Low education levels were defined as no formal qualifications in Germany, illiterate or primary schooling only in Spain, no qualifications in Sweden, no qualifications in the United Kingdom, and less than four years of high school (that is, less than a high school degree) in the United States. High education levels were defined as some post-upper-secondary education in Sweden and as a university degree everywhere else. For details, see Nickell and Layard (1999).

8. The definitions are mutually exclusive, so the category short-term workers does not include those who were employed by temporary-

help agencies or were on call. It also does not include those who were independent contractors or worked for a company that contracted out services. The latter two categories comprised 1.0 and 1.3 percent of workers, respectively (Houseman 2001). Note that the non-U.S. averages shown in the table differ from those cited earlier in the text (from Bentolila and Dolado 1994) for the European Community because the latter are employment weighted and include only the EC countries.

9. For earnings definitions and exclusions, see appendix table 2A.2. The source for the earnings information discussed here is an unpublished spreadsheet compiled by the OECD. We are grateful to Jonas Pontusson for his help in obtaining these data.

10. We use the PCE deflator rather than the CPI because the latter has come under fire in recent years due to its failure to account for consumer substitution adequately as well as for new products and improved product quality. According to a prestigious commission, these limitations result in an overestimation of the rate of inflation of 1.1 percent per year (Boskin et al. 1998). However, the methods used to construct this estimate have also been criticized (Abraham, Greenlees, and Moulton 1998). We, therefore, employ the PCE deflator, which is believed to do a better job of accounting for consumer substitution than the CPI does (Boskin et al. 1998). However, even the PCE deflator may incorrectly assess the extent of inflation, suggesting that we must be careful about making strong conclusions about the extent of real-wage changes. While there may be some controversy about the direction and magnitude of changes in U.S. real wages over this period, we are most interested in the behavior of real wages in the United States compared to that of other countries. As long as we use the same deflator for all countries, such relative comparisons are unaffected by the particular deflator used. Of course, index-number problems may still remain to the extent that U.S. weights are inappropriate for other countries. These issues will affect any comparison of real wages across countries.

11. Had we used the CPI, all our conclusions about absolute changes in real wages in table 2.11 would have been more pessimistic. For example, we would have concluded that, from 1979 to 1996, U.S. men's real wages fell 13 percent while U.S. women's real wages rose 6 percent.

12. We note that these measures of productivity differences can be somewhat noisy, particularly those on GDP per hour worked in

1994 and 1992, which come from different sources. For example, Australia's productivity per hour ranged from 79 (1994) to 93 (1992) percent of that in the United States, that of Italy ranged from 87 to 111 percent. Moreover, the purchasing-power correction undoubtedly lowers measured productivity in a country like Japan, which has a high cost of living.

13. The countries were Canada, Belgium, France, Germany, Italy, Japan, the Netherlands, Norway, Sweden, and the United Kingdom. See the BLS website (accessed October 15, 2001, on the World Wide Web at: *www.bls.gov*).

14. An additional factor that could conceivably explain higher or more rapidly growing U.S. wage inequality is that the employment-to-population ratio is higher in the United States and has been rising there relative to the other countries (see the discussion earlier in this chapter). We do not observe wage offers for those who are not employed, and such individuals constitute a larger and more rapidly growing portion of the population in other countries than in the United States. If the nonemployed are less skilled than are the employed, we observe a larger portion of the distribution of wage offers to low-skilled workers in the United States than in other countries. What appears to be higher wage inequality in the United States may simply reflect our greater ability to observe the bottom portion of the distribution of wage offers there. In our earlier work (Blau and Kahn 1996a, 2000a), we explicitly took account of this truncation problem in comparing U.S. wage inequality with that in other countries in the 1980s and the 1990s. In each case, we found that wage inequality among a comparably selected group of workers was much higher in the United States than in other countries. Thus, the differences in wage inequality between the United States and other countries shown in table 2.12 are likely to be qualitatively accurate representations of differences in the inequality of wage *offers* as well as observed wages.

15. In the United States, the 50–10 ratio was 28.1 percent higher than in other countries in 1989 to 1990, and the 90–50 ratio 16.7 percent higher. The 50–10 ratio was 32.7 percent higher than in the other countries in 1994 to 1998, and the 90–50 ratio 17.2 percent higher.

16. France is included in the list of countries for which we examine wage inequality (tables 2.12 and 2.13) but not wage levels (table 2.11). This is because the wage data for France are net of payroll taxes, which were considerable there, at 38.8 percent of wages during the period 1989 to 1994 (Nickell and Layard 1999, 3038).

Chapter 3

1. This discussion of recent trends is based on Harry Katz (1993), Per-Anders Edin and Bertil Holmlund (1995), Per-Anders Edin and Robert Topel (1997), and OECD (1989).
2. Recognizing the potential job losses to be incurred by the young if minimum-wage laws are enforced, several countries have instituted youth subminima (see Katz and Krueger 1992; Dolado et al. 1996; and OECD 1998b). As we discuss in chapter 6, evidence is mixed on the employment effects of minimum wages generally and the subminimum in particular.
3. Using the CPI, the 1998 value of the 1979 U.S. minimum wage was $6.51, or 26 percent above the actual 1998 minimum wage in real terms.
4. Note that, in many cases, the OECD figures reported in tables 3.4 to 3.6 understate the restrictions on employers' utilization of labor. For example, in Germany, collective-bargaining contracts place strict limitations on collective dismissals (Heseler and Mückenberger 1999).
5. Edward Lazear (1990) makes this theoretical argument but finds evidence suggesting that mandated severance pay does affect employment. His study suggests that the expected compensating differentials are either nonexistent or incomplete.
6. Several countries require that, after a particular duration of benefit collection, one must shift from the regular UI system to an alternative unemployment-assistance system, with, in many cases, an indefinite benefit duration. These unemployment-assistance systems typically are means tested and have an eligibility requirement that is usually independent of one's work history, unlike the regular UI programs (Gornick 1999, 58).

Chapter 4

1. For further discussions, see Laurence Ball (1997, 1999), Rebecca Blank and Richard Freeman (1994), Olivier Blanchard and Lawrence Summers (1986), or Richard Layard, Stephen Nickell, and R. Jackman (1991).
2. For a thorough discussion of various models of trade unionism, see Henry Farber (1986).
3. Of course, the payroll taxes that finance UI and other benefits may

restrain union wage demands since employer taxes shift the labor demand curve downward. We consider the overall effect of such taxes in more detail later in this chapter.

4. This notion goes back to Wassily Leontief (1946).

5. This framework assumes that union members are risk neutral, although the basic reasoning holds even if union members are risk averse. It is helpful to think of the firm as having some market power over its customers, which allows it to survive even if it is the only firm in the labor market that is unionized. To make the model more general, one can think of household production as the alternative activity of union members or of UI benefits as their alternative source of income in the event that they lose their jobs.

6. In general, economists expect that, as additional workers are added to a fixed amount of capital (that is, plant and equipment), the marginal product of labor will eventually decrease because each additional worker has less capital to work with than do previous workers.

7. However, Layard and Nickell (1990) point out that, even if unions raise the employment of particular bargaining units in these efficient bargains, the overall level of employment in the economy may still fall.

8. This is clearly true if UI benefits are financed out of income-tax revenues. In the more likely case in which payroll taxes pay for UI benefits, union members' incomes will be lowered to the extent that some of the taxes are shifted to wages, a likely outcome (see the discussion later in this chapter). Note that, where the UI system is experience rated, union members may be affected even in a decentralized system. However, the United States is virtually the only country with experience rating, and, even in the U.S. case, experience rating is imperfect, so the higher UI costs will to some extent be borne by other firms and their workers.

9. By *corporatism* is meant highly centralized, coordinated labor-management relations in which central labor and employer organizations, often in partnership with the government, have considerable authority to impose contract terms throughout the country.

10. A study by Jane Friesen (1996) of the effect of advance-notice and severance-pay mandates in Canada suggests that the assumption of less-than-complete adjustment of wages is realistic. Friesen finds that such protection lowers the starting wages of nonunion workers but not of union workers, which suggests that, at least for union workers, starting pay does not fully adjust in response to job protection. Of course, the negative effects on the initial wages of non-

union workers may or may not be fully offsetting with respect to the costs of protection. And, as noted in the previous chapter, Lazear's (1990) finding that mandated severance pay reduces employment also suggests less-than-complete adjustment of wages.

11.   The natural-experiment approach has become widely used in labor economics when examining the effect of policy changes, such as immigration, compulsory-school-attendance laws, or minimumwage laws. For a thorough discussion of the research-design issues associated with the approach, see Joshua Angrist and Alan Krueger (1999).

Chapter 5

1.   Because there can clearly be reverse causality from unemployment to spending on active labor market policy, Nickell and Layard instrumented this variable by using its predicted value based on the 1977 to 1979 unemployment rate, a period occurring well in advance of that included in their regressions.

2.   For an analysis of this issue, see Blanchard and Katz (1999).

3.   The existing literature on the effect of employment protection is largely inconclusive as to the issue of its effect on unemployment or overall employment, perhaps reflecting the theoretical ambiguity just discussed. Some authors find that protection raises unemployment, while others find that it has no effect. Results appear to be sensitive to econometric technique. For cross-national studies, see Lazear (1990), John Addison and Jean-Luc Grosso (1996), and John Addison, Paulino Teixeira, and Jean-Luc Grosso (2000). Among single-country studies, Jennifer Hunt (2000) finds that Germany's 1985 reduction of firing costs had little effect on employment adjustment. However, Dertouzos and Karoly (1993) found that, in the United States, states whose courts permitted workers to sue for wrongful discharge had lower employment growth after these court decisions, all else equal. While this latter finding suggests that firing costs lower employment, it is also possible that other aspects of a state's legal structure and environment could have been contributing factors.

4.   That is, the antilog of the other-country average log unemployment rate is 7.0 percent, which is about 13 percent higher than the U.S. rate of 6.2 percent.

5.   While the United States has higher levels of home ownership, it also has higher rates of labor mobility (Bertola 1998), so one may

question whether the homeownership difference really raises the U.S. unemployment rate compared to that in other countries. Following the logic of Oswald's (1996) argument, however, labor mobility in the United States would be even higher if the United States had a smaller incidence of owner-occupied housing.

6. This estimate assumes that labor taxes and inflation stay the same, so, in order to increase spending on active labor-market policies, we would need to reallocate some government spending or raise nonlabor taxes. Implicitly, such a reallocation is already accounted for in the coefficient on active labor-market policies since the regression controls for the change in inflation and labor taxes.

7. Nickell and Layard (1999) also examined the determinants of productivity growth from 1976 to 1992. They found that, after controlling for where a country stood relative to the United States in 1976, institutions were not important factors explaining international differences in productivity growth. This finding implies that the slower rate of U.S. productivity growth, which we documented in chapter 2, is largely a catching-up phenomenon for the other countries. Moreover, the recent rise in U.S. productivity growth in the 1990s, both absolutely and relative to other countries, could be a significant new development.

8. While the Japanese economy has been hard hit by the Asian crisis that began in the late 1990s, its unemployment rate has remained low by international standards. Although its measured unemployment rate may mask considerable underemployment, it is still noteworthy that Japan was able to keep measured unemployment down to 4 to 5 percent of its labor force.

9. We thank Olivier Blanchard and Justin Wolfers for graciously making available the data and programs used in Blanchard and Wolfers (2000), which we built on to conduct the analyses reported here.

10. While one might also consider the oil shocks to be worthy of inclusion, their effect may be subsumed by the TFP change. Moreover, Blanchard and Wolfers (2000) show that the magnitude of the effect of the TFP slowdown on labor markets dwarfs that of the oil shocks.

11. If there is an aggregate Cobb-Douglas production function, shifts in labor share track shifts in labor demand. Note that the labor-share measure is adjusted so that it is purged of the effects of factor prices in the presence of a low elasticity of substitution in the short run (Blanchard and Wolfers 2000).

12. This equilibrium unemployment rate is best thought of as a kind of medium-term equilibrium that corresponds to a particular set of

macroeconomic shocks and a constant inflation rate (Blanchard 1997; Blanchard and Wolfers 2000). How long it takes the economy to adjust to changes in TFP growth, real interest rates, and labor-demand shifts (the major shocks considered here) is an empirical question.

13. For details on the specification of the interaction model, see the notes to table 5A.1. Following Blanchard and Wolfers (2000), we interact a linear combination of the shocks with each institution, rather than each shock individually, in order to estimate a relatively parsimonious model, given limited degrees of freedom.

14. When Blanchard and Wolfers (2000) tried to account for changing institutions, their results became worse. However, we have augmented their list of changing institutions and obtain stronger results from specifications that allow institutions to change.

15. The countries are Australia, Canada, Finland, France, Italy, Japan, Spain, Sweden, and the United Kingdom.

16. The additional countries are Belgium, Denmark, Ireland, the Netherlands, New Zealand, Norway, Portugal, and West Germany. Each country is included for the time period(s) for which data are available.

17. In the linear combination of the shocks, the weights are the main effects of each shock.

18. In such models (that is, excluding period effects), the coefficient on birth/population is negative and insignificant.

19. The effect of employment protection contrasts with Nickell and Layard's (1999) insignificant main effect for the periods 1983 to 1988 and 1989 to 1994. Our findings suggest that, with high levels of unemployment-inducing shocks, protection has a larger effect on unemployment than it does with low levels of these shocks. Whether this is due to reduced hiring or more-aggressive union wage-setting behavior is an open question.

20. To compute the non-U.S. averages in table 5.3, we took the averages of the changes in the individual predicted unemployment rates among the non-U.S. countries. We take this average, rather than merely predicting the change in non-U.S. unemployment evaluated at the intercountry average values of the changes in the explanatory variables, because of the nonlinearity of the interactions model.

21. As mentioned earlier, it is possible that institutions affect macroeconomic policy responses. For example, highly unionized economies may have a different monetary-policy response to global events than less highly unionized economies do (see Cukierman

and Lippi 1999 and the references cited therein, as well as Iversen, Pontusson, and Soskice 1998). This issue is considered in greater detail in Bertola, Blau, and Kahn (2002).

22. Even the shocks-interactions model, however, underpredicts the 1970 to 1996 divergence between unemployment in the United States and that elsewhere. Recall that the Nickell and Layard (1999) model overpredicts the degree to which other countries' unemployment rates exceed that in the United States in the period 1989 to 1994. These two conclusions are not necessarily contradictory since the former examines levels at one period in time while the latter examines changes over time.

23. For details on these data, see Bertola, Blau, and Kahn (2002).

24. We thank Jonas Pontusson and David Rueda for providing additional union-density data beyond that available in Visser (1996).

25. There were some individual exceptions to the pattern suggested by the nine-country average. Benefit systems became less generous in the 1980s and 1990s in specific countries such as the Netherlands and the United Kingdom (Nickell and van Ours 2000), and collective-bargaining coverage fell dramatically after 1980 in the United Kingdom (OECD 1997) and after 1991 in New Zealand (Maloney 1994).

26. The coordination measure clearly does not take into account the fact that, even in the United States, bargaining became less coordinated in the 1980s and 1990s (Katz 1993).

27. Country dummies were included in the regressions, so the effect of institutions reflects only the effect of changes within countries. Period effects were not included in order to give shocks their best chance of explaining the results, although the findings were not greatly affected by including period dummies. The main effects of the institutions are typically positive, as one would expect (recall that the effects of employment protection are theoretically ambiguous), although the interaction effects are mixed.

28. These are the same twenty countries used in Nickell and Layard's (1999) study (see table 5.1).

29. Questions of endogeneity arise here, as they also do in Blanchard and Wolfers's (2000) framework. Specifically, increases in the natural rate may affect macro policy. As Gregory Mankiw (1999) argues in his comments on Ball (1999), a falling natural rate may enable the government to pursue a more-expansionary monetary policy. The regression results that show a negative effect of inflation on the natural rate may, thus, reflect the effect of the natural rate on inflation. Note that Blanchard and Wolfers's (2000) analysis of the actual

unemployment rate implies the opposite reverse-causality bias from the one that Mankiw (1999) emphasizes. When the actual unemployment falls relative to the natural rate, we expect compensating monetary policy.

30. Ball estimated regression specifications for models in which UI benefits were interacted with the inflation variables one at a time and for models in which interactions of UI benefits are interacted with both inflation variables but no UI-benefit main effect is included.

31. When we estimated a model including only the inflation variables and a UI duration main effect, we explained 57 percent of the U.S.-other country difference. Thus, interactions between UI and macro shocks are very important in raising the explanatory power to 95 percent, although UI duration is also important in its own right.

Chapter 6

1. Recent work by political scientists using macro-level data finds that union coverage and the centralization of wage setting are associated with lower wage inequality, other things equal, a result that is consistent with the studies using micro data that we review later in this chapter (see Rueda, Way, and Pontusson 1998; and Wallerstein 1999).

2. This framework was developed by Chinhui Juhn, Kevin M. Murphy, and Brooks Pierce (1993) in their study of changes in U.S. wage inequality from the 1960s to the 1980s.

3. In addition, this unexplained portion of international differences in wage inequality includes differences in the distribution of measurement errors.

4. Union-membership information was not available for Australia, Italy, or Sweden. In each case, a U.S. wage equation was estimated that had the same explanatory variables as were available for the country in question, allowing for comparisons of the pay structure between the United States and each of the other countries.

5. In performing the decomposition, we used the U.S. wage coefficients and residual distribution to obtain the measured-characteristics effect and the other-country distribution of measured characteristics to obtain the wage-coefficients and wage-equation-residual effects. It would also be possible to perform the decomposition using the opposite set of weights (that is, evaluating the U.S.–other-country difference in measured characteristics at the other country's

wage equation and residual distribution and the wage coefficients and wage residual effects at the U.S. distribution of personal characteristics). When we used these opposite weights, we obtained results very similar to those presented in table 6.1. The decomposition is described in greater detail in Francine Blau and Lawrence Kahn (1996a).

6. While union status is treated here (see table 6.1, panel B) as a measured characteristic, it could be considered part of the wage-setting institutions. The effects of collective bargaining are discussed in more detail later in this chapter.

7. For example, while several have argued that at least a portion of these wage differentials represents unequal pay for equally qualified workers, that is, efficiency wages (Krueger and Summers 1988; Gibbons and Katz 1992), others argue that such wage differentials are largely caused by unmeasured differences in labor quality (Murphy and Topel 1990).

8. For further details on the technique employed to estimate these effects and consideration of related methodological issues, see Krueger and Summers (1988), John Haisken-DeNew and Christoph Schmidt (1997), and Kahn (1998b).

9. For further description of the IALS, see OECD (1998c).

10. All reported correlations are based on calculations using sampling weights.

11. In addition to the countries listed in table 6.3, the IALS collected test-score data for Germany, Northern Ireland, and Poland, and data on earnings were available in the IALS for Germany and Poland. We excluded Germany because, in our version of the IALS data, the sample size was extremely small for cases in which earnings data were available, no distinction was made between East and West Germany, and the earnings distributions that we obtained were not comparable to those available from other sources. We excluded Poland because of its status as a transition economy. We show test scores for Britain alone rather than including Northern Ireland in order to have a more homogeneous sample.

12. These standard deviations are computed on the pooled men's and women's regression samples, where each country is given the same weight. That is, each individual is given a weight of $s/(Ns_a)$, where s is the individual's sampling weight, N is the sample size for the individual's country, and s_a is the average sampling weight for the individual's country. The standard-deviation effects reported in the text correspond to log wage coefficients on education for the United States of 0.0469 (men) and 0.0744 (women) and averages for the non-U.S. countries of 0.0181 (men) and 0.0290 (women).

13. Similar results are reported by Dan Devroye and Richard Freeman (2001).

14. Unfortunately, the IALS does not have consistent information on race or ethnicity across countries, so we were not able to control for this factor.

15. This correction is similar in spirit to that used by Hunt (forthcoming).

16. Much of this higher U.S. union-nonunion wage differential is due to a higher ceteris paribus (other things equal) U.S. union-nonunion wage gap rather than to differences in the personal characteristics of union and nonunion workers (Blanchflower and Freeman 1992; Blanchflower 1996). Thus, a strong causal role for the industrial-relations system is suggested.

17. This will be the case if union "threat" effects dominate any negative "crowding" effects in the nonunion sector caused by the adverse employment effects of unionism. Lawrence Kahn and Michael Curme (1987) found that, other things equal, nonunion wage dispersion in the United States was lower in highly unionized than in less-unionized industries.

18. For further details on this method of decomposing the variance, see Freeman (1980), where it was used to assess the role of unionism in U.S. wage inequality; Blau and Kahn (1996a), where it was used to compare wage inequality in the United States with that in several other countries; or Juhn, Murphy, and Pierce (1993), where it was used to measure the effect of industry on wage inequality in the United States.

19. The decomposition in table 6.5 uses specific weights in order to exhaust the U.S.–other-country differential in log wage variance. For example, the first term uses the U.S. union and nonunion employment proportions to weight the within-sector wage variances, while the within-sector employment term uses the other-country within-sector wage variances to weight the U.S.–other-country differences in union density, and so on. We obtained very similar results when we used an alternative set of weights composed of other-country union- and nonunion-employment proportions for the first term, the U.S. within-sector variances for the second term, and so on.

20. These countries include Australia, Italy, the United Kingdom, the United States, and West Germany (Katz 1993).

21. The fact that the 1980 to 1983 recession was weaker than the 1987 to 1991 slump could have contributed to the worse employment outcome for less-educated workers in the latter period.

22. Sylvia Dixon (1998) did not report evidence on changes in residual inequality for the subperiods 1984 to 1990 or 1990 to 1997.

23. This is much larger than the effect of union density of 5 percent implied by the results reported in table 6.5 if we sum the within-sector and the between-sector composition effects for men. One way to view this difference is that Lemieux's estimate allows for an effect of union density on within-sector wage dispersion but that the accounting in table 6.5 holds within-sector wage dispersion constant in estimating the effect of union density. Comparing the two estimates suggests a sizable effect of union density on within-sector wage dispersion. Lemieux did not present results for women.

24. In a related study, John DiNardo and Thomas Lemieux (1997) attempted to explain Canada's slower growth in men's log wage inequality compared to that in the United States over the period 1981 to 1988. Using a methodology similar to that employed by John DiNardo, Nicole Fortin, and Thomas Lemieux (1996), DiNardo and Lemieux attributed about one-third of Canada's slower increase in the log wage variance of men to the combined effects of its greater unionization rate and its more-equalizing union pay effects; another third was attributed to the declining real value of the minimum wage in the United States. Again, institutions were important in explaining the different outcomes in Canada and the United States.

25. An exception is Alida Castillo-Freeman and Richard Freeman's (1992) study of the U.S. decision to bring minimum-wage coverage to Puerto Rico starting in 1974. By 1988, about 28 percent of workers in Puerto Rico were paid within 5 cents of the U.S. minimum wage of $3.35 per hour; on the mainland, roughly 25 percent of teenagers were paid within 5 cents of the minimum at this time (Card and Krueger 1995). And, in 1987, the U.S. minimum wage was about 63 percent of the average manufacturing wage in Puerto Rico but only 34 percent on the mainland. Thus, the high minimum in Puerto Rico had the potential greatly to disrupt its labor market. Castillo-Freeman and Freeman (1992), in fact, find large disemployment effects, but Krueger (1995) finds that this result is very sensitive to econometric issues such as weighting.

26. That is, in most cases, a small, statistically insignificant effect whose standard errors make an effect that is large in magnitude unlikely.

27. The countries were Austria, Denmark, Finland, France, Germany, Italy, the Netherlands, Portugal, Switzerland, and the United Kingdom.

28. The demand index was essentially a measure of the degree to which the industrial structure of the country changed favorably with respect to a particular education group.

29. Data were not available for each country for every year.

30. As noted earlier, the skill groups were chosen to comprise thirds of the distribution of individuals pooled across countries. Therefore, in a particular country, the size of, for example, the low-skilled men's group can deviate from one-third of the country's male population.

31. This point applies most strongly if layoffs are randomly distributed. In fact, in the United States, layoffs are distributed by inverse seniority. So the European system could actually increase the probability of income loss for more senior workers while providing considerably more income insurance for junior workers.

32. This is, in fact, likely to be an additional reason (besides less-generous UI systems) for a shorter duration of unemployment in the United States.

33. For discussions of public-sector employment, see Anders Björklund and Richard Freeman (1997), Edin and Topel (1997), Blank (1994), Blau and Kahn (2000b), and Kahn (1998a). Data discussed in chapter 3 show a lower incidence of public-sector employment in the United States than elsewhere, while, in 1991, the United States ranked last among twenty OECD countries in relative spending on active labor-market programs.

34. The positive effects of unions on enrollment suggest the possibility that higher education subsidies in heavily unionized economies could be responsible for both the enrollment and the employment effects obtained for young men. However, when Kahn (2000) excluded the enrolled from the analysis of employment, he still found that unionization and collective bargaining were associated with lower relative employment among both young men and young women. In addition, since categories in the ISSP are meant to capture an individual's major activity, that of school enrollment is not likely to include those in dual apprenticeship programs if they are also currently employed, as is common in Germany. Thus, the positive effects of collective bargaining on school attendance are not being driven solely by the high incidence of apprenticeship in highly unionized countries like Austria and Germany.

Chapter 7

1. Later in this chapter we consider evidence on these employment effects.

2. Switzerland incorporated the principle of equal pay for work of equal value into its constitution in 1981 (Simona 1985), but there is no indication that it has been implemented as yet. And, in 1991,

Ontario required virtually all employers to practice the principles of comparable worth, but other Canadian provinces did not pass such legislation (Gunderson and Robb 1991).

3. Waldfogel (1998a) finds that this conclusion holds even when data on total actual experience are available and experience is controlled for. Thus, in this context, the family penalty could reflect the loss of seniority (as just argued) or a lower quality of work experience among women with children.

4. An example of this is provided by the case of Australia, where the adoption of comparable worth by the labor courts produced a rapid increase in the gender earnings ratio (for example, Gregory and Daly 1991; Killingsworth 1990).

5. These estimates come from OECD (1998a), and they do not include time spent in apprentice training programs. These programs are more prevalent in countries like Germany than in the United States, and men are far more likely to participate in them than are women (Blau and Kahn 2000b). Thus, focusing on formal education alone understates the shortfall in women's schooling in countries such as Germany.

6. The index of segregation is calculated as $\frac{1}{2}\Sigma_i |m_i - f_i|$, where m_i = the percentage of all male workers employed in occupation i, and f_i = the percentage of all female workers employed in occupation i. Examples of the seventy-five occupations that Anker (1998) used include jurist, teacher, mail clerk, and protective-service worker.

7. For details on the wage data in the ISSP, see Blau and Kahn (forthcoming).

8. For each country, the average female percentile is obtained by assigning each woman a percentile ranking of her wage in the *male* wage distribution and then finding the female mean of these percentiles.

9. For details, see Blau and Kahn (1996b, forthcoming).

10. For each country, the adjusted wage ratio is $\exp(X_f\beta_f)/\exp(X_f\beta_m)$, where X_f is a vector of means of the explanatory variables for women, and β_m and β_f are vectors of estimated coefficients from log wage regressions estimated for men and women separately.

11. For each country, the mean female percentile in the male residual distribution is obtained by assigning each woman a percentile ranking of her wage residual (from the male wage regression) in the distribution of male wage residuals (from the male wage regression) and finding the female mean of these percentiles. The residual is defined as a woman's actual log wage minus her predicted log wage based on the male wage regression.

12. This potential problem was noted by Juhn, Murphy, and Pierce (1991), as well as by Blau and Kahn (1992, 1995, 1996b), and is discussed formally by Wing Suen (1997).

13. For evidence on the effect of occupational segregation, see, for example, Elaine Sorensen (1990) and David Macpherson and Barry Hirsch (1995). For evidence on the importance of firm segregation, see, for example, Blau (1977), Erica Groshen (1991), and Kimberly Bayard et al. (1999). The latter study found a larger role for within-firm and -industry pay gaps, but it used more aggregated occupation categories than did the other two.

14. Specifically, over the period 1985 to 1994, for Western countries (Australia, Austria, Britain, Canada, Ireland, Israel, Italy, Japan, the Netherlands, New Zealand, Norway, Sweden, Switzerland, the United States, and western Germany), the coefficient on the male log standard deviation in an equation with the average female percentile as dependent variable was -2.180 (standard error $=$ 17.117), while, for Eastern countries or regions (Bulgaria, the Czech Republic, eastern Germany, Hungary, Poland, Russia, and Slovenia), it was 14.514 (standard error $=$ 15.859).

15. The countries included were Australia, Austria, Britain, Canada, Ireland, Israel, Italy, Japan, the Netherlands, New Zealand, Norway, Sweden, Switzerland, the United States and western Germany as well as the following Eastern European countries or regions: Bulgaria, the Czech Republic, eastern Germany, Hungary, Poland, Russia, and Slovenia.

16. For further discussion of the implementation of comparable worth, see Robert Gregory and Anne Daly (1991), Mark Killingsworth (1990), or Morley Gunderson and Roberta Robb (1991).

17. Shortly, we will discuss an alternative view of employment responses to mandated wage increases in the presence of employer monopsony (Manning 1996).

18. Mark Meitzen (1986) also analyzed U.S. data on men's and women's quit behavior. However, he included several measures of pay (for example, starting wages, top pay level in the job, market wages), and men's and women's relative responsiveness differed by type of pay variable; thus, his results do not allow one to determine which group's labor supply is more sensitive to wages overall.

Chapter 8

1. This information on the EITC is taken from the Internal Revenue Service website (*www.irs.gov*).

2. Nada Eissa and Jeffrey Liebman (1996) find modest positive effects of the EITC on the labor supply of female household heads in the 1980s.
3. James Heckman (1999) makes an especially forceful case for greater investment in early-intervention programs.

———— References ————

Abowd, John M., Francis Kramarz, Thomas Lemieux, and David Margolis. 2000. "Minimum Wages and Youth Unemployment in France and the U.S." In *Youth Employment and Joblessness in Advanced Countries,* edited by David G. Blanchflower and Richard B. Freeman, 427–72. Chicago: University of Chicago Press.

Abraham, Katharine G., John S. Greenlees, and Brent R. Moulton. 1998. "Working to Improve the Consumer Price Index." *Journal of Economic Perspectives* 12(1): 27–36.

Abraham, Katharine G., and Susan N. Houseman. 1994. "Does Employment Protection Inhibit Labor Market Flexibility? Lessons from Germany, France, and Belgium." In *Social Protection versus Economic Flexibility,* edited by Rebecca Blank and Richard B. Freeman, 59–93. Chicago: University of Chicago Press.

———. 1995. "Earnings Inequality in Germany." In *Differences and Changes in Wage Structures,* edited by Richard B. Freeman and Lawrence F. Katz, 371–403. Chicago: University of Chicago Press.

Abraham, Katharine G., and James L. Medoff. 1985. "Length of Service and Promotions in Union and Nonunion Work Groups." *Industrial and Labor Relations Review* 38(3): 408–20.

Addison, John T., and Jean-Luc Grosso. 1996. "Job Security Provisions and Employment: Revised Estimates." *Industrial Relations* 35(4): 585–603.

Addison, John T., Paulino Teixeira, and Jean-Luc Grosso. 2000. "The Effect of Dismissals Protection on Employment: More on a Vexed Theme." *Southern Economic Journal* 67(1): 105–22.

Agell, Jonas, and Kjell Erik Lommerud. 1992. "Union Egalitarianism as Income Insurance." *Economica* 59(August): 295–310.

———. 1997. "Minimum Wages and the Incentives for Skill Formation." *Journal of Public Economics* 64(1): 25–40.

Albaek, Karsten, Mahmood Arai, Rita Asplund, Erling Barth, and Strøjer Marsden. 1996. "Inter-Industry Wage Differentials in the Nordic Coun-

285

tries." In *Wage Differentials in the Nordic Countries,* edited by Niels Westergård-Nielsen. Amsterdam: North-Holland.

Allen, Steven G., Adriana Cassoni, and Gaston J. Labadie. 1996. "Wages and Employment after Reunionization in Uruguay." *Cauadernos de economia* 33(August): 277–93.

Angrist, Joshua D., and Alan B. Krueger. 1999. "Empirical Strategies in Labor Economics." In *Handbook of Labor Economics,* edited by Orley C. Ashenfelter and David Card, 3A: 1277–1366. Amsterdam: Elsevier.

Anker, Richard. 1998. *Gender and Jobs: Sex Segregation of Occupations in the World.* Geneva: International Labour Organization.

Atkinson, Anthony B., and John Micklewright. 1991. "Unemployment Compensation and Labor Market Transitions: A Critical Review." *Journal of Economic Literature* 29(4): 1679–1727.

Baker, Michael, Dwayne Benjamin, and Shuchita Stanger. 1999. "The Highs and Lows of the Minimum Wage Effect: A Time-Series Cross-Section Study of the Canadian Law." *Journal of Labor Economics* 17(2): 318–50.

Ball, Laurence. 1997. "Disinflation and the NAIRU." In *Reducing Inflation: Motivation and Strategy,* edited by Christina Romer and David Romer, 167–85. Chicago: University of Chicago Press.

———. 1999. "Aggregate Demand and Long-Term Unemployment." *Brookings Papers on Economic Activity* (2): 189–251.

Barth, Erling, and Harald Dale-Olsen. 1999. "Monopsonistic Discrimination and the Gender Wage Gap." *NBER* working paper no. 7197. Cambridge, Mass.: National Bureau of Economic Research, June.

Barth, Erling, and Josef Zweimüller. 1992. "Labour Market Institutions and the Industry Wage Distribution: Evidence from Austria, Norway, and the U.S." *Empirica—Austrian Economic Papers* 19(2): 181–201.

Bayard, Kimberly, Judith Hellerstein, David Neumark, and Kenneth Troske. 1999. "New Evidence on Sex Segregation and Sex Differences in Wages from Matched Employee-Employer Data." *NBER* working paper no. 7003. Cambridge, Mass.: National Bureau of Economic Research, March.

Beller, Andrea H. 1979. "The Impact of Equal Employment Opportunity Laws on the Male/Female Earnings Differential." In *Women in the Labor Market,* edited by Cynthia B. Lloyd, Emily Andrews, and Curtis Gilroy. New York: Columbia University Press.

Bentolila, Samuel, and Juan Dolado. 1994. "Labour Flexibility and Wages: Lessons from Spain." *Economic Policy* (18): 53–99.

Bertola, Giuseppe. 1992. "Labor Turnover Costs and Average Labor Demand." *Journal of Labor Economics* 10(4): 389–411.

———. 1998. "Labor Demand, Institutions, and Tenure Lengths." *European University Institute* working paper.

———. 1999. "Microeconomic Perspectives on Aggregate Labor Markets." In *Handbook of Labor Economics,* edited by Orley C. Ashenfelter and David Card, 3C: 2985–3028. Amsterdam: Elsevier.

Bertola, Giuseppe, Francine D. Blau, and Lawrence M. Kahn. 2002. "Comparative Analysis of Labor-Market Outcomes: Lessons for the United States from International Long-Run Evidence." In *The Roaring Nineties: Can Full Employment Be Sustained?,* edited by Alan B. Krueger and Robert Solow. New York: Russell Sage Foundation.

Bewley, Truman F. 1999. *Why Wages Don't Fall During a Recession.* Cambridge, Mass.: Harvard University Press.

Björklund, Anders, and Richard B. Freeman. 1997. "Generating Equality and Eliminating Poverty, the Swedish Way." In *The Welfare State in Transition: Reforming the Swedish Model,* edited by Richard B. Freeman, Robert Topel, and Birgitta Swedenborg, 33–78. Chicago: University of Chicago Press.

Blackburn, McKinley L., and David E. Bloom. 1993. "The Distribution of Family Income: Measuring and Explaining Changes in the 1980s for Canada and the United States." In *Small Differences That Matter,* edited by David Card and Richard B. Freeman, 233–65. Chicago: University of Chicago Press.

Blanchard, Olivier Jean. 1997. "The Medium Run." *Brookings Papers on Economic Activity* (2): 89–141.

Blanchard, Olivier Jean, and Lawrence F. Katz. 1999. "Wage Dynamics: Reconciling Theory and Evidence." *American Economic Review* 89(2): 69–74.

Blanchard, Olivier, and Pedro Portugal. 2000. "What Hides behind an Unemployment Rate: Comparing Portuguese and U.S. Labor Markets." Unpublished paper. Massachusetts Institute of Technology, April.

Blanchard, Olivier Jean, and Lawrence H. Summers. 1986. "Hysteresis and the European Unemployment Problem." *NBER Macroeconomics Annual,* 15–78.

Blanchard, Olivier Jean, and Justin Wolfers. 2000. "The Role of Shocks and Institutions in the Rise of European Unemployment: The Aggregate Evidence." *Economic Journal* 110(March): 1–33.

Blanchflower, David G. 1996. "The Role and Influence of Trade Unions in the OECD." Working paper. Dartmouth College, September.

Blanchflower, David G., and Richard B. Freeman. 1992. "Unionism in the U.S. and Other Advanced OECD Countries." *Industrial Relations* 31(1): 56–79.

———. 1994. "Did the Thatcher Reforms Change British Labour Performance?" In *The U.K. Labour Market: Comparative Aspects and Institutional Developments,* edited by Ray Barrell, 51–92. Cambridge: Cambridge University Press.

———, eds. 2000. *Youth Employment and Joblessness in Advanced Countries.* Chicago: University of Chicago Press.

Blank, Rebecca M., ed. 1994. *Social Protection Versus Economic Flexibility.* Chicago: University of Chicago Press.

———. 1997. "Is There a Trade-Off between Unemployment and Inequality? No Easy Answers: Labor Market Problems in the United States versus Europe." *Levy Economics Institute* public policy brief no. 33. Annandale-on-Hudson, N.Y.: Levy Economics Institute.

Blank, Rebecca M., and Richard B. Freeman. 1994. "Evaluating the Connection between Social Protection and Economic Flexibility." In *Social Protection versus Economic Flexibility,* edited by Rebecca M. Blank, 21–41. Chicago: University of Chicago Press.

Blau, Francine D. 1977. *Equal Pay in the Office.* Lexington, Mass.: Lexington.

Blau, Francine D., and Andrea H. Beller. 1988. "Trends in Earnings Differentials by Gender: 1971–1981." *Industrial and Labor Relations Review* 41(4): 513–29.

Blau, Francine D., and Marianne A. Ferber. 1992. *The Economics of Women, Men, and Work.* 2d ed. Englewood Cliffs, N.J.: Prentice-Hall.

Blau, Francine D., Marianne A. Ferber, and Anne E. Winkler. 1998. *The Economics of Women, Men, and Work.* 3d ed. Englewood Cliffs, N.J.: Prentice-Hall.

Blau, Francine D., and Lawrence M. Kahn. 1981. "Race and Sex Differences in Quitting by Young Workers." *Industrial and Labor Relations Review* 34(4): 563–77.

———. 1992. "The Gender Earnings Gap: Learning from International Comparisons." *American Economic Review* 82(2): 533–38.

———. 1995. "The Gender Earnings Gap: Some International Evidence." In *Differences and Changes in Wage Structures,* edited by Richard B. Freeman and Lawrence F. Katz, 105–43. Chicago: University of Chicago Press.

———. 1996a. "International Differences in Male Wage Inequality: Institutions versus Market Forces." *Journal of Political Economy* 104(4): 791–837.

———. 1996b. "Wage Structure and Gender Earnings Differentials: An International Comparison." *Economica* 63(May): S29–S62.

———. 1997. "Swimming Upstream: Trends in the Gender Wage Differential in the 1980s." *Journal of Labor Economics* 15(1, pt. 1): 1–42.

————. 1999. "Institutions and Laws in the Labor Market." In *Handbook of Labor Economics,* edited by Orley C. Ashenfelter and David Card, 3A: 1399–1461. Amsterdam: Elsevier.

————. 2000a. "Do Cognitive Test Scores Explain Higher U.S. Wage Inequality?" Working paper. Cornell University, June.

————. 2000b. "Gender and Youth Employment Outcomes: The U.S. and West Germany, 1984–1991." In *Youth Unemployment and Joblessness in Advanced Countries,* edited by David G. Blanchflower and Richard B. Freeman, 107–67. Chicago: University of Chicago Press.

————. 2000c. "Gender Differences in Pay." *Journal of Economic Perspectives* 14(fall): 75–99.

————. Forthcoming. "Understanding International Differences in the Gender Pay Gap." *Journal of Labor Economics.*

Blöndal, Sveinbjörn, and Mark Pearson. 1995. "Unemployment and Other Non-Employment Benefits." *Oxford Review of Economic Policy* 11(1): 136–69.

Boskin, Michael J., Ellen R. Dulberger, Robert J. Gordon, Zvi Griliches, and Dale W. Jorgenson. 1998. "Consumer Prices, the Consumer Price Index, and the Cost of Living." *Journal of Economic Perspectives* 12(1): 3–26.

Brown, Charles. 1999. "Minimum Wages, Employment, and the Distribution of Income." In *Handbook of Labor Economics,* edited by Orley C. Ashenfelter and David Card, 3B: 2101–63. Amsterdam: Elsevier.

Brown, Charles, and James L. Medoff. 1989. "The Employer Size Wage Effect." *Journal of Political Economy* 97(5): 1027–59.

Brunello, Giorgio, Simona Comi, and Claudio Lucifora. 2000. "The College Wage Gap in Ten European Countries: Evidence from Two Cohorts." Unpublished paper. University of Padova, October.

Bulow, Jeremy, and Lawrence Summers. 1986. "A Theory of Dual Labor Markets with Application to Industrial Policy, Discrimination, and Keynesian Unemployment." *Journal of Labor Economics* 4(3, pt. 1): 376–414.

Burkhauser, Richard V., Kenneth A. Couch, and David C. Wittenburg. 2000. "A Reassessment of the New Economics of the Minimum Wage Literature with Monthly Data from the Current Population Survey." *Journal of Labor Economics* 18(4): 653–80.

Burkhauser, Richard V., Douglas Holtz-Eakin, and Stephen E. Rhody. 1997. "Labor Earnings Mobility and Inequality in the United States and Germany during the Growth Years of the 1980s." *NBER* working paper 5988. Cambridge, Mass.: National Bureau of Economic Research.

Calmfors, Lars. 1993. "Centralisation of Wage Bargaining and Macroeconomic Performance—a Survey." *OECD Economic Studies* (21): 161–91.

Calmfors, Lars, and John Driffill. 1988. "Centralization of Wage Bargaining." *Economic Policy* (3): 14–61.

Calmfors, Lars, and Anders Forslund. 1991. "Real Wage Determination and Labour Market Policies: The Swedish Experience." *Economic Journal* 101(September): 1130–48.

Card, David. 1999. "The Causal Effect of Education on Earnings." In *Handbook of Labor Economics*, edited by Orley C. Ashenfelter and David Card, 3A: 1801–63. Amsterdam: Elsevier.

Card, David, Lawrence F. Katz, and Alan B. Krueger. 1994. "Employment Effects of Minimum and Subminimum Wages: Panel Data on State Minimum Wage Laws: Comment." *Industrial and Labor Relations Review* 47(3): 487–97.

Card, David, Francis Kramarz, and Thomas Lemieux. 1999. "Changes in the Relative Structure of Wages and Employment: A Comparison of the United States, Canada, and France." *Canadian Journal of Economics* 32(4): 843–77.

Card, David, and Alan B. Krueger. 1995. *Myth and Measurement: The New Economics of the Minimum Wage.* Princeton, N.J.: Princeton University Press.

———. 2000. "Minimum Wages and Employment: A Case Study of the Fast-Food Industry in New Jersey and Pennsylvania: Reply." *American Economic Review* 90(5): 1397–1420.

Carrington, William J., and Kenneth R. Troske. 1995. "Gender Segregation in Small Firms." *Journal of Human Resources* 30(3): 503–33.

Castillo-Freeman, Alida, and Richard B. Freeman. 1992. "When the Minimum Wage Really Bites: The Effect of the U.S. Level Minimum on Puerto Rico." In *Immigration and the Work Force,* edited by George J. Borjas and Richard B. Freeman, 177–211. Chicago: University of Chicago Press.

Cowen, Penelope J. Brook. 1993. "Labor Relations Reform in New Zealand: The Employment Contracts Act and Contractual Freedom." *Journal of Labor Research* 14(1): 69–83.

Crafts, N. F. R. 1997. "Economic Growth in East Asia and Western Europe since 1950: Implications for Living Standards." *National Institute Economic Review* 162(October): 75–84.

Crawford, Aaron, Raymond Harbridge, and Pat Walsh. 1999. "Unions and Union Membership in New Zealand: Annual Review for 1998." *New Zealand Journal of Industrial Relations* 24(3): 383–95.

Cukierman, Alex, and Francesco Lippi. 1999. "Central Bank Independence, Centralization of Wage Bargaining, Inflation, and Unemployment: Theory and Some Evidence." *European Economic Review* 43(7): 1395–1434.

Danthine, Jean-Pierre, and Jennifer Hunt. 1994. "Wage Bargaining Structure, Employment, and Economic Integration." *Economic Journal* 104(May): 528–41.

Daveri, Francesco, and Guido Tabellini. 2000. "Unemployment, Growth, and Taxation in Industrial Countries." *Economic Policy* (30): 47–88.

Davis, Steven J., and John Haltiwanger. 1991. "Wage Dispersion between and within U.S. Manufacturing Plants." *Brookings Papers on Economic Activity: Microeconomics*: 115–80.

———. 1999. "Gross Job Flows." In *Handbook of Labor Economics,* edited by Orley C. Ashenfelter and David Card, 3B: 2711–2805. Amsterdam: Elsevier.

Davis, Steven J., and Magnus Henrekson. 1997. "Explaining National Differences in the Size and Industry Distribution of Employment." Working paper. University of Chicago, Graduate School of Business, August.

———. 2000. "Wage-Setting Institutions as Industrial Policy." *NBER* working paper no. 7502. Cambridge, Mass.: National Bureau of Economic Research, January.

de la Rica, Sara, and Thomas Lemieux. 1994. "Does Public Health Insurance Reduce Labor Market Flexibility or Encourage the Underground Economy? Evidence from Spain and the United States." In *Social Protection versus Economic Flexibility: Is There a Trade-Off?* edited by Rebecca M. Blank, 265–99. Chicago: University of Chicago Press.

Deere, Donald, Kevin M. Murphy, and Finis Welch. 1995. "Employment and the 1990–1991 Minimum-Wage Hike." *American Economic Review* 85(2): 232–37.

Demleitner, Nora V. 1992. "Maternity Leave Policies of the United States and Germany: A Comparative Study." *New York Law School Journal of International and Comparative Law* 13(1): 229–55.

Dertouzos, James N., and Lynn A. Karoly. 1993. "Employment Effects of Worker Protection: Evidence from the United States." In *Employment Security and Labor Market Behavior: Interdisciplinary Approaches and International Evidence*, edited by Christoph F. Buechtemann, 215–27. Ithaca, N.Y.: ILR Press.

Devroye, Dan, and Richard B. Freeman. 2001. "Does Inequality in Skills Explain Inequality in Earnings across Advanced Countries?" *NBER* working paper no. W8140. Cambridge, Mass.: National Bureau of Economic Research, February.

DiNardo, John E., Nicole M. Fortin, and Thomas Lemieux. 1996. "Labor Market Institutions and the Distribution of Wages, 1973–1992: A Semiparametric Approach." *Econometrica* 64(5): 1001–44.

DiNardo, John E., and Thomas Lemieux. 1997. "Diverging Male Wage

Inequality in the United States and Canada, 1981–1998: Do Institutions Explain the Difference?" *Industrial and Labor Relations Review* 50(July): 629–51.

Dixon, Sylvia. 1998. "The Growth of Earnings Inequality, 1984–1997: Trends and Sources of Change." Paper presented at the Eighth Conference on Labour, Employment, and Work, Victoria University of Wellington, November.

Dolado, Juan, Francis Kramarz, Stephen Machin, Alan Manning, David Margolis, and Coen Teulings. 1996. "The Economic Impact of Minimum Wages in Europe." *Economic Policy* (23): 319–72.

Dolton, Peter, and Donal O'Neill. 1996. "Unemployment Duration and the Restart Effect: Some Experimental Evidence." *Economic Journal* 106(March): 387–400.

Dolton, Peter, Donal O'Neill, and Olive Sweetman. 1996. "Gender Differences in the Changing Labor Market." *Journal of Human Resources* 31(3): 549–65.

Edin, Per-Anders, and Bertil Holmlund. 1995. "The Swedish Wage Structure: The Rise and Fall of Solidarity Wage Policy." In *Differences and Changes in Wage Structures,* edited by Richard B. Freeman and Lawrence F. Katz, 307–43. Chicago: University of Chicago Press.

Edin, Per-Anders, and Katerina Richardson. Forthcoming. "Swimming with the Tide: Solidarity Wage Policy and the Gender Earnings Gap." *Scandinavian Journal of Economics.*

Edin, Per-Anders, and Robert Topel. 1997. "Wage Policy and Restructuring: The Swedish Labor Market since 1960." In *The Welfare State in Transition: Reforming the Swedish Model,* edited by Richard B. Freeman, Robert Topel, and Birgitta Swedenborg, 155–201. Chicago: University of Chicago Press.

Edin, Per-Anders, and Johnny Zetterberg. 1992. "Interindustry Wage Differentials: Evidence from Sweden and a Comparison with the United States." *American Economic Review* 82(5): 1341–49.

Ehrenberg, Ronald G. 1994. *Labor Markets and Integrating National Economies.* Washington, D.C.: Brookings Institution.

Ehrenberg, Ronald G., Leif Danziger, and Gee San. 1983. "Cost-of-Living Adjustment Clauses in Union Contracts: A Summary of Results." *Journal of Labor Economics* 1(3): 215–45.

Ehrenberg, Ronald G., and Robert S. Smith. 2000. *Modern Labor Economics.* 6th ed. Reading, Mass.: Addison Wesley Longman.

Eissa, Nada, and Jeffrey B. Liebman. 1996. "Labor Supply Response to the Earned Income Tax Credit." *Quarterly Journal of Economics* 111(2): 605–37.

Erickson, Chris, and Andrea Ichino. 1995. "Wage Differentials in Italy: Market Forces and Institutions." In *Differences and Changes in Wage Structures,* edited by Richard B. Freeman and Lawrence F. Katz, 265–305. Chicago: University of Chicago Press.

Evans, Lewis, Arthur Grimes, Bryce Wilkinson, and David Teece. 1996. "Economic Reform in New Zealand, 1984–95: The Pursuit of Efficiency." *Journal of Economic Literature* 34(4): 1856–1902.

Farber, Henry S. 1986. "The Analysis of Union Behavior." In *Handbook of Labor Economics,* edited by Orley C. Ashenfelter and Richard Layard, 2: 1039–89. Amsterdam: North-Holland.

Flanagan, Robert J. 1973. "The U.S. Phillips Curve and International Unemployment Rate Differentials." *American Economic Review* 63(3): 114–31.

———. 1999. "Macroeconomic Performance and Collective Bargaining: An International Perspective." *Journal of Economic Literature* 37(1): 1150–75.

Forslund, Anders, and Alan B. Krueger. 1997. "An Evaluation of the Swedish Active Labor Market Policy: New and Received Wisdom." In *The Welfare State in Transition: Reforming the Swedish Model,* edited by Richard B. Freeman, Robert Topel, and Birgitta Swedenborg, 267–98. Chicago: University of Chicago Press.

Fortin, Nicole M., and Thomas Lemieux. 1998. "Rank Regressions, Wage Distributions, and the Gender Gap." *Journal of Human Resources* 33(3): 610–43.

Foster, Ann C. 2000. "Private Sector Employee Benefits, 1996–97." *Compensation and Working Conditions* 5(2): 17–22.

Freeman, Richard B. 1976. *The Overeducated American.* New York: Academic.

———. 1980. "Unionism and the Dispersion of Wages." *Industrial and Labor Relations Review* 34(1): 3–23.

———. 1982. "Union Wage Practices and Wage Dispersion within Establishments." *Industrial and Labor Relations Review* 36(1): 3–21.

———. 1988. "Contraction and Expansion: The Divergence of Private Sector and Public Sector Unionism in the United States." *Journal of Economic Perspectives* 2(2): 63–88.

———. 1994. "How Labor Fares in Advanced Economics." In *Working Under Different Rules,* edited by Richard B. Freeman, 1–28. New York: Russell Sage Foundation.

———. 1996. "Why Do So Many Young American Men Commit Crimes, and What Might We Do About It?" *NBER* working paper no. 5451. Cambridge, Mass.: National Bureau of Economic Research.

———. 1999. "The Economics of Crime." In *Handbook of Labor Economics,* edited by Orley C. Ashenfelter and David Card, 3C: 3529–71. Amsterdam: Elsevier.

Freeman, Richard B., and Robert S. Gibbons. 1995. "Getting Together and Breaking Apart: The Decline of Centralized Collective Bargaining." In *Difference and Changes in Wage Structures,* edited by Richard B. Freeman and Lawrence F. Katz, 345–70. Chicago: University of Chicago Press.

Freeman, Richard B., and Lawrence F. Katz, eds. 1995. *Differences and Changes in Wages in Wage Structures.* Chicago: University of Chicago Press.

Freeman, Richard B., and Jeffrey Pelletier. 1990. "The Impact of Industrial Relations Legislation on British Union Density." *British Journal of Industrial Relations* 28(2): 141–64.

Freeman, Richard B., and Ronald Schettkat. 2000. "The Role of Wage and Skill Differences in U.S.-German Employment Differences." *NBER* working paper no. 7474. Cambridge, Mass.: National Bureau of Economic Research, January.

Friesen, Jane. 1996. "The Response of Wages to Protective Labor Legislation: Evidence from Canada." *Industrial and Labor Relations Review* 49(2): 243–55.

Gibbons, Robert, and Lawrence F. Katz. 1992. "Does Unmeasured Ability Explain Inter-Industry Wage Differentials?" *Review of Economic Studies* 59(3): 515–35.

Glyn, Andrew, and Wiemer Salverda. 2000. "Does Wage Flexibility Really Create Jobs?" *Challenge* 43(January–February): 32–43.

Golden, Miriam, and Michael Wallerstein. 1995. "The Fragmentation of the Bargaining Society: Changes in the Centralization of Wage-Setting in the Nordic Countries, 1950–1992." Paper presented at the Cornell University Conference "Macroeconomic Regimes, Wage Bargaining, and Institutional Change in Corporatist Political Economies," October.

Goldin, Claudia. 1990. *Understanding the Gender Gap: An Economic History of American Women.* New York: Oxford University Press.

Goldsmith, Arthur H., Jonathan R. Veum, and William A. Darity Jr. 1996. "The Psychological Impact of Unemployment and Joblessness." *Journal of Socio-Economics* 25(3): 333–58.

Gornick, Janet C. 1999. "Income Maintenance and Employment Supports for Former Welfare Recipients: The United States in Cross-National Perspective." In *Rethinking Income Support for the Working Poor,* edited by Evelyn Ganzglass and Karen Glass, 49–90. Washington, D.C.: National Governors' Association.

Gornick, Janet C., Marcia K. Meyers, and Katherin E. Ross. 1997. "Supporting the Employment of Mothers: Policy Variation across Fourteen Welfare States." *Journal of European Social Policy* 7(1): 45–70.

Gregory, Robert G., and Jeff Borland. 1999. "Recent Developments in Public Sector Labor Markets." In *Handbook of Labor Economics,* edited by Orley C. Ashenfelter and David Card, 3C: 3573–3630. Amsterdam: Elsevier.

Gregory, Robert G., and Anne E. Daly. 1991. "Can Economic Theory Explain Why Australian Women Are So Well Paid Relative to Their U.S. Counterparts?" In *Women's Wages: Stability and Changes in Six Industrialized Countries,* edited by Steven L. Willborn, 81–125. Greenwich, Conn.: JAI.

Gregory, Robert G., and R. C. Duncan. 1981. "Segmented Labor Market Theories and the Australian Experience of Equal Pay for Women." *Journal of Post Keynesian Economics* 3(3): 403–28.

Groshen, Erica L. 1991. "The Structure of the Female/Male Wage Differential: Is It Who You Are, What You Do, or Where You Work?" *Journal of Human Resources* 26(3): 457–72.

Gruber, Jonathan. 1994. "The Incidence of Mandated Maternity Benefits." *American Economic Review* 84(June): 622–41.

———. 1997a. "The Consumption Smoothing Benefits of Unemployment Insurance." *American Economic Review* 87(1): 192–205.

———. 1997b. "The Incidence of Payroll Taxation: Evidence from Chile." *Journal of Labor Economics* 15(3, pt. 2): S72–S101.

Gruber, Jonathan, and Alan B. Krueger. 1990. "The Incidence of Mandated Employer-Provided Insurance: Lessons from Workers' Compensation Insurance." *Industrial Relations Section* working paper no. 279. Princeton University, November.

Gunderson, Morley, and Roberta Robb. 1991. "Equal Pay for Work of Equal Value: Canada's Experience." In *Advances in Industrial and Labor Relations,* edited by D. Sockell, D. Lewin, and D. Lipsky, 5: 151–68. Greenwich, Conn.: JAI.

Haisken-DeNew, John P., and Christoph Schmidt. 1997. "Inter-Industry and Inter-Region Differentials: Mechanics and Interpretation." *Review of Economics and Statistics* 79(3): 516–21.

Hall, Peter, and Robert Franzese. 1998. "Central Bank Independence and Coordinated Wage Bargaining." In *Unions, Employers, and Central Banks: Wage Bargaining and Macro-Economic Policy in an Integrating Europe,* edited by Torben Iversen, Jonas Pontusson, and David Soskice. Ann Arbor: University of Michigan Press.

Hall, Robert. 1970. "Why Is the Unemployment Rate So High at Full Employment?" *Brookings Papers on Economic Activity* (3): 369–410.

Hamermesh, Daniel S. 1993a. "Employment Protection: Theoretical Implications and Some U.S. Evidence." In *Employment Security and Labor Market Behavior,* edited by C. Buechtemann, 126–47. Ithaca, N.Y.: ILR Press.

———. 1993b. *Labor Demand.* Princeton, N.J.: Princeton University Press.

Harbridge, Raymond, and James Moulder. 1993. "Collective Bargaining and New Zealand's Employment Contracts Act: One Year On." *Journal of Industrial Relations* 35(March): 62–83.

Hashimoto, Masanori. 1990. "Employment and Wage Systems in Japan and Their Implications for Productivity." In *Paying for Productivity,* edited by Alan S. Blinder, 245–94. Washington, D.C: Brookings Institutions.

Heckman, James. 1999. "Policies to Foster Human Capital." *NBER* working paper no. 7288. Cambridge, Mass.: National Bureau of Economic Research, August.

Hendricks, Wallace E., and Lawrence M. Kahn. 1982. "The Determinants of Bargaining Structure in U.S. Manufacturing Industries." *Industrial and Labor Relations Review* 35(2): 181–95.

Heseler, Heiner, and Ulrich Mückenberger. 1999. "The Case of Germany." *Labour* 13(1): 183–235.

Heylen, Fred. 1993. "Labour Market Structures, Labour Market Policy, and Wage Formation in the OECD." *Labour* 7(2): 25–51.

Hibbs, Douglas A. 1990. "Wage Compression under Solidarity Bargaining in Sweden." *Trade Union Institute for Economic Research* economic research report no. 30. Stockholm.

Hibbs, Douglas A., Jr., and Håkan Locking. 2000. "Wage Dispersion and Productive Efficiency: Evidence for Sweden." *Journal of Labor Economics* 18(4): 755–82.

Houseman, Susan N. 2001. "Why Employers Use Flexible Staffing Arrangements: New Evidence from an Establishment Survey." *Industrial and Labor Relations Review* 55(1): 149–78.

Howell, David R. 1999. "Increasing Earnings Inequality and Unemployment in Developed Countries: A Critical Assessment of the Unified Theory." Unpublished paper. New School University, December.

Hunt, Jennifer. 1995. "The Effect of Unemployment Compensation on Unemployment Duration in Germany." *Journal of Labor Economics* 13(1): 88–120.

———. 2000. "Firing Costs, Employment Fluctuations, and Average Employment: An Examination of Germany." *Economica* 67(May): 177–202.

———. Forthcoming. "The Transition in East Germany: When Is a Ten Point Fall in the Gender Wage Gap Bad News?" *Journal of Labor Economics.*

Iversen, Torben, Jonas Pontusson, and David Soskice, eds. 1998. *Unions, Employers, and Central Banks: Wage Bargaining and Macro-Economic Policy in an Integrating Europe.* Ann Arbor: University of Michigan Press.

Jeffreys, Stephen. 2000. "A 'Copernican Revolution' in French Industrial Relations: Are the Times a'Changing?" *British Journal of Industrial Relations* 38(June): 241–60.

Johnson, George E., and Gary Solon. 1986. "Estimates of the Direct Effects of Comparable Worth Policy." *American Economic Review* 76(5): 1117–25.

Juhn, Chinhui, Kevin M. Murphy, and Brooks Pierce. 1991. "Accounting for the Slowdown in Black-White Wage Convergence." In *Workers and Their Wages,* edited by Marvin H. Kosters, 107–43. Washington, D.C.: AEI.

———. 1993. "Wage Inequality and the Rise in Returns to Skill." *Journal of Political Economy* 101(June): 410–42.

Kahn, Lawrence M. 1998a. "Against the Wind: Bargaining Recentralisation and Wage Inequality in Norway, 1987–1991." *Economic Journal* 108(May): 603–45.

———. 1998b. "Collective Bargaining and the Interindustry Wage Structure: International Evidence." *Economica* 65(November): 507–34.

———. 2000. "Wage Inequality, Collective Bargaining, and Relative Employment, 1985–94: Evidence from 15 OECD Countries." *Review of Economics and Statistics* 82(4): 564–79.

Kahn, Lawrence M., and Michael Curme. 1987. "Unions and Nonunion Wage Dispersion." *Review of Economics and Statistics* 69(4): 600–7.

Katz, Harry C. 1993. "The Decentralization of Collective Bargaining: A Literature Review and Comparative Analysis." *Industrial and Labor Relations Review* 47(1): 3–22.

Katz, Harry C., and Thomas A. Kochan. 1992. *An Introduction to Collective Bargaining and Industrial Relations.* New York: McGraw-Hill.

Katz, Lawrence F., and David H. Autor. 1999. "Changes in the Wage Structure and Earnings Inequality." In *Handbook of Labor Economics,* edited by Orley C. Ashenfelter and David Card, 3A: 1463–1555. Amsterdam: Elsevier.

Katz, Lawrence F., and Alan B. Krueger. 1992. "The Effect of the New Minimum Wage Law in a Low-Wage Labor Market." *Industrial and Labor Relations Review* 46(1): 6–21.

———. 1999. "The High-Pressure U.S. Labor Market of the 1990s." *Brookings Papers on Economic Activity* (1): 1–65.

Katz, Lawrence F., Gary W. Loveman, and David G. Blanchflower. 1995. "A Comparison of Changes in the Structure of Wages in Four OECD

Countries." In *Differences and Changes in Wage Structures,* edited by Richard B. Freeman and Lawrence F. Katz, 25–65. Chicago: University of Chicago Press.

Katz, Lawrence F., and Kevin M. Murphy. 1992. "Changes in Relative Wages, 1963–1987: Supply and Demand Factors." *Quarterly Journal of Economics* 107(1): 35–78.

Kidd, Michael P., and Michael Shannon. 1996. "The Gender Wage Gap: A Comparison of Australia and Canada." *Industrial and Labor Relations Review* 49(4): 729–46.

Killingsworth, Mark. 1983. *Labour Supply.* Cambridge: Cambridge University Press.

———. 1990. *The Economics of Comparable Worth.* Kalamazoo, Mich.: W. E. Upjohn Institute for Employment Research.

Knoester, Anthonie, and Nico Van de Windt. 1987. "Real Wages and Taxation in Ten OECD Countries." *Oxford Bulletin of Economics and Statistics* 49(1): 151–69.

Korenman, Sanders, and David Neumark. 2000. "Cohort Crowding and Youth Labor Markets: A Cross-National Analysis." In *Youth Employment and Joblessness in Advanced Countries,* edited by David G. Blanchflower and Richard B. Freeman, 57–105. Chicago: University of Chicago Press.

Krueger, Alan B. 1995. "The Effect of the Minimum Wage When It Really Bites: A Reexamination of Evidence from Puerto Rico." In *Research in Labor Economics,* edited by Soloman Polachek, 1–22. Greenwich, Conn.: JAI.

———. 2000. "From Bismarck to Maastricht: The March to European Union and the Labor Compact." *NBER* working paper no. 7456. Cambridge, Mass.: National Bureau of Economic Research, January.

Krueger, Alan B., and Jörn-Steffen Pischke. 1997. "Observations and Conjectures on the U.S. Employment Miracle." *Industrial Relations Section* working paper no. 390. Princeton University, August.

Krueger, Alan B., and Lawrence Summers. 1988. "Efficiency Wages and Inter-Industry Wage Structure." *Econometrica* 56(2): 259–93.

Lang, Kevin. 1998. "The Effect of Trade Liberalization on Wages and Employment: The Case of New Zealand." *Journal of Labor Economics* 16(4): 792–814.

Layard, Richard, and Stephen Nickell. 1990. "Is Unemployment Lower if Unions Bargain over Employment?" *Quarterly Journal of Economics* 105(3): 773–87.

Layard, Richard, Stephen Nickell, and R. Jackman. 1991. *Unemployment.* Oxford: Oxford University Press.

Lazear, Edward P. 1990. "Job Security Provisions and Employment." *Quarterly Journal of Economics* 105(3): 699–726.

Leion, Anders. 1985. "Sweden." In *Industrial Relations in Europe,* edited by B. C. Roberts. London: Croom Helm.

Lemieux, Thomas. 1993. "Unions and Wage Inequality in Canada and the United States." In *Small Differences That Matter,* edited by David Card and Richard B. Freeman, 69–107. Chicago: University of Chicago Press.

Leonard, Jonathan S., and Marc Van Audenrode. 1993. "Corporatism Run Amok: Job Stability and Industrial Policy in Belgium and the United States." *Economic Policy* no. 17 (October): 356–400.

Leontief, Wassily. 1946. "The Pure Theory of the Guaranteed Annual Wage Contract." *Journal of Political Economy* 54(February): 76–79.

Leuven, Edwin, Hessel Oosterbeek, and Hans van Ophem. 1998. "Explaining International Differences in Male Inequality by Differences in Demand and Supply of Skill." Unpublished paper. Universiteit Van Amsterdam.

Levine, David I., and Laura D'Andrea Tyson. 1990. "Participation, Productivity, and the Firm's Environment." In *Paying for Productivity,* edited by Alan S. Blinder, 183–243. Washington, D.C.: Brookings Institution.

Lewis, H. Gregg. 1986. "Union Relative Wage Effects." In *Handbook of Labor Economics,* edited by Orley C. Ashenfelter and Richard Layard, 2: 1139–81. Amsterdam: North-Holland.

Light, Audrey, and Manuelita Ureta. 1992. "Panel Estimates of Male and Female Job Turnover Behavior: Can Female Nonquitters Be Identified?" *Journal of Labor Economics* 10(2): 156–81.

Lindbeck, Assar, Sten Nyberg, and Jorgen W. Weibull. 1999. "Social Norms and Economic Incentives in the Welfare State." *Quarterly Journal of Economics* 114(1): 1–35.

Lindbeck, Assar, and Dennis J. Snower. 1986. "Wage Setting, Unemployment, and Insider-Outsider Relations." *American Economic Review* 76(2): 235–39.

Ljungqvist, Lars. 1995. "Wage Structure as Implicit Insurance on Human Capital in Developed versus Underdeveloped Countries." *Journal of Development Economics* 46(1): 35–50.

Ljungqvist, Lars, and Thomas J. Sargent. 1998. "The European Unemployment Problem." *Journal of Political Economy* 106(3): 514–50.

Machin, Stephen, and Alan Manning. 1994. "The Effects of Minimum Wages on Wage Dispersion and Employment: Evidence from the U.K. Wage Councils." *Industrial and Labor Relations Review* 47(2): 319–29.

———. 1999. "The Causes and Consequences of Long-Term Unemployment in Europe." In *Handbook of Labor Economics,* edited by Orley C. Ashenfelter and David Card, 3C: 3085–3139. Amsterdam: Elsevier.

Macpherson, David A., and Barry T. Hirsch. 1995. "Wages and Gender Composition: Why Do Women's Jobs Pay Less?" *Journal of Labor Economics* 13(3): 426–71.

Madden, Janice Fanning. 1973. *The Economics of Sex Discrimination.* Lexington, Mass.: D. C. Heath.

Maloney, Tim. 1994. "Estimating the Effects of the Employment Contracts Act on Employment and Wages in New Zealand." *Australian Bulletin of Labour* 20(4): 320–43.

Mankiw, N. Gregory. 1999. "Comments and Discussion [on Ball 1999]." *Brookings Papers on Economic Activity* (2): 237–41.

Manning, Alan. 1996. "The Equal Pay Act as an Experiment to Test Theories of the Labour Market." *Economica* 63(May): 191–212.

McDonald, Ian, and Robert M. Solow. 1981. "Wage Bargaining and Employment." *American Economic Review* 71(5): 896–908.

Meitzen, Mark E. 1986. "Differences in Male and Female Job-Quitting Behavior." *Journal of Labor Economics* 4(2): 151–67.

Meyer, Bruce D. 1995. "Lessons from the U.S. Unemployment Insurance Experiments." *Journal of Economic Literature* 33(1): 91–131.

Mincer, Jacob, and Solomon Polachek. 1974. "Family Investments in Human Capital: Earnings of Women." *Journal of Political Economy* 82(2, pt. 2): S76–S108.

"Minimum Pay in 18 Countries." 1992. *European Industrial Relations Review* (225): 14–21.

Murphy, Kevin M., W. Craig Riddell, and Paul M. Romer. 1998. "Wages, Skills, and Technology in the United States and Canada." *NBER* working paper no. 6638. Cambridge, Mass.: National Bureau of Economic Research, July.

Murphy, Kevin M., and Robert H. Topel. 1990. "Efficiency Wages Reconsidered: Theory and Evidence." In *Advances in the Theory and Measurement of Unemployment,* edited by Y. Weiss and G. Fishelson, 204–40. New York: Macmillan.

Neal, Derek A., and William R. Johnson. 1996. "The Role of Premarket Factors in Black-White Wage Differences." *Journal of Political Economy* 104(5): 869–95.

Neumark, David, and William Wascher. 1992. "Employment Effects of Minimum and Subminimum Wages: Panel Data on State Minimum Wage Laws." *Industrial and Labor Relations Review* 46(October): 55–81.

———. 1999. "A Cross-National Analysis of the Effects of Minimum

Wages on Youth Employment." *NBER* working paper no. 7299. Cambridge, Mass.: National Bureau of Economic Research, August.

————. 2000. "Minimum Wages and Employment: A Case Study of the Fast-Food Industry in New Jersey and Pennsylvania: Reply." *American Economic Review* 90(5): 1362–96.

Nickell, Stephen. 1987. "Why Is Wage Inflation in Britain So High?" *Oxford Bulletin of Economics and Statistics* 49(1): 103–28.

————. 1997. "Unemployment and Labor Market Rigidities: Europe versus North America." *Journal of Economic Perspectives* 11(3): 55–74.

————. 1998. "Unemployment: Questions and Some Answers." *Economic Journal* 108(May): 802–16.

Nickell, Stephen, and Richard Layard. 1999. "Labor Market Institutions and Economic Performance." In *Handbook of Labor Economics,* edited by Orley C. Ashenfelter and David Card, 3C: 3029–84. Amsterdam: Elsevier.

Nickell, Steve, and Jan van Ours. 2000. "The Netherlands and the United Kingdom: A European Unemployment Miracle?" *Economic Policy* (30): 137–80.

OECD. 1983. *Employment Outlook: September 1983.* Paris: OECD.

————. 1988. *Employment Outlook: September 1988.* Paris: OECD.

————. 1989. *Employment Outlook: July 1989.* Paris: OECD.

————. 1990. *Employment Outlook: July 1990.* Paris: OECD.

————. 1993. *Employment Outlook: July 1993.* Paris: OECD.

————. 1994a. *Employment Outlook: July 1994.* Paris: OECD.

————. 1994b. *The OECD Jobs Study: Evidence and Explanations.* Paris: OECD.

————. 1995. "The Transition from Work to Retirement." Social Policy Studies no. 16. Paris: OECD.

————. 1996. *Employment Outlook: July 1996.* Paris: OECD.

————. 1997. *Employment Outlook: July 1997.* Paris: OECD.

————. 1998a. *Education at a Glance: OECD Indicators.* Paris: OECD.

————. 1998b. *Employment Outlook: July 1998.* Paris: OECD.

————. 1998c. *Human Capital Investment: An International Comparison.* Paris: OECD.

————. 1998d. *Purchasing Power Parities and Real Expenditures.* Paris: OECD.

————. 1999. *Employment Outlook: June 1999.* Paris: OECD.

————. 2000. *Employment Outlook: June 2000.* Paris: OECD.

O'Neill, June, Michael Brien, and James Cunningham. 1989. "Effects of Comparable Worth Policy: Evidence from Washington State." *American Economic Review* 79(2): 305–9.

O'Neill, June, and Solomon Polachek. 1993. "Why the Gender Gap in

Wages Narrowed in the 1980s." *Journal of Labor Economics* 11(1): 205–28.

Oswald, Andrew. 1996. "A Conjecture on the Explanation for High Unemployment in the Industrialized Nations: Part 1." *Department of Economics* economic research paper no. 475. University of Warwick, December.

Pelling, Henry. 1960. *American Labor.* Chicago: University of Chicago Press.

Reskin, Barbara, and Heidi I. Hartmann, eds. 1986. *Women's Work, Men's Work.* Washington D.C.: National Academy of Sciences.

Riddell, W. Craig. 1993. "Unionization in Canada and the United States: A Tale of Two Countries." In *Small Differences That Matter,* edited by David Card and Richard B. Freeman, 109–47. Chicago: University of Chicago Press.

Rosen, Sherwin. 1985. "Implicit Contracts: A Survey." *Journal of Economic Literature* 23(3): 1144–75.

Rowthorn, R. E. 1992. "Centralisation, Employment, and Wage Dispersion." *Economic Journal* 102(May): 506–23.

Rubin, D. B. 1987. *Multiple Imputation for Nonresponse in Surveys.* New York: John Wiley and Sons.

Rueda, David, Christopher Way, and Jonas Pontusson. 1998. "Gendered Patterns of Wage Inequality in OECD Countries." Paper presented at the annual meeting of the American Political Science Association, September 3–6, Boston.

Ruhm, Christopher J. 1998. "The Economic Consequences of Parental Leave Mandates: Lessons from Europe." *Quarterly Journal of Economics* 113(1): 285–317.

Ruhm, Christopher J., and Jackqueline L. Teague. 1997. "Parental Leave Policies in Europe and North America." In *Gender and Family Issues in the Workplace,* edited by Francine D. Blau and Ronald G. Ehrenberg, 133–56. New York: Russell Sage Foundation.

Saint-Paul, Gilles. 1996. "Exploring the Political Economy of Labor Market Institutions." *Economic Policy* (23): 265–315.

Scarpetta, Stefano. 1996. "Assessing the Role of Labour Market Policies and Institutional Settings on Unemployment: A Cross-Country Study." *OECD Economic Studies* (26): 43–98.

Schmitt, John. 1995. "The Changing Structure of Male Earnings in Britain, 1974–1988." In *Differences and Changes in Wage Structures,* edited by Richard B. Freeman and Lawrence F. Katz, 177–204. Chicago: University of Chicago Press.

Sen, Amartya. 1997. "Inequality, Unemployment, and Contemporary Europe." *International Labor Review* 136(2): 155–72.

Shapiro, Carl, and Joseph Stiglitz. 1984. "Equilibrium Unemployment as a Worker Discipline Device." *American Economic Review* 74(3): 433–44.

Sheldon, George. 1997. "Unemployment and Unemployment Insurance in Switzerland." In *Economic Policy in Switzerland*, edited by Philippe Baccetta and Walter Wasserfallen, 62–92. New York: St. Martin's.

Shimer, Robert. 1999. "The Impact of Young Workers on the Aggregate Labor Market." *NBER* working paper no. 7306. Cambridge, Mass.: National Bureau of Economic Research, August.

Siebert, Horst. 1997. "Labor Market Rigidities: At the Root of Unemployment in Europe." *Journal of Economic Perspectives* 11(3): 37–54.

Simona, Ilda. 1985. "Switzerland." In *Women Workers in Fifteen Countries,* edited by Jenny Farley, 147–53. Ithaca, N.Y.: ILR Press.

Sorensen, Elaine. 1990. "The Crowding Hypothesis and Comparable Worth Issue." *Journal of Human Resources* 25(1): 55–89.

Soskice, David. 1990. "Wage Determination: The Changing Role of Institutions in Advanced Industrialized Countries." *Oxford Review of Economic Policy* 6(4): 36–61.

Statistics Canada. 1998. *International Adult Literacy Survey Microdata Package*. CD Rom. Ottawa.

Stiglitz, Joseph. 1974. "Alternative Theories of Wage Determination and Unemployment in LDCs: The Labor Turnover Model." *Quarterly Journal of Economics* 88(2): 194–227.

Suen, Wing. 1997. "Decomposing Wage Residuals: Unmeasured Skill or Statistical Artifact?" *Journal of Labor Economics* 15(3, pt. 1): 555–66.

Summers, Lawrence H., Jonathan Gruber, and Rodrigo Vergara. 1993. "Taxation and the Structure of Labor Markets: The Case of Corporatism." *Quarterly Journal of Economics* 108(2): 385–411.

Teulings, Coen, and Joop Hartog. 1998. *Corporatism or Competition? Labour Contracts, Institutions, and Wage Structures in International Comparison*. Cambridge: Cambridge University Press.

Thorsrud, Einar. 1985. "Norway." In *Industrial Relations in Europe,* edited by B. C. Roberts, 180–203. London: Croom Helm.

Tomandl, Theodor, and Karl Fuerboeck. 1986. *Social Partnership*. Ithaca, N.Y.: ILR Press.

Topel, Robert H. 1997. "Factor Proportions and Relative Wages: The Supply-Side Determinants of Wage Inequality." *Journal of Economic Perspectives* 11(spring): 55–74.

Tyrväinen, Timo. 1995. "Real Wage Resistance and Unemployment: Multivariate Analysis of Cointegrating Relations in 10 OECD Economies." *OECD Jobs Study* working paper no. 10. Paris: OECD.

Van Audenrode, Marc A. 1994. "Short-Time Compensation, Job Security, and Employment Contracts: Evidence from Selected OECD Countries." *Journal of Political Economy* 102(1): 76–102.

Viscusi, W. Kip. 1980. "Sex Differences in Working Quitting." *Review of Economics and Statistics* 62(3): 388–98.

Visser, Jelle. 1996. "Unionisation Trends Revisited." Research Paper 1996/2. Amsterdam: Centre for Research of European Societies and Industrial Relations, February.

Waldfogel, Jane. 1998a. "The Family Gap for Young Women in the United States and Britain: Can Maternity Leave Make a Difference?" *Journal of Labor Economics* 16(3): 505–45.

———. 1998b. "Understanding the 'Family Gap' in Pay for Women with Children." *Journal of Economic Perspectives* 12(1): 157–70.

Wallerstein, Michael. 1999. "Wage-Setting Institutions and Pay Inequality in Advanced Industrial Societies." *American Journal of Political Science* 43(3): 649–80.

Western, Bruce, and Katherine Beckett. 1999. "How Unregulated Is the U.S. Labor Market? The Penal System as a Labor Market Institution." *American Journal of Sociology* 104(4): 1030–60.

Zabalza, A., and Z. Tzannatos. 1985. "The Effect of Britain's Anti-Discriminatory Legislation on Relative Pay and Employment." *Economic Journal* 95(September): 679–99.

——— Index ———

Numbers in **boldface** refer to figures and tables.